DATE DUE

MAR 0 7 1995	
NOV 2 2 1995	
DEC 1 4 1995	
JAN 0 4 1996	
FEB 2 0 1996	
APR - 9 1996	
MAR 3 1997	
JUN - 5 1997	
NOV 2 8 1997	
NOV 1 5 1998	
OCT 3 0 2003	
RGW-1016805	

BRODART.   Cat. No. 23-221

Sex and Love

51
54

SEX and *Love*

ADDICTION, TREATMENT, and RECOVERY

Eric Griffin-Shelley

PRAEGER

New York
Westport, Connecticut
London

Library of Congress Cataloging-in-Publication Data

Griffin-Shelley, Eric.
   Sex and love : addiction, treatment, and recovery / Eric Griffin-
Shelley.
      p.   cm.
   Includes bibliographical references and index.
   ISBN 0–275–93794–1 (alk. paper)
   1. Sex addiction. 2. Relationship addiction.   I. Title.
RC560.S43G75   1991
616.86—dc20   90–21283

British Library Cataloguing in Publication Data is available.

Library of Congress Catalog Card Number: 90–21283
ISBN: 0–275–93794–1

First published in 1991

Praeger Publishers, One Madison Avenue, New York, NY 10010
An imprint of Greenwood Publishing Group, Inc.

Printed in the United States of America

The paper used in this book complies with the
Permanent Paper Standard issued by the National
Information Standards Organization (Z39.48–1984).

10 9 8 7 6 5 4 3 2 1

Contents

Acknowledgments

Many people have helped in the development of this book, but no one else has had anywhere near the impact of my wife, Helen Griffin-Shelley. She provided the nurturing environment and support that allowed me to go to graduate school, which led to employment opportunities that taught me about addictions. She literally suggested my writing a book. Her patience, encouragement, understanding, and most of all, love allowed the creative process to take place. Finally, she provided invaluable and persistently positive thinking during the search for a publisher. Without her, none of this would have been possible.

I would also like to thank the many professionals who have contributed to my learning, especially Dr. Patrick Carnes and David Henrich, M.S.S. My special appreciation goes to the many patients with whom I have worked and the generous members of the Augustine Fellowship of Sex and Love Addicts Anonymous—all of whom have helped me grow in love and understanding. I would like to acknowledge my son, "Griff," who gives me joy and love every day. Finally, I would like to thank my Higher Power for His many gifts, the many people who love me, and the therapeutic and writing talents that daily keep me in touch with His grace.

Sex and Love

1

Introduction

When I began my work in the addiction field almost 20 years ago, sex and love addiction was unknown. Even today, the concept that a person could be "hooked" on love or sex is unsettling to most people. Some professionals scoff at the idea outright. Most are skeptical. However, as more is written and taught about this painful illness, many, laypersons and professionals alike, are starting to open their eyes, and in fact to see the magnitude of the problem.

The purpose of this book is twofold. It is directed at both professional and nonprofessional audiences. My intent is to help those in clinical practice identify and assist the sex and love addicts who make up their patient load and to provide hope and direction for those suffering from this long-ignored addiction.

Ever since Patrick Carnes's ground-breaking book, *Out of the Shadows: Understanding Sexual Addiction*, was published in 1983, there have been an increasing number of books and articles that address this topic. Robin Norwood's 1985 book, *Women Who Love Too Much*, hit a popular chord for many, and sold millions of copies. These books taught us much about this new area of addictionology, but they still dealt with love and sex as separate problem areas. This is similar to the views of alcohol and drug addiction of two decades ago. Most clients and clinicians saw the addicts as different, but the differences tended to be age- and social group-related (drug addicts were more often young and street-wise). Today, most people see both drug and alcohol dependence as examples of chemical dependency. The same will be true eventually with love and sex addiction. Some individuals have already suggested that both are problems with intimacy. In any case, in this book love and sex addictions will be considered together as they are in the Twelve Step recovery program in the Philadelphia area, the Augustine Fellowship of Sex and Love Addicts Anonymous.

Until a couple of years ago, most of my training and experience had been in the area of chemical dependency. I had heard references to sexual addiction and even had heard of Patrick Carnes, but it was not until I ran into a sexually addicted patient that I really began to learn about and understand the nature of this addiction. The client in question had been engaged in sadomasochistic sexual activities prior to admission to a psychiatric hospital. As we talked about his experiences, it became increasingly obvious to me that there was a clear pattern of escalation in terms of both the danger and the proximity. For example, he started out going to New York City to act out, but as his illness progressed, he began to find partners closer to home. I hesitated to call the problem an addiction, but it nonetheless seemed to me to be exactly like the many stories that I had heard in my work with drug addicts and alcoholics.

My experience with drug and alcohol addicts had taught me that a crucial aspect of recovery was connecting with a support group like Alcoholics Anonymous, so I began to look for a similar group for the client with sexual compulsions. Groups were hard to find because they were so anonymous, but eventually we found Sex and Love Addicts Anonymous (S.L.A.A.), and his recovery and my education were both well underway.

Since that time, I repeatedly have my eyes opened to the prevalence and extent of this potentially fatal illness. I see public figures like politicians and religious leaders who appear to have a compulsion to act out sexually. I see teenagers who are obsessed with love relationships that actually put their lives in danger. I see pornographic bookstores and massage parlors that cater to the sickness in my clients. I hear love songs that "program" teenagers to become love addicts. I read articles in my local paper about people whose addictions have progressed to the point where they are experiencing legal consequences. I wonder if we are not somehow becoming an addicted society.

Over ten years ago, the National Institute of Health identified sexual addiction as a priority for research. At the time, they estimated that 15 million Americans had this problem. Now, conservative estimates indicate that the prevalence rate is about 5 percent, and most experts would guess that 10 percent is a more realistic figure. In fact, in a recent article on university students who were asked to self-identify their own addictions, over 30 percent indicated that they had a problem with compulsive love and sex relationships.

Sex and love addictions have been around for centuries. The Roman emperor Caligula was probably a sex addict. The S.L.A.A. program also calls itself the Augustine Fellowship because they suspect that St. Augustine was addicted to love and sex. Casanova is another historical example. In fact, I recently had a client referred to me who wanted to find out if he had a "Casanova Complex" such as he had read about in a popular magazine. In my view, sex and love addictions will be the "disease of the 90s"; that is as the next decade progresses, increasing amounts of evidence will surface to confirm and expand our understanding of this complex and hurtful disease.

The time is right. Until recently, most people had trouble considering love and sex addictions as potentially fatal problems. Now, especially with the presence of human immunodeficiency virus (HIV), people are beginning to respect the potential lethality of unsafe sexual activity. In the Sex and Love Addicts Anonymous program, there is a saying that when you have sex with someone, you are also having sex with all the other people that person has had sex with. The threat of sexually transmitted diseases (STDs) and AIDS are real and frightening to these sex and love addicts. Many become suicidal or place their lives in dangerous situations, hoping that they will somehow be removed from their tortured existence. As professionals and as a society, we need to be sensitive to their pain and to find more and better ways to help those who are suffering from a love or sex addiction.

What Is a Sex and Love Addiction?

Most of us are quite hesitant to label someone an addict. We are more able to admit that we and others have "bad habits," but we shy away from saying that we are "hooked on" someone or something. I think that part of this fear comes from our stereotype of addicts. Most of us think of alcoholics, for example, as "skid row bums" when, in fact, only about 5 or 10 percent of alcoholics are that severely debilitated by their disease. Most alcoholics work, and many are not obvious to the public eye.

In the field of chemical dependency, we have come a long way from the moralistic view that people addicted to chemicals simply lack willpower and are morally weak. A major step along this path was the recognition by the American Medical Association in 1954 that alcoholism is a disease. Nowadays, most Americans see alcoholism as an illness, and are aware of treatment options as well as support groups like Alcoholics Anonymous (A.A.). We have even had a president's wife obtain help for drug and alcohol dependence and lend her name to a treatment facility, the Betty Ford Center.

Still, we are afraid to say we think someone might be an addict. In addition to the social stigma and moral judgments involved, another basis for these reservations is the poor success rate associated with addictions. Some 25 years ago, when the only residential treatment program for heroin addicts was in Lexington, Kentucky, their recovery rate was estimated to be an abysmal 4 percent. Heroin addiction was like a death sentence. The problem was considered to be incurable, much like the current situation with AIDS. Under these conditions, then, it was understandable that diagnosing oneself or someone else as an addict was a heavy burden and, perhaps, a fatal curse.

The circumstances are entirely different today. Success rates for treatment programs have gradually improved from an average of 30 percent ten years ago to 50 percent or better today. We have found that the abstinence rate for people who regularly attend Alcoholics Anonymous for one to five years is about 86 percent. After more than five years of A.A. attendance, the rate of continued abstinence from alcohol is around 92 percent (Vejnoska, 1983). This is the exact opposite of the 4 percent quoted above. In psychological research, we use 5 percent as the cutoff point for the effects of chance; in other words, anything with a rate better than 95 percent or less than 5 percent did not happen by accident. The 4 percent recovery rate for heroin addicts means that they have "no chance" of success, while the 92 percent abstinence rate for alcoholics regularly attending their support group for five or more years means they have almost "no chance" of failure. This is indeed a dramatic turnaround, and indicates great hope for addicted people and for those who care about them. In light of this new information and the help now available for those who suffer from addictive diseases, the label of "addict" should be less aversive.

DEFINITION OF ADDICTION

Many people have struggled with trying to define addiction. This in part is due to our growing knowledge of addicts, and the people and things on which they become hooked. The word addict has a Latin root, *ad dictum*, which means "to the dictator." When people were captured and sent into slavery, they were sent *ad dictum*. The idea of addiction as enslavement is something to which most addicts would readily agree. When you are addicted to a person, whiskey, prostitutes, or cigarettes, you feel that you have no choice and are powerless to stop. You cannot get the person or thing off your mind, and you are somehow its captive. Often the power of the captivity is disguised by the addict both to him- or herself and to the rest of the world; addicts tell us, "I can quit any time I want." In other cases there may be an irregular pattern with apparent periods of control. However, the telling factor is the power that the activity, person, or thing has to draw the addict back into use and abuse.

Consequently, part of the definition of addiction has to do with the issue of power and control. Most of us, especially Americans, hate the idea that someone or something has power or control over us. Freedom has an extremely high value for us. We view dependence as something distasteful, immature, weak, immoral, and unnecessary, and we strive for independence in all areas of our lives. The truth is that we are all interdependent on each other and our environment. Problems come about when we are out of balance somehow, for example, either too independent or too dependent. Addicts are out of balance. Love and sex are too important to them, and the rest of their lives suffer because of this overemphasis. Therefore, being out of control and out of balance are parts of the definition.

As an addiction progresses, it gradually becomes more and more important in the addict's life. The activity, substance, or person takes over center stage, and all the other things in the person's life move into the backstage or off the stage completely. In the language of Gestalt Psychology, the addiction becomes stuck in the foreground, and there is less and less ability to shift it into the background. As a result, the centrality and value of the activity, thing, or person is another element of the definition.

Not only is the addiction central and important, it is also unhealthy and pathological. When running becomes an addiction rather than a means of maintaining good health, it becomes destructive to the individual. Similarly, most people these days would agree that masturbation is a normal and healthy form of sexuality, yet there are people who are so hooked on masturbating that they actually hurt themselves physically. Some even die when their erotic contraptions fail and they suffocate. Another aspect of our definition, then, is that in addiction, sex and love have become destructive and unhealthy rather than joyful and life-enhancing.

The American Medical Association's definition of alcoholism states that it is "a chronic, progressive, and potentially fatal disease." Addictions, then, are seen as "chronic" or incurable. This means that the person will have to manage the illness for the rest of his or her life. Due especially to the high rate of relapse, addictive diseases are considered chronic. Addicts themselves are well aware that the temptation to return to the addiction will always be part of them, although with time it will have less pull.

Progression means that an ailment gets worse over time, especially when untreated. Some drug addicts and alcoholics believe that their chemical dependency continues to get worse even when they are in a period of abstinence. Stories of addicts who pick up a drug or a drink and immediately begin where they had left off or beyond are not uncommon in A.A. Progression can be a confusing idea because the course of an addiction can vary from person to person, with some who pick up pornography and rapidly go down hill, some who have an up-and-down pattern with periods of improvement as well as periods of decline, and some who gradually slip into more and more degrading and humiliating love relationships. Consequently, a downward trend needs to be part of our definition.

Sex and love addictions are not often seen as life-threatening or, at least, not as obviously dangerous as drug addiction or cigarette smoking. This is far from the truth. The arrival of AIDS has made unsafe sex potentially fatal. Moreover, love and sex addicts have a high rate of suicidal ideation, and often are admitted to psychiatric hospitals for depressions accompanied by suicidal thoughts or actions. Even driving while under the influence of a sexual or love addiction can be dangerous if not fatal.

Our definition has become rather complex so far: An addiction is an enslavement to an activity, person, or thing that is characterized by imbalance, lack of control, loss of power, distortion of values, inflexible centralness to the person's life, unhealthiness, pathology, chronicity, progression, and potential fatality. More simply put, an addict is a person who cannot say "no." A sex and love addict cannot say "no" to his or her impulses to have sex or get into a love relationship. An addict is a person whose thoughts and behaviors are causing problems but who cannot stop them. In addition to these definitions, a sex and love addiction involves a high, tolerance, craving, dependence, withdrawal, obsession, compulsion, secrecy, and a personality change. These nine characteristics of sex and love addictions will be elaborated in the next nine sections.

THE HIGH

An extremely important and often overlooked aspect of an addiction is the high. After all, this is the thing that gets the person hooked in the first place. There is a "good-feeling fix" with which the person falls in love and that he or she then wants more and more. For some addictions, the high is fairly obvious; for example, the intoxication of a drink, the "rush" of cocaine, or the "mellow" feeling of marijuana. The "fix" an addict gets from nicotine or caffeine is not so powerful but can be just as habit-forming. We have even been able to observe such a thing as a "runner's high." All these good feelings are the result of chemical changes in the brain—some ingested and some produced by our own bodies. Some of us just enjoy these good feelings and do not get hooked, while others (about 10 percent) get addicted to them.

What is it on which love and sex addicts get hooked? Some people might think this is a silly and obvious question, but it is not. Certainly the pleasure of a sexual orgasm is part of what the addict seeks, but orgasm is a relatively brief experience. Most people cannot sustain a multiply orgasmic state, so there has to be more that the addict seeks. In fact, there is. Most sex and love addicts spend a good deal of time in fantasy, during which they are in a state of mild arousal. In this state of preoccupation, their excitement can grow and their pleasure can increase. Most get quite good at developing and sustaining this high. For example, I treated a lawyer who was fired for not getting his work done because he spent much of his day in preoccupation. Another love addict that I worked with only acted out once each week, but she spent hours thinking about what she would wear and fixing her makeup.

"Cruising" and "intriguing" are ways that sex and love addicts build up sexual energy. For some, the excitement of "the chase" or the seduction is more addicting than the sexual part of the encounter. An exhibitionist I knew would spend hours driving around in his car looking for girls that he could "flash" before he would actually expose himself. Bars, pornographic bookstores, and street corners are all places where sex and love addicts will look for action.

Many addicts, however, are not involved in any public activities that would enhance their level of arousal. Instead, they spend hours reading or watching pornography, with eventual masturbation as only a part of their activity. Similarly, they will primp in front of a mirror or spend all day thinking of the romantic, charming dinner they will produce, including the flowers, candles, and atmosphere. They may be obsessed with helping their mate develop his or her career or be planning ways that their partner can patch things up with the boss.

The key element in all these activities is the good feeling they produce. This is what addicts get attached to, and what they must give up. Too many professionals with whom I have worked do not recognize the significance of the high, and therefore underestimate the power of the addiction, alienate their client through a lack of compassion or understanding, or blame the addict for not trying hard enough to change. Addicts are generally very sensitive people and quite tuned-in to facades and cover-ups. If they perceive the professional as not knowing or caring about their pain, they will never be open and honest. Appreciating the power of the high is essential to understanding the addict and the addiction.

Most addicts will say that their sex or love fix is more dependable than people. Addicts know how to get the feeling that they want, and can create a relatively predictable, repeatable high. If they give up depending on sex or love for their good feelings, they will have to turn to other people and to themselves—both of which are less reliable or under their control. Thus, to the addict, giving up sex and love addictions feels like relinquishing control and power, even though the opposite is really true.

Most so-called normal people react with shock or disgust at the severity or extent of a sex addict's "perversion" or a love addict's dependence. This moral judgment and lack of ability to identify with the addicted person taps the addict's already severely impaired self-esteem, and the addict will run for cover. Most of us, if we try, can identify bad habits or obsessions and compulsions in ourselves. To understand the addict, we need to connect with these problems and place ourselves in his or her shoes. What would we do if we felt ourselves compelled to have affairs, read or view pornographic materials, "look for love in all the wrong places," be sexual with children, masturbate, or go to prostitutes or massage parlors? These are all behaviors that human beings act out. If they are addicts, they have a sense that their high has gone out of control. They did not start out this way, and they never intended to become addicted, but this is where they have ended up.

A physician that I worked with traced his obsession with sex to his early teens. His mother was alcoholic and had many affairs. His father would become frustrated and enraged with his spouse, but he would take it out on his son instead. He beat him regularly, and almost killed him when he was 11. As a youth, my client found solace and what he thought was friendship with older males in his neighborhood. They introduced him to oral sex, and he felt wanted and cared for in their company, feelings unlike the hatred and violence that he experienced at home. He developed his own alcohol and drug addiction. After he recovered, he expected that his sexuality would come under control.

In fact, the opposite was true. He became more and more obsessed with cruising the homosexual "pick-up" district in town and having oral sex performed on him. This was his high. This is what he looked forward to and lived for. He thought that giving it up would be equivalent to dying. On the other hand, he began to so hate himself that he became intensely suicidal. His high had turned on him. Life with sex was not working, and life without sex was impossible to even contemplate.

Other highs are more subtle and difficult to observe. For example, I had a client who became extremely dependent on her therapy. Her life came to center around our sessions, and she began to have fewer and fewer outside social contacts. At one point she even stopped working, and only came out of the house to attend her therapy sessions. This is what gave her her good feelings, and the idea of stopping felt like ending her life. She did not have the energetic high of cocaine, but rather a more mellow euphoria like a marijuana high. (Many chronic marijuana users do not appear high to people who know them because these people have never really seen them straight; so too with my client.)

Another sex and love addict with whom I worked would often come to our initial sessions high. That is, before the sessions he would have some sort of encounter with a woman that was intriguing and potentially sexual, and he would become excited and energized. In these sessions, he would be talkative and engaging. When he was not high, he was much more depressed, and put on a "poor me" act to try to get me to sympathize with him about how tough his life was and how abusive his father had been to him.

Just like for other addicts, there is no one type of high that captures all addicts. Even the same type of romantic or sexual encounter may produce differing types of highs for different people. The same is true for drug or alcohol highs; in other words, alcohol can calm some and stimulate others, marijuana "turns on" some people and makes others sleepy, and cocaine excites users and makes others irritated and jumpy. We have learned that the type of high experienced is a combination of the chemistry and psychology of the person. With love and sexual highs, the same is true. What turns some people on turns others off. Whatever the turn-on is, however, is important, since it indicates both the physiological and the psychological basis for the addiction.

The study of unusual sexual highs has been termed the study of paraphilias. In the *Diagnostic and Statistical Manual (DSM-III)* of the American Psychiatric Association, there is a long list that includes fetishism, sexual masochism, transvestic fetishism, voyeurism, telephone scatologia (lewdness), necrophilia (eroticism toward corpses), and klismaphilia (enemas), among others. Unfortunately, the focus has too often been on the origin or elimination of the specific source of sexual excitement. Some treatment programs, for example, only treat exhibitionism, and neglect to see that for the sexually addicted person, there are many forms of sexual arousal, with something like exhibitionism as only the most favorite of many channels of excitement.

For instance, I worked with an exhibitionist who also was involved in compulsive masturbation and pornography. I was consulted by another sex addict who had transvestite impulses but also could not stop masturbating and had begun to visit prostitutes prior to coming to see me. In fact, there is what has been termed informally among treatment specialists the "rule of threes." That is, for most love and sex addicts, there are usually three areas of sexual or romantic arousal. They have a main preference, but when this is unavailable for some reason, they have other outlets to satisfy their compulsion. For example, a sex addict who expected to "score" at a conference, after cruising for awhile, might be unable to find a partner among the conferees. He then might go to the hotel bar in search of a sexual encounter. If this failed, he would settle for watching the X-rated movie channel in his room or might purchase some form of erotic literature. In any case, he would feel compelled to act out sexually in some way, and would justify it to himself in terms of needing a release to relax him so that he could go to sleep.

The highs that love and sex addicts seek vary both for the individual and among addicts generally. However, that is constant is the intense feeling that this need *must* be satisfied. Underestimating or judging the addict's high serves as an indication to the addict who is seeking help that he or she will not be understood and that his or her pain and struggle will not be appreciated.

TOLERANCE

One important aspect of addictions about which we have known for a long time is the existence of tolerance. What tolerance means is that the person becomes accustomed to an activity, person, or substance and it no longer has the same capacity to create the high that it did originally. Another way of saying this is that it takes more and more of the addictive substance to produce the same results.

For example, a love addict might get a big "kick" out of a simple phone call from a potential partner. After a few calls, however, the addict will have developed some tolerance and will need more to get the same fix, for example, he or she may need flowers or a romantic dinner date. A sex addict might get his or her rush from a mildly explicit magazine or ads for underwear in a store circular, but when viewed more frequently, they lose their power to stimulate the addict and he or she moves on to "hard-core" pornography. A sex and love addict with whom I worked and who was into sadomasochistic sexual encounters with whips, leather, and bondage eventually was no longer satisfied with the victim role and needed to become the victimizer (the sadist) in order to achieve the type of sexual arousal and orgasm that he had come to expect from these sex scenes.

Most of us think of tolerance in terms of drugs and alcohol. We discovered when we learned to drink that we started out with a certain level of tolerance for alcohol (which was usually quite low). With experience and exposure, we learned we could increase our tolerance or capacity for alcohol if we drank more. For men especially, having a high tolerance was a sign of prowess. Heavy drinkers were seen as more manly than those with little or no tolerance for liquor. In bars and fraternity houses, men have contests to see who can consume the most liquor, with the winner being the only person still standing at the end of the evening. Most of us, then, associate tolerance with the body's ability to accommodate increasing doses of a given chemical such as alcohol. Often we minimize or do not even recognize the psychological aspect of tolerance.

For sex and love addicts there is a definite amount of physical tolerance involved in an escalating addiction. The chemicals are not ingested from a source outside the self but are instead produced entirely from within. Our bodies have, essentially, two nervous systems, the sympathetic and the para-sympathetic. The sympathetic nervous system wakes us up, turns us on, alerts us, arouses us, and stimulates us. It is our adrenalin system. It makes us feel alive and ready to engage. On the other hand, our parasympathetic nervous system calms us down, puts us to sleep, helps us to relax, turns us off, and lets us disengage from the world. It is our soothing system, and makes us feel peaceful and content.

In a sex and love addiction, the addict is overusing the sympathetic system. The quest for sexual highs produces adrenalin and excitement. It is like driving your car with the accelerator pedal to the floor. As you get used to this pace, it becomes a common, normal, everyday feeling. In other words, tolerance develops. You need more speed to create more excitement. The love and sex addict is in the same bind. He or she must find ever more ways to be turned on. An exhibitionist may find that exposing him- or herself is not enough, and may come to do it more often or in riskier situations. A love addict may learn to tolerate more and more danger and physical abuse because he or she feels the intensity of the relationship more when there are more frequent conflicts and reconciliations. The fights are worse, but making-up is better.

While the sympathetic nervous system is being overtaxed, the parasym-pathetic system is also working overtime. After the addict has overstimulated him- or herself, it takes more and more to calm down. Sleep, then, can become a problem. At one point one orgasm may have been enough to bring on a sense of relief and relaxation, but over time, the addict may need more and more orgasms or may start using other ways of inducing sleep like ingesting drugs or alcohol. Two addictions, namely, chemicals and sex, can then interact with each other and produce increasing tolerance in both areas.

DEPENDENCE

In addition to the idea of increasing tolerance as one aspect of an addiction, we need to understand more about dependence. Hopefully, it is clear at this point that anyone can develop tolerance to a thing, person, or activity. This does not mean that everyone who develops a tolerance to buying lottery tickets or playing bingo will become a gambling addict. A person may have to overcome some discomfort to participate initially (perhaps having been taught that any form of gambling was wrong or immoral), but it is possible to be a "social user" of gambling activities without becoming a gambling addict, just as it is possible to be a "social drinker" without being an alcoholic. Likewise, we all need to be social users of food to survive, and most of us choose to have love relationships and sex as an important part of our lives. Where then does a person draw the line? Is every romance a potential love addiction? It is definitely not.

One of the important characteristics differentiating addicted people from normal people is the aspect of dependence. Someone who depends on sex or love to survive is dependent. In other words, a sex and love addict feels that he or she cannot live without constant involvement in sexual or romantic thoughts, feelings, or behaviors. Normal people may want love and sex in their lives to greater or lesser degrees, but they also know that they can live without it for a while.

The concepts of tolerance and dependence in addictions came about in regard to alcohol and drug addiction. Dependence was considered to mean physiological dependence. That is, alcohol, narcotics, and central nervous system depressant–type drugs create physical dependence. Our bodies not only develop a tolerance for these chemicals, but actually become dependent on them in order to function normally. The absence of a regular dose will produce a withdrawal syndrome that is unpleasant and, for some chemicals, potentially life-threatening. Thus, an alcoholic will "need" a drink in order to prevent symptoms like agitation, difficulty concentrating, anxiety, problems eating and sleeping, seizures, and hallucinations such as delirium tremens or "d.t."s.

Addicts who are physically dependent on chemicals need chemicals (1) to feel "normal" and function, and (2) to postpone the symptoms of withdrawal. More recently, we have come to realize that people who are chemically dependent on drugs such as stimulants (amphetamines and cocaine) and hallucinogens (LSD and marijuana) experience these same dependencies (namely, needing the drugs to feel "normal" or function and to avoid withdrawal), even though the drugs on which they are hooked are generally not considered physically addictive. We no longer see a difference between a heroin addict and a marijuana addict in terms of their potential for being dependent on their drug of choice. In fact, the Surgeon General recently compared cigarette addiction to heroin addiction, even though there are also obvious differences.

Consequently, it should not be too hard for us to see that sex and love addiction involves a dependency that is both physical and psychological. The physiological dependency is similar to the physical dependency of cocaine addicts; in other words, the addict "needs" the drug, activity, or person in order to feel "normal" and function, and the fix postpones withdrawal symptoms like depression or difficulty sleeping. Sex and love addicts have rearranged their bodies' normal patterns of stimulation and relaxation to the point where only a sexual or romantic encounter will prevent the feeling of discomfort that signals the beginning of withdrawal and loss of functioning.

Examples of dependency for sex and love addicts abound. In terms of physical dependence, many sex addicts have programmed their bodies to the point where they cannot fall asleep without an orgasm. Similarly, many love addicts cannot sleep without a romantic fantasy of some kind. Sex addicts can experience agitation and anxiety that may increase to the point of a panic attack if they sense that they will be unable to get their sexual fix. A sex addict who came to see me said he did not feel normal unless he was involved in some intrigue or affair, even though he desperately wanted to have a "normal," committed relationship. Love addicts can feel dizzy, unable to concentrate, and nauseous or crampy if they find that their love dependency is threatened.

Psychological dependence involves being "unable to live" without thoughts of sex or the love object; without patterns of friendships, leisure activities, and sex toys; without the excitement and so-called freedom of the addictive lifestyle; without the glamour and stimulation; and without the lying and secrecy. In most recovery programs, a great emphasis is placed on changing "people, places, and things" associated with the addiction. The purpose of this sort of guideline is to help break the psychological dependency. Most addicts are highly resistant to suggestions like these and find many ways to justify holding onto old patterns and connections, arguing, for example, "They really are friends," "I never had sex in a bookstore," or "I like to collect things like these magazines for research for my teaching."

The love and sex addict's psychological dependence is quite strong; in addition to the physical withdrawal symptoms he or she may have, there will be profound and powerful psychological withdrawal symptoms as well. The psychological withdrawal symptoms include boredom, depression, anxiety, suicidal ideas, guilt, and shame. The addict does everything in his or her power to avoid these feeling states because he or she has no way of coping with them other than acting out sexually or romantically. Addicts have little tolerance for boredom due to the high level of excitement and secrecy with which they are involved on a daily basis. They are terrified of the emptiness and dysphoria that will set in if they are not involved with their addiction, and they fear the feelings of worthlessness and guilt that will come over them. They have had periods of abstinence before, and are familiar with all these psychological complications.

Letting go is hard. One love-addicted woman who came to me held onto a relationship with a man with whom she had been involved because "We are such good friends." Rather than facing the pain of having to relinquish someone that she cared about, she chose to make herself vulnerable by keeping the friendship alive. She rationalized her behavior, and felt justified because the man was a traveling salesman and was seldom available. However, once when he was available, she had a slip that shook her self-esteem and self-confidence. She was able to avoid a full-blown relapse by telling her sponsor and me about what had happened, but still she wanted to hold on to this idealized "friendship," and was not willing to admit how she was being victimized, and how she was participating in her own victimization.

Another addict, whose addiction had had profound effects on his life due to his compulsive pedophilia, was highly resistant to any suggestions that he was overly dependent. He maintained a strong attachment to his parents, and often visited them on weekends. He held on to a demeaning clerical job that did not allow him to grow because he was afraid to go on job interviews. One weekend, on his way to visit his parents and play a tennis game with a friend, it began to rain. Despite six months of sobriety, he ended up wandering around in a shopping mall and having anonymous sex with someone in the men's room. Then he went to a pornographic bookstore. Afterwards, he felt terrible at losing his half year of sobriety. He resented the interpretation that he had set himself up by his pattern of refusing to solve his dependency issues. He also resisted using the phone to ask for help when he felt like acting out. Thus, he was avoiding developing healthy dependencies while holding on to his unhealthy dependencies. This pattern of keeping up old coping styles makes addicts vulnerable to slips and relapse. Breaking the psychological dependency is, then, an essential part of the recovery process.

CRAVING

Craving is the intense experience of wanting the activity, person, or substance on which the addict depends. Cravings are different from dependency and from compulsion in terms of the strength of the desire. Most addicts fear their cravings because they are well aware of the strength of their desire. Addicts also fool themselves into thinking that they are not addicts because they have periods of time when they do not experience cravings. Addicts, like most of us, expect that there will be an intense craving for sex or love. Cravings are not as predictable or consistent as most of us anticipate, but they indeed can make the difference between a successful recovery and a painful relapse, and consequently they need to be understood and appreciated.

Like dependency issues, cravings are both physical and psychological. That is, cravings can be triggered on the physical level, and they can also be started by environmental cues, emotional needs, or stress. Physically, craving comes from an abundance of receptor sites in the brain that are "expecting" the chemicals produced by the sex and love addict's high. Psychologically, cravings are the result of the addict's being stimulated by outside cues such as an unhealthy and erotically stimulating environment or internal cues such as unsatisfactory emotional states like boredom, depression, or stressful situations, all of which the addict may feel incapable of handling.

If we return to the analogy that sex and love addiction is similar to cocaine addiction, we can get some idea of the neurochemistry that may be producing the cravings. When large amounts of stimulant drugs are ingested, the brain is taxed beyond its capacity to absorb the chemicals at its receptor sites, so the body produces more. Now when more chemicals are ingested, the addict will have more tolerance and need more drugs. When there are periods when no drugs are available, the abundant unused receptors start clamoring to be filled and craving results.

A sex and love addiction produces its own internal flood of good-feeling chemicals, and thus increases the number of receptor sites in the brain. When the addict goes into a period of abstinence, for whatever reason, his or her body will begin to have cravings because it has become used to a high level of stimulation. This often happens two or three days after the last acting out, although it may be sooner or later for a variety of reasons. For example, it is not unusual for a sex and love addict to feel no intense cravings during residential treatment, which may be four or five weeks. However, upon returning home, the cravings return with a vengeance. This is probably due to inhibition on the addict's part during treatment, as well as the stimulation of other good-feeling chemicals during treatment through sharing and getting support from other addicts and the professional staff.

Some addicts experience strong cravings after only short periods of abstinence. I worked with one sex addict who was so caught up in his addiction that he could not resist his cravings even during inpatient treatment, and who was asked to leave the program because he could not comply with the expectation that he not act out sexually while in residence. He had no sense that his cravings would eventually subside if he did not give in to them. Cravings usually are relatively short-term, namely, from a few minutes to an hour or so. When the cravings are not indulged, the body begins its own adaptation process, which will eventually result in the reduction of receptor sites. All receptor sites will not be eliminated, so there will always be cravings, but their duration and intensity will be diminished to the point where they are passing annoyances instead of life-threatening confrontations between the addiction and health.

The process of building up the hope and confidence that cravings will be less difficult is an important part of the recovery process, and other sober, recovering people are often the best and most trusted resource for addicts struggling with the problem of cravings early in recovery. The basic message that needs to be communicated is, "It gets better." In some ways, learning to cope with cravings by saying "no" to them is the foundation of a good recovery. It may be a minute-by-minute, hour-by-hour, or day-by-day process, especially in the beginning, but it is essential and can be a model for future success. The S.L.A.A. program is well aware of how overwhelming it seems in the beginning to think of months or even years of recovery, so it emphasizes the need to work day by day. Small victories are what big recoveries are made of, and they need to be encouraged and reinforced. Sometimes it is helpful to remind the addict that his or her addiction was not created in a day, that it mostly was made of small steps that built up over time. Recovery, then, can be framed as a reversal of this process, which will not take as long nor be as painful.

There are psychological aspects of craving that need to be touched on as well. Some cravings come from the internal physiology of the addict, but others are triggered by environmental and emotional cues. The addict's environment can be a major source of temptation and stimulation of urges to act out romantically or sexually. Seasonal changes, for example, are often the source of increased cravings. The first spring I worked with sex and love addicts, I was surprised to hear them complaining about the coming of warm weather until one of them reminded me that people shed their clothing as the temperature rises. Summer, then, can be a very difficult time for a sex and love addict because there are many more environmental cues and temptations.

Emotional upheavals and needs can also initiate cravings for the sex and love addict. For some it might be anxiety and for others depression; for some it is boredom and for others embarrassment. Love and sex addicts have learned to sexualize and romanticize their feelings, so the answer to an emotional problem or need is to get a sexual or romantic fix. An exhibitionist who does not know what to do with himself on a rainy day when he cannot go to his construction job may go cruising at a mall or burrow into his pornography collection. A cleric who feels overworked and neglected may try to get more out of that friendly hug with a parishoner or may feel the urge to give the parishoner a "friendly" kiss. A love addict who is feeling insecure or anxious will experience a craving for a romantic encounter.

Many sex and love addicts use their addiction as their primary coping mechanism; for example; if they are happy, a sexual or romantic fix will make them even happier; if they have had some sort of success like closing a deal or earning a degree, a fix is the way to celebrate; if they are down or blue, a fix will bring them up; if they are just plain bored or have nothing to do, a fix will change things. Romantic and sexual fixes are also their way to handle stress. Many addicts come to me and tell me that sex is the way they handle stress: "It relaxes me." Good stresses like promotions or special projects and bad stresses like losses or moving all get the same response. "Love or sex will remove me from reality, at least for a while, and give me the good feeling that I need in order to continue" is how the addict rationalizes giving in to his or her cravings.

In order to break the cycle of responding to internal physical or emotional states or environmental cues or stressors, the love and sex addict needs to learn to let the cravings go, and not respond or dwell on them. An analogy about cravings for alcohol seems to embody the message that the addict needs to hear: When the craving for a drink comes knocking on your door, as it will, you need to shut the door quickly and get about other business; if you allow the craving into your living room and entertain it for a while, it will begin to gain more and more power over you until, in the end, you will give in to its illusive call.

WITHDRAWAL

As with tolerance, dependence, and craving, the withdrawal from a sex and love addiction has both physiological and psychological components. Most addicts who have also gone through food, cigarette, drug, alcohol, gambling, spending, or work addictions have indicated that the withdrawal process is lengthier and more painful than for any of the other addictions they have experienced. Most lay people underestimate the severity and intensity of the withdrawal for sex and love addicts, and in the process alienate them due to their lack of appreciation or compassion.

Part of the reason for the severity of the withdrawal is the length of the addiction. Most sex and love addictions have their roots in adolescence, if not earlier. It is not unusual for a sex and love addict to have discovered the mood-altering benefits of masturbation or fantasy as early as age 5, 6, or 7. A 31-year-old man recently consulted me who had been acting out since age 6, which meant that his addiction had been going on for 25 years. He could not remember a time when he was not preoccupied with or fantasizing about relationships or sex. As a preadolescent, he was fascinated with male authority figures like presidents and popular idols like singers. His addiction progressed to the point where he was suicidally depressed because he could not imagine living without acting out. He was obsessed with an abusive lover, felt compelled to visit male "hustlers," went to pornographic bookstores for anonymous sex, and masturbated even though he did not want to. He was terrified of withdrawal, and felt that recovery was "too hard."

Another addict lived in a large but detached family. His parents had a poor marriage and his father was sexually addicted. His parents slept in different bedrooms, and his father used the money that they had saved to buy their own home to go by himself to Italy. The addict tried to be the family "hero" and to live down the suggestion by his father that he was illegitimate. At a young age he found that masturbation would reduce his feelings of isolation and emptiness. He also discovered that self-inflicted flagelation, a technique that he learned reading the lives of the saints, would improve the intensity of his orgasm. Clearly, the roots of his later sadomasochistic acting out went very deep.

One love addict reported experiencing rejection from her alcoholic mother and unexpressed incestuous feelings toward her father, which had existed as long as she could remember. She was good at academics and sports, but failed to be the "feminine" daughter that her mother wanted. She felt that her mother wanted her to take on the "wife role" with the father. However, her father indicated that he harbored a deep hatred of and lack of respect for her sex by making derogatory comments about other women. Therefore, my client grew up with profound conflicts about her sexuality as well as terrible self-esteem. When adolescence hit, she felt betrayed not only by her family but also by her own body. Her peer relationships deteriorated, as she found it quite difficult to relate to other women and was afraid of men. Her love addiction escalated in her 20s and 30s with a series of destructive and dangerous relationships with males which gave her a number of venereal diseases and put her in the company of a boyfriend who would randomly fire his gun while she was in the room, and finally into a suicidal depression that resulted in hospitalization. She was terrified of going through withdrawal because she did not have a sense that she could survive and had no recall of life before her intense need for approval and love.

Another reason for the intensity of the withdrawal from sex and love addictions is that sex and love are seen as so much a part of who we are. Letting go of sex and love, even for a short amount of time, seems like giving up our whole identity. When an addict discards drugs, drink, cigarettes, spending, work, or gambling, it is easier to see these things as external. They are important parts of an addict's life, but not all that he or she is. Food addictions are more similar to sex and love addictions in that we cannot put down food and survive. We need to eat, so food addicts need to learn to manage their food intake. A drug addict, alcoholic, or smoker does not need to continue to ingest destructive chemicals, even though, when the cravings are strong, this is how it feels. It is harder to put down sex because it is so much a part of us.

Sex and love are both a physical and a psychological part of our identity. Hormones are an essential part of our physiology, and regulate growth and mood as well as sex drive and secondary sex characteristics. When our hormones are out of balance, (for example, during menopause), our entire life is affected, including our mood, concentration, and appetite, to a greater or lesser degree. Our sexuality, including our sense of our own masculinity or femininity, is an essential part of our identity. In fact, the first question asked about us at birth is; "Is it a boy or a girl?" The world begins to respond to us in terms of our sexual organs from the start. With modern technology, many parents know the sex of their child even before birth, and decorate the child's environment with sex-related cues such as blue for boys and pink for girls. Consequently, withdrawal from a sex and love love addiction feels like having your heart cut out or your genitals removed.

For many sex and love addicts, the addictions have periods of increased intensity or activity and times of abstinence or quiescence. Addicts will have been both hypersexual and sexually anorexic. They will have been in love and have given up on love. They are used to living in extremes with no sense of what is normal or of how to achieve a healthy balance. Their idea of withdrawal and recovery is, therefore, distorted, and resembles a life of isolation, emptiness, boredom, rigidity, and deprivation. Many of them grew up with these feelings, and discovered that love and sex would remove them, at least temporarily. Withdrawal, then, has psychological associations with childhood neglect, abuse, and deprivation, and feels too painful to live through again.

On a biological level, the sex and love addict's body, which is used to high levels of stimulation, will start to reestablish its metabolic balance when it goes through withdrawal. Our bodies have a wonderful ability to achieve homeostasis, that is, a balance or equilibrium, if we allow the natural process to operate unencumbered by an addiction. The process takes at least a month, and for some people it may be three months, six months, or even a year before they are completely normal again.

The physical systems that are affected include eating, sleeping, concentration, energy level, body fluids, and nerves. Usually the person will have an extreme reaction in one direction or the other. That is, in withdrawal, the addicts either cannot eat or cannot stop eating. They cannot sleep, or they cannot get out of bed and all they want to do is sleep. They are unable to concentrate or they are afraid unless they bury their head in something like work. They have too much energy, cannot sit still, and are agitated and hyperactive, or they have no energy, cannot move, and are listless and passive. They are sweaty or feel dried-up. They feel like a "raw nerve" or they are strangely "numb." Some may have periods where they go back and forth between both extremes. Some experience other physical symptoms more commonly associated with drug or alcohol withdrawal, like increased or decreased heartbeat, nausea, vomiting, or muscle cramping. With their bodies going through all this, it is no wonder that many sex and love addicts feel like they are "going crazy" during withdrawal.

In addition to the physical withdrawal, there is also a psychological withdrawal that takes place, although the emotional detoxification from a sex and love addiction takes longer than the biological adjustment. The psychological withdrawal involves a readjustment of the person's emotional and coping systems which are also out of balance. Moreover, there is a grief, loss, and mourning process that needs to be attended to since, in some ways, addiction has been the addict's "best friend" and most reliable companion.

On an emotional level, addicts seem to come out of an addiction either emotionally hypersensitive (namely, the "raw nerve") or emotionally dead (numb). They tend to have mood swings that include anxiety, anger, and depression, which may seem out of control at times, or else they do not feel anything. Both extremes bother the addicts themselves as well as those who care about them. Withdrawing addicts may seem irritable, impatient, sarcastic, critical, and demanding. They also may express hopelessness, worthlessness, and a lack of motivation.

Depression is a quite frequent component of withdrawal, and often is accompanied by suicidal ideas. Dysphoria and thoughts of "ending it all" need to be taken quite seriously at this point since the addict is quite vulnerable during the withdrawal period and will be subject to unpredictable mood swings. Anger at the self, guilt, shame, and embarrassment all aggravate the addict's depression. Not only does the sex and love addict feel like he or she cannot live without the addiction, but he or she will also be starting to feel unable to live with it either. The obvious choice, then, is suicide, and any threats or thoughts must be perceived as potentially fatal.

Dangerous depressions, panic attacks, and rage are all part of the psychological withdrawal. There is also a mourning process that begins, which involves all the classic aspects of grief and loss. There are periods of shock, denial, anger, bargaining (for example, "If I can only masturbate, I will not go to any more bookstores"), blaming (for example, "It's all God's fault"), and eventually acceptance and a working through.

Obviously, the withdrawal process can be difficult for the addict and those around him or her. However, it is also a time of hope and renewal. New coping mechanisms begin to be established with the addict's self, friends, family, and work. A metamorphosis is starting which will create change in the addict physically, mentally, emotionally, socially, and spiritually. Support needs to come from other recovering addicts who are in a Twelve Step program like Sex and Love Addicts Anonymous, from family and friends who have educated themselves about this type of problem, and from professionals who have had training in sex and love addictions.

Talking is the treatment of choice for withdrawal at this time. Talking means sharing with other recovering addicts at S.L.A.A. meetings, calling sponsors daily, and reaching out when you feel like indulging the craving for a sexual or romantic fix. Talking means telling the people about whom you care, and who care about you, what you are going through. Talking means finding a therapist or professional counselor whom you can trust and who knows about addictions, especially sex and love addictions.

Medically, there is little available as of this writing to ease the withdrawal process. Unlike chemical dependencies, for which there are many detoxification units, there are no inpatient treatment programs for sex and love addiction withdrawal. The residential programs that treat sex and love addicts expect their patients to go through withdrawal during the initial part of their stay. They offer much support for the psychological aspects of withdrawal, and even assist with the management of the physical symptoms. For example, a turkey sandwich and a glass of milk taken an hour or so before bedtime can promote sleep. Generally, these units are wary of using medications such as sleeping medicines or benzodiazipines (namely, Valium, Librium, and others in this class, which are typically used with drug and alcohol withdrawals) because many sex and love addicts are also chemically dependent. We may see efforts to try drugs like Clonodine or Naltraxone, which appear helpful in cocaine and opiate addictions. Antidepressants may also be used at some point, since depression and suicidal ideas are so prevalent. This is only speculation, however, and as yet there is no accepted medical management profile available for treating the withdrawal from sex and love addiction.

OBSESSION

So far, we have examined how the high, tolerance, dependence, craving, and withdrawal are aspects of sex and love addictions. Another important consideration in defining and diagnosing an addiction is the mental obsession involved. Traditionally, obsessive/compulsive disorders have been considered confined to people who are obsessed with germs or danger and compulsively wash or check things. These "checkers" or "washers" can get so hung up in their own minds that they will compulsively wash their hands or check to see if the stove is off or the door is locked 50 or 100 times in a row, or more. As we have learned more about this problem, it has become more obvious that these people have difficulty managing their anxiety. Instead of learning that their anxiety will increase to a certain point and then level off (and not escalate to the point where they will explode or "go crazy"), they have interrupted the normal curve with an anxiety-reducing ritual. Unfortunately, this strategy only works for a short time, and then their anxiety returns. Another anxiety-reducing ritual then is needed, and the cycle or repetition becomes established.

This pattern of obsessive thinking and compulsive behaviors to cope with fear and anxiety is similar to what happens in an addiction. There is a short-term gain that is powerfully reinforcing to the obsessive/compulsive individual, but the long-term effects are disastrous. These people can become so invested in their repetitive rituals that they physically harm themselves, such as by washing even when their hands are raw from soap and previous rubbing. They cannot think of anything else; they are emotionally numb or hypersensitive. They are socially isolated; they cannot function at work or in relationships with family or friends, and they are spiritually dead. This account is surprisingly similar to the description of the effects of an addiction.

Sex and love addicts are not as obviously obsessed as these traditional obsessive/compulsive patients, but their minds are just as "stuck" and they are in just as deep a mental rut. Sex and love addicts do much to conceal the extent of their mental obsession both from themselves and from others, but their minds are never far from their favorite subject. Sometimes the extent of their obsession comes out in subtle ways. For instance, a chemically dependent teenager with whom I worked never spoke to me about sex and minimized his involvement when I questioned him. With his peers, however, sex was "all that he talked about." A lawyer whom I saw was fired for his lack of productivity at work. The real problem was not laziness but his preoccupation with sex. A middle-aged housewife who is love-addicted spent hours preparing to "to out with the girls" while her marriage became completely celibate. None of these addicts thought that they spent an inordinate amount of time thinking about love and sex.

Preoccupation and fantasy are the major components of obsession. Preoccupation or thinking a good deal about sex and love can involve a great deal of planning with regard to what sort of activity will be undertaken and with whom, how the addict will get the money needed, and how to cover his or her tracks in terms of time and expense. It takes a great deal of effort to lead a second, usually secret, life, so much planning is needed. For example, a sexually addicted doctor frequently would go cruising for a homosexual partner for oral sex right after his regular meeting of Alcoholics Anonymous so that his wife would not suspect him, and he would spend the hour in the A.A. meeting preoccupied with what would transpire next.

Fantasy is another aspect of the addict's obsessive thinking. Many addicts spend hours each day fantasizing about past or potential romantic or sexual encounters. A sex and love addict in his mid-30s had lost a number of jobs because he could not stop fantasizing at work. He was a tennis instructor at private clubs, and would imagine sexual and romantic encounters with the women that he was supposed to be instructing. His pupils would become uncomfortable with his staring and his overt attitude, and he would find himself fired for some seemingly minor difficulty like coming in late. He was frequently late to work because he was busy masturbating and could not stop in time. He also found that he became interested in younger and younger women as older women were turned off by his increasingly obvious sexual preoccupation. His fantasy life was so out of control that he ended up unable to function in his chosen profession because no one would hire him. His job skills were also impaired due to the extent of his preoccupation.

A seminarian who was a recovering alcoholic spent hours each day fantasizing about finding a partner with whom it would be safe to act out his dreams of dressing in women's clothing. When he discovered a prostitute who catered to men with transvestite fantasies, he became so obsessed with finding out what this experience would be like that he stole money from the church's collection for the poor to finance a session with her. Moreover, for many years he had found it almost impossible to concentrate and study due to his sexual preoccupations.

In order to normalize their fantasies and preoccupations with love and sex, addicts develop distorted thought processes. Many of these take the form of traditional mechanisms of defense: denial, rationalization, minimization, and projection. Obsessions are denied through the use of thoughts like "Everyone does it," "It's only normal for men to think a lot about sex," "Love makes the world go 'round," "It's not hurting anyone," or "Life is to be lived, not wasted." There is a fair amount of support for the idea that our culture is preoccupied with sex. Certainly sex is used to sell all sorts of products. Advertisers know our culture's fascination with sex, and make it an important part of their marketing strategies. Love is the dominant theme of music, books, and magazines geared toward women because, again, producers "know what the public wants." Addicts notice these preoccupations in our larger culture and use them to deny the existence of their own problems.

When denial does not work, rationalization takes over. To rationalize is to make up a pseudo-reason or excuse to justify a thought, feeling, or behavior. It is "all right" to do something if you have a good reason, and addicts are masters at making excuses or coming up with reasons for how and why they think and act the way they do. For instance, one of the favorite excuses for compulsive masturbation is that it "reduces stress." In our stress-filled society, this sounds almost logical. However, the rationalization begins to fall apart when it is learned that the sex and love addict in question ran up a phone bill of over $1,600 in a two- or three-month period of so-called stress reduction.

When rationalizations are challenged, the usual addict's response is minimization, which is the opposite of exaggerating. Thus, the hill that is exaggerated into a huge mountain, when minimized becomes a barely perceptible rise in the surface of the land. A hysteric may "make a mountain out of a molehill," while an addict "makes a molehill out of a mountain." Thus, a love addict will minimize his obsession with a female coworker, saying she's "only a friend," and a sex addict will minimize his obsession with prostitutes as "not hurting anyone."

Another thought distortion that sex and love addicts use is projection. When we project, we place the blame or responsibility for our thoughts, feelings, or actions onto someone or something other than ourselves. For example, a common projection for embarrassing or uncomfortable behavior is, "The devil made me do it." Rather than accepting the responsibility for our own actions, we blame some unseen spirit like the devil. Addicts love to blame others for their obsessions. They do not want to admit their own lack of control over their thoughts, so they project blame onto others. For instance, a sex addict might say, "My wife does not really understand me" to rationalize having an affair. Rather than dealing with his own problems with his marriage, he finds an easy scapegoat in his wife and her alleged lack of understanding.

Addicts have confessed to me that they have wanted to act out so badly that they will intentionally pick fights with their wives in order to have an excuse to leave the house and act out sexually. A love addict whom I treated projected blame on her husband for her acting out because he was no longer interested in her sexually. She could not see that her attitudes and behaviors concerning her sexuality may have actually been hurtful and a "turn-off" to him.

All these defenses—denial, rationalization, minimization, and projection—enable the sex and love addict to continue to nurture obsessions. Excessive amounts of preoccupation and fantasy can actually produce a trance-like state, especially when combined with rituals. This trance-like state intensifies the addict's tendency to objectify people and to numb his or her own emotions. Sex and love addicts, despite their great skill at seduction and the chase, do not see people as real human beings. Rather, they perceive others as objects. To them another person is an object that may provide the sexual or romantic high that is sought. Since most people do not enjoy being treated like objects, sex and love addicts become quite good at deception. In order to be a good "con artist," you need to believe your own "cons," at least to some extent. Consequently, sex and love addicts come to believe their own lies, like "I am a pioneer in sexual freedom." Freedom is one of the great cons that sex and love addicts use. Another is "true love." I had a teenage sex addict write a new female patient, one day after she had come into treatment, that he loved her deeply and wanted to "spend the rest of our lives together." After this touching, seemingly typical, teenage romance, he proceeded to tell her that he fantasized about having sex with her "until [she would] scream."

Sadomasochistic (S/M) sex is a somewhat extreme example of the objectification of people that sex and love addicts practice. In these encounters, the players dress in costumes, often leather, and act out "scenes" of torture such as shackling someone to a bed or chaining him or her in a cellar. There is little or no expression of tenderness or love; rather, the sexual passion is enhanced by fear and pain. Pornography, adult bookstores with sex shows, exotic dancers, anonymous sex, multiple affairs, massage parlors, obscene phone calls, exhibitionism, voyeurism, and indecent liberties (inappropriate touching), as well as the most extreme forms—rape, incest, and pedophilia—are all examples of objectified sex and love relationships. There is no personal contact involved. What counts is the fulfillment of the perpetrator regardless of what happens to the other participant.

In order not to care or think about what is really going on, addicts turn themselves off. One of the primary characteristics of addicts is that they "don't care." Through their trance-like preoccupation and their fantasies, sex and love addicts have come to numb their own emotional life. They are obsessed with sex and love, but they cannot afford to let themselves feel the emotional pain of their enslavement so they cut off their feelings. They may be able to resemble people who are quite emotional, especially as part of their seduction routine, but in fact their feelings are deeply buried within them. This may be simply the result of their addiction, or it may have been complicated by a neglectful or abusive childhood that forced them to disown their emotions. In any case, addicts do not feel deep emotions, so it is relatively easy for them to objectify others.

Despite their obsessiveness, addicts do have what they call in the program, "moments of sanity." These are periods when they can see things realistically and can be rational. Unfortunately, these periods of insight can create intense conflicts for addicts. Unless they are at the point where they are ready to seek help or undergo some sort of change process, they will need to detach from these "moments of sanity." This process of detaching is a way of numbing thoughts. Programs for co-dependents, people who are overly involved in the lives of active addicts and become unhealthy themselves, teach them to "detach with love." This is true of Alanon, the program for those who care about alcoholics, and Co-S.L.A.A., the program for people who care about sex and love addicts. The addict, on the other hand, uses detachment destructively. Rather than using it as a way to prevent getting overly involved, the sex and love addict learns to use detachment to be indifferent about others and removed from his or her own inner conflicts and pain. Detachment, then, is a way to allow the obsession to continue and grow. Detachment makes it possible to "sexualize" or objectify another human being while feeling no guilt about using him or her as a sex object.

COMPULSION

The compulsive aspect of an addiction is, of course, more obvious because it involves behavior. Where mental obsessions can be kept secret easily, compulsive behaviors are harder to hide. Still, most sex and love addicts are masters at hiding their addictions. They deserve partial credit for their ability to be deceptive, but we also deserve part of the blame for not noticing the "tip of the iceberg" and for accepting their denials, rationalizations, minimizing, and blaming of other things, events, and people. This goes back to what I spoke of earlier in terms of our reluctance to label a person addicted. We have not known what to do with sex and love addiction until fairly recently, so part of our blindness is due to the avoidance that comes from feeling powerless to do anything and being bereft of resources for help.

The compulsion is the driving force behind the behavior. I have heard it described as having the power and might of a "runaway locomotive." Addicts, in their trance-like state, feel compelled to complete their missions no matter who or what is in their way. In fact, many times people who are somewhat naive about addictions cannot believe the power of the compulsion. Nonaddicts look at the addict in disbelief and ask, "Why can't you stop?" One exhibitionist I treated was from a small nearby town. He had red hair, so he was relatively easy to identify. He was first picked up for exposing himself when he was 16. After that, he was known by the local authorities. Every time someone reported a man exposing himself, the police would ask if he had red hair, and then would call my client and tell him to come in. Most people—including addicts themselves—underestimate the power of the compulsion. In the S.L.A.A. program, there is a saying that addiction is a "cunning, baffling, and powerful disease." In fact, I use the addict's respect for the power of his or her illness as a guidepost for determining growth in recovery. Addicts with good sobriety have a healthy respect for the power of their compulsions.

In addition to the obsessive thoughts and fantasies, part of what sets the compulsion in motion is the addict's use of ritual. Rituals enhance the trance-like state of mind and encourage repetition. We all use healthy rituals that enhance trance-like states. Hypnotists, clergy, and yoga teachers know that rituals increase the production of a desired mental state, be it hypnosis, prayer, or meditation. Sex and love addicts may develop rather extensive and elaborate rituals, or there may be simple routines that they go through to get into the "right frame of mind." Some of the more extreme examples of sexual addictions provide examples of rituals, but the routines need not be as elaborate or as destructive.

A few years ago, before I knew anything about sexual addiction, I read the story of the "Boston Strangler." As I learned more about the compulsive and ritualistic nature of this illness, his story kept coming back to me. His wife allegedly thought that he was "oversexed," and he reported a great sexual appetite. In order to satisfy his growing hunger for sex, he began to rape women. He always had a fixed routine. As his behavior escalated out of control, he began to tie his victims to their beds with silk scarves. When rape was no longer enough of a sexual high, he began to murder his victims. Again he always used the same ritual, and the police could identify his victims from his pattern.

In a recent edition of a popular magazine, a college professor was allegedly accused of having an incestuous relationship with his adopted twin daughters as well as at least ten other children whom he had befriended. He denied the charges. His friends and colleagues could not believe it was true, since he seemed like "such a nice man." The pattern of abuse would allegedly begin in the morning, when he would enter his daughters' bed for fondling and oral sex. He progressed to the point where he was photographing the acting out and allegedly sexually abusing children when he would ritualistically take them to process the film in his photo lab at the school where he was so respected.

A teenager that I interviewed at 17 had had an ongoing sexual relationship with the live-in maid that his parents employed. He had a routine of having sex when he came home from school, which would have continued unnoticed had we not encouraged him to share this with his parents as part of his recovery from chemical dependency. His sex and love addiction only came to light because of his difficulty concentrating in treatment. He eventually admitted that he was totally preoccupied with sex and that he was not even able to pay attention in his groups and meetings because his mind was on the genitals of the females in the room.

Certainly these are extreme examples, but they highlight the ritualistic aspect of the compulsive behavior. Most of us get upset when our rituals are interrupted. Can you imagine someone standing up in the middle of your Sunday church service and saying, "I don't think that this is the right order of service" or "I would like to make a few comments at this time"? (The only place that such behavior would be deemed appropriate would be at a Quaker meeting.) Our rituals are well-worn ruts that make us feel comfortable and secure. So, too, the addict's rituals produce a false sense of security and reduce his or her anxiety. They enhance the sense of power and control when, in reality, the addict is out of control. Addicts delude themselves into thinking that they are actually in control and that they have a choice to resist their compulsion.

Another example of this delusional thinking and the power of the compulsion comes from a client who had a heart condition. He was playing the role of victim in a dungeon S/M scene, and was chained hand and foot. He had carefully instructed the sadist in the scene not to use any electrical equipment. However, when he was completely helpless, his partner brought out an electric cattle prod and began to shock him with it. The client was convinced that he would die on the spot from a heart attack, yet despite his fear, his shame kept him from asking for help even at this life-threatening stage. His compulsion would have driven him to still more acting out had an outside force not intervened and brought him into treatment.

The compulsive part of the addiction needs to be seen as impulsive as well. The obsessive aspect of the illness does not bring about a well-thought-out plan of action that is then put into place. Rather, the obsession serves to build up the energy that is impulsively and, often explosively, expressed in the compulsive behavior. For example, the sex and love addict who enjoys making obscene phone calls may obsess about the act for hours and then impulsively act out, or there may be little obsessing and much more impulsivity. The obscene caller knows that the calls can be traced and that he or she is at a high risk for being discovered, but the combination of compulsion and impulse doom him or her to act out anyway.

Another example of this impulsivity involved a pedophile who had acted out homosexually while he was in the seminary. He had developed the delusion that his problems with compulsive sexuality would end after he was ordained. However, what actually happened was that he impulsively acted out with a male friend on the day of his ordination after the services had been completed. He made the fatal error of underestimating the power of his compulsion and the danger of impulsively acting out should the opportunity present itself.

SECRECY

An important part of an addiction is secrecy. Assessing the extent of and investment in covering up the truth can be a useful diagnostic tool as well as providing motivation for treatment. All addicted people are dishonest to some degree in their addictions, at least until they get into a recovery process. They keep secrets and lie a great deal. They are most dishonest with themselves and most deceitful with others. Sex and love addicts appear to be the most dishonest and secretive of the addict populations with whom I have worked. This is partially due to the great shame and embarrassment that they feel about having a problem in an area that is supposed to be so natural. Most people joke about problems with love or sex. Men are socialized to act "macho," which involves being oversexed. Women are taught that their self-esteem should be based on their physical attractiveness to men, and especially to the man they "catch." However, while some bragging about affairs and sexual exploits may occur among sex and love addicts (mostly among the males), most of their thoughts and actions are kept well under cover.

It is not unusual for a sex and love addict to tell me that his or her spouse knows nothing about the addiction. For example, an office furniture salesman came to see me and described an ongoing problem of being compelled to visit prostitutes. He had done a number of things to try to gain some control over this difficulty, and felt quite ashamed and embarrassed that he was depriving his children of the money that he could save for them if it weren't for his need to go to these prostitutes. He had even undergone analytic psychotherapy for about five years to try to get some control over these impulses. He gained a good deal from the therapy in terms of resolving issues concerning his parents, but nothing changed in terms of his need to get a sexual fix, especially after making a big sale. He had analyzed his behavior in terms of his desire to be better than his father or to make up for being better than his father financially, but neither of these interpretations seemed to have any impact on his actual behavior. In fact, after hearing me give a presentation on sexual addiction, his analyst had suggested that he contact me. At the end of our session, the salesman made a big issue of where I was to send the bill. He did not want me to have his home phone number or address because I might tell his wife the nature of his problem. I was to call him only at his office and write him only at a post office box. Having a post office box is one of the ways that sex and love addicts keep their secrecy.

A love addict that I treated conducted a six-year series of extramarital affairs right under her husband's nose but with complete secrecy. The couple had tried "swinging" with another couple, but her husband had been turned off by the sexual escapade. Therefore, my client proceeded to go "out with the girls" (a cover for acting out sexually) on the weekends right in front of her husband and with his approval. He rationalized that he was "being supportive and liberal." Despite sexually transmited diseases and back problems due to her acting out, both she and her husband kept their heads in the sand like ostriches, and maintained a pact of silence and secrecy. Even in recovery, during which she was told that "honesty is the key to sobriety," she continued to want to keep secrets.

Secrecy, of course, heightens the excitement as well as the intrigue, and therefore improves the high or kick of the romantic or sexual encounter. For instance, a sexual fix can double the power of a big business deal or sports success, and the secrecy can be the "icing on the cake." Babe Ruth was infamous for being a "womanizer," but the press and public conspired with him to keep his excesses secret and revered him as macho.

Addicts are skillful at getting other people to participate in the cover-up. Often, spouses and family members are embarrassed about the out-of-control sexual behavior and are only too willing to make excuses and invent lies in order to keep the family secret. Incest perpetrators and pedophiles often threaten and intimidate their young victims in order to get them to maintain the code of silence. One love addict patient of mine manipulated me into conspiring with her to keep her family uninformed and uninvolved in her treatment, using the excuse of patient-therapist "privilege" and confidentiality. Actually, she was ensuring that they would not intrude on her dependency on me, since they were quite concerned about her overdependency on therapy and her lack of other social outlets or activities. As I was uninformed about love addiction at the time and had diagnosed her as a borderline personality, nurturing seemed to be the treatment of choice. Supportive, nonconfrontive therapy was my approach. However, she did not improve. I began to work more aggressively on her family issues. After trips to visit each parent were unfruitful in terms of identifying further issues on which to work, I began to suspect that the real problem was her dependency on me. Shortly after she started to attend S.L.A.A., her sponsor recommended that she terminate therapy, which she did.

Another love-dependent patient used her 15 years of analytic therapy to avoid dealing with her love addiction. She constantly would bring up unresolved issues with her parents rather than working on her need to get affirmation from other people. She stubbornly clung to the hope that some day, somehow, things would change and her parents would love her the way that she wanted and needed. She also constantly tried to manipulate me into giving her "fixes" of good feelings, like an approving nod or smile of acknowledgment. She kept her underlying problem a secret, and to others appeared only a bit needy and insecure. Her sex and love addiction thus was hidden beneath her people-pleasing exterior.

The cost of all this lying and secrecy is high for the addict, even though on the surface it appears to work and to add to the excitement of living a double life. The price of all this dishonesty is self-esteem. In their hearts, addicts know that they are not being truthful with themselves or with anyone else. Even though they act as if they believed their own lies, they feel phony inside. Even people who come into an addiction with fairly solid feelings of self-worth cannot survive the daily erosion caused by all the dishonesty. By the time most addicts ask for help, their sense of self-worth has been almost completely destroyed.

PERSONALITY CHANGE

A final area of commonality among addicted people is that of personality change. A majority of families of addicts identify and complain about this aspect of the addiction the most. They frequently describe it as a "split personality" or "Dr. Jekyll and Mr. Hyde." They say things like, "When he is sober, he is the nicest guy in the world, and when he is drinking, he is a complete bastard." For sex and love addicts, this same sort of transformation occurs, but often it is subtle or unidentified because of the secrecy involved in the sex and love addict's world.

For years people have been searching for the "addictive personality" without success. Researchers and professionals have operated under the assumption that a certain type of personality is drawn to addictions. However, research and clinical experience have failed to find it. In fact, those who know or work with addicts know that there are all sorts of personalities among recovering people. There are passive people and aggressive people. There are narcissistic as well as unselfish people. There are overly controlled as well as overly impulsive people. Addicts may be either sensitive or insensitive, and caring or cold. In other words, addicts have all types of personality. In essence, then, the personality does not cause the addiction.

On the other hand, an addiction has a profound effect on the person who suffers from it. In fact, what most people consider the addictive personality is the result of the addictive process, not the cause. What people are identifying would more appropriately be called the "addict personality." As we become more familiar with addictive disorders, we are better able to see the similarities between drug addicts and alcoholics, between heroin addicts and smokers, between sex and love addicts and food addicts, and between overworkers and the overly religious. "Fanatics," "drunks," "perverts," and "junkies"—the pejorative nicknames for some of these addicts—all have some personality traits in common.

The powerful reinforcement of the sexual, romantic, chemical, food, or work fix creates the belief in a quick resolution to uncomfortable experiences. The high will also make good times better and uneventful times interesting. The seeds for the "instant gratification syndrome" have been planted if they did not already exist in the person. Eventually, a personality develops that expects quick, predictable fixes. In some ways, the addict's personality has regressed to the infantile, demanding stages of childhood. In fact, the program of S.L.A.A. recovery refers to this personality as "His (or Her) Majesty the

Baby." Addicts point out this "character defect" to one another with sayings like "You want what you want when you want it."

The narcissistic addict personality is characterized by self-centeredness, grandiosity, impulsivity, and low tolerance for frustration. The addict hates to hear the word "no," much like the small infant who expects to receive instant gratification. Often, addicts become enraged and unreasonably demanding when they do not get their way. They can be aggressive, domineering, manipulative, obnoxious, egotistical, insensitive, irritable, rigid, judgmental, and passive/aggressive; just the sort of person you would love to spend time with! Actually, the addict personality serves another important function for the addict. It keeps people from getting too close, so they cannot really tell what the addict is like or up to.

Sex and love addicts develop the same sort of childish, demanding, self-centered personality. Some can be very grandiose, like the sex addict in Florida who was chairman of the state's Pornography Commission by day and visited prostitutes and pornographic book stores by night, or the school-bus driver who, after he was finally caught for giving children drugs, was also discovered to be involved in pedophilia. He participated in about six months' worth of outpatient counseling and came to think of himself as a safe person. He wanted to find some other form of work with children. With a male authority figure, he was passive, superficially compliant, and cooperative. Underneath (and with children), he was narcissistic, demanding, manipulative, and highly unsafe. When confronted with his two personalities, he exhibited a great deal of denial. He felt like the victim rather than the victimizer; the latter is what he really was with the children. He complained about his own victimization, and used it as an excuse to justify his behavior rather than a motivation to get better. He himself was unaware of the shift in his personality from victim to aggressor. In a good recovery process, this is one of the areas in which the addict learns about him- or herself.

Another example of this personality change, or the two sides of the addict personality, comes from an alcoholic nun with whom I worked. She presented herself to the world as asexual. She wore clothing that was modest and not at all revealing (her order no longer wore habits). She did not make sexual references in her speech, and seemed embarrassed when sex was the subject of conversation. She complained about men "coming on" to her and feeling unable to cope with this other than by running away. On the other hand, she had a secret sexual life that included periods of compulsive masturbation, affairs with men, and romantic and sexual encounters with other religious women in her community. These secrets were told only to me and her confessor. To the rest of the world, this addict appeared unselfish, controlled, modest, and able to tolerate frustration, but inside, there was a person who was impulsive, self-centered, judgmental, and demanding, and who used alcohol and sex to numb herself or as a reward for working hard.

For some families and friends of sex and love addicts, the transformation of their loved one is rather obvious. A wife told me that her husband had been a warm, tender, kind, and loving man when they were married five years earlier. As he sank deeper into his sex and love addiction, however, he became more withdrawn, irritable, demanding, self-centered and, finally, verbally and physically abusive to her and to their children. His decision making and judgment became worse and more impulsive as he became more irrational and desperate. Other transformations are less obvious but just as compelling. For instance, there is the business man who prides himself as a good husband and father but finds increasingly more excuses to pull away from them and frequent the prostitutes that he feels will fill his sexual needs. As he has to make up more lies and excuses, he becomes more distant, critical, and touchy. His wife and children blame themselves because he tells them that they are bothering him and that he "needs his space." They have no idea what is going on in the other half of his life. He lives in fear that he will be arrested or that somehow his secret will come out and destroy his family's relationships with him. On one level, his family knows that something is going wrong, but they assume that it is their fault because the husband cannot tell them the truth about his own personality change and his addiction.

GETTING IT ALL TOGETHER: DIAGNOSTIC CRITERIA

Now that we have reviewed the various aspects of sex and love addiction, it is time to try to put it all together into a picture that makes sense. Being able to see the big picture is what makes it possible for us to fully comprehend addiction. When we only see bits and pieces, it is possible to overlook the obvious. For most addictions, this is what happens. The person and the people around him or her are involved in so much denial and defensiveness that they do not see the reality of the addictive process even when it is before their very eyes. Lots of factors contribute to this ignorance, such as shame, lack of education or resources, and other addictions. Sex and love addicts make a great effort to cover up the existence and effects of their obsessions and compulsions, which make identification and treatment all the more difficult. Hopefully, as we become more knowledgeable about addictions in general and this addiction in particular, we will be able to spot the problem in ourselves and in others, and to get help for those who suffer.

We cannot help a sex and love addict if we do not have a proper concept of addiction. An addiction is a combination of all the aspects that we have just reviewed. That is, the big picture of what is involved in having an addiction includes a high, tolerance, dependence, craving, withdrawal, obsession, compulsion, secrecy, and personality change. These nine elements give a broad view of what to look for when trying to decide if an addiction is present. The person does not have to have all nine elements, but if they have two or three, you ought to suspect that you are looking at only the tip of the iceberg. Remember, most addictions are hidden. Even when they are visible, like overeating, we tend to give a person the "benefit of the doubt." We need to be less generous and more suspicious that if we see some elements, more are really there. Addicts rarely ask for help. Most need to be pushed into treatment by someone who can see the forest for the trees. Addicts will be happy to focus on the trees because they tend to have lots of excuses or plans for remediation. Changes in small aspects of the addiction will not bring about the big change that is needed.

Sex and love addicts usually hide the truth, the big picture, especially early in treatment and recovery. I worked with a priest who was referred because a friend of a parishoner had gone to another priest and told him that my client had kissed him after a counseling session. When the priest came to see me, he was still in a moderate state of denial, and failed to tell the "whole truth." He did not consider this lying, he just felt too embarassed to reveal the extent of his addiction. He admitted to having started hugging parishoners during the movement in the 1970s that encouraged more openness and involvement with laity. This was contrary to his seminary training, which had emphasized no physical contact between clergy and parishoners, and had even encouraged "custody of the eyes" to avoid visual stimulation. After a few sessions, he admitted to a number of encounters with young men who had sought his counsel, in which he had even gone so far as to invite them in to talk. He also acknowledged a problem with compulsive masturbation that had begun in his 20s, had disappeared for about 30 years, and had come back in the past 10 years or so. About six months later he added to his story (in a written inventory, because he was too ashamed to talk about it) that he was involved in mutual masturbation and visiting pornographic movie theaters. It is not uncommon for the truth to take months and even years to come out fully. Attendence at Twelve Step programs like Sex and Love Addicts Anonymous helps open addicts up through exposure to others sharing the truth on a regular basis.

Another example of how difficult it is for some addicts to tell the truth occurred to me about a year ago. A client was referred because another treatment program had failed for him. He had had 18 months of intensive therapy, and had worked on issues of depression, poor self-esteem, and family problems. He had been born with a cleft palate, and had suffered from teasing and rejection by his peers. He had been initially referred for inappropriate touching of young boys but had managed to keep the majority of his addiction a secret from his therapist and other members of his treatment team. In a meeting with one of his religious superiors, the broader question of pedophilia was raised, and he admitted that he had been holding back the truth. His therapist felt his own trust to have been irreparably damaged, and he referred the client to me. When this man came to see me, he allegedly told me the whole story. However, after he began attending some S.L.A.A. meetings, he said he felt the need to be completely honest with me, and revealed some additional information. Part of his treatment was to make up a list of all the people with whom he was sexually involved, and we went over each experience in detail. Again, after about six months, "true confessions" occurred again, and more of his story was revealed. The addict justified withholding information by telling himself he would be hurt if other people found out the truth. What he failed to see was that his withholding style had already given others the message that he was not being completely open and honest. Despite hearing in his own religious training that "the truth shall make you free," he was afraid that people would discover the extent of his sex and love addiction and somehow punish him for it.

In terms of deciding if someone has an addiction based on a review of these nine elements—the high, tolerance, dependence, craving, withdrawal, obsession, compulsion, secrecy, and personality change—it needs to be remembered that each individual's addiction will vary in terms of extent and severity. Some people develop addictive disorders at a young age, and have all or most of the elements as teenagers. Others show a more gradual development process. Some addicts have ups and downs, with periods of activity and periods of abstinence. Some do not develop their problem until later in life. Just like other illnesses, such as diabetes, addictions show themselves at various ages and with differing degrees of severity. Usually, the sooner they are caught the better the prognosis, except where there is a high level of denial. Unfortunately, because we do not see the big picture, oftentimes early warning signs are overlooked.

For instance, when I spoke with the best friend of the priest who eventually was confronted with hugging and kissing the young males he counseled, his friend acknowledged his awareness of this man's infatuation with young men. He had noticed that his friend would pay unusual attention to young men on television and that he would stare at them when they were out shopping. He never thought of this as only the tip of the iceberg, thus ignoring the indicators of potential trouble. He could have said something to his friend or to his religious superiors. Instead, he did what he probably thought was the Christian thing to do, in a sense, "turning the other cheek." What addicts need is for all of us to be more aware of the various elements of addictive diseases and to ask questions when we see potential danger signs. Recovering people are extremely helpful in being able to identify the early signs that uneducated people might miss.

In fact, the client I discussed who had kept his addiction a secret during 18 months of therapy knows of other people who may also be suffering but is unwilling to speak up. Addicts in general have an unspoken code of not "ratting" on anyone else. They feel a great loyalty to other addicts, and fail to see how they are helping to maintain their fellow addicts' suffering by keeping the code of silence. This particular client knew of other addicts because he had met them in pornographic book stores and X-rated movie theaters. He had also observed the romantic looks and touches that these people had directed toward others. He felt that talking to these people about what he had observed or sharing his concerns with other people who cared about them would victimize the addicts. He could not yet get himself out of the role of victim. He did not yet see that helping others is a healthy role as neither victim or victimizer (his role with children in his addiction). As addicts progress in their recovery, they become more willing and able to help others. In fact, the Twelfth and last step in their program is: "Having had a spiritual awakening as a result of these steps, we tr[y] to carry the message to sex and love addicts." All of us can and need to "carry the message."

Since love and sex addictions are relatively new concepts, there are no formal diagnostic criteria, although this is an area that is being rapidly developed by professionals and recovering people in the field. The revised *DSM-III* (Diagnostic and Statistical Manual of the American Psychiatric Association, third edition) makes a brief and somewhat confusing reference to sexual addiction. The entry is located in the Sexual Disorders section, after the list of paraphilias mentioned before, in a subheading titled "Sexual Disorder Not Otherwise Specified," between "marked feelings of inadequacy" about body parts and "persistent and marked distress about one's sexual orientation." The entry reads: "Distress about a pattern of repeated sexual conquests or other forms of nonparaphilic sexual addiction, involving a succession of people who exist only as things to be used." Love addiction is not listed anywhere. Certainly this categorization gives us little to go on, although I am also aware that there is an effort underway to get more detailed and accurate diagnostic criteria for the next edition of the diagnostic manual.

The Institute for Behavioral Medicine in Golden Valley, Minnesota, has developed a set of diagnostic criteria for sexual addiction. From the institute's experience, a person ought to have five or more of the following criteria:

1. Sexual obsession and fantasy as a primary coping strategy.
2. Sexual behavior as a central organizing principle of daily life.
3. Inordinate amounts of time spent in obtaining sex, being sexual, or recovering from sexual experience.
4. Amount, extent, or duration of sexual behavior often in excess of what the person had intended.
5. Severe mood shifts involving sexual acting out.
6. Escalating pattern of increasing amounts of sexual experience because the current level of activity is no longer sufficient (exemplified by more of current sexual behavior, addition of new sexual behavior, or initiation of new, high-risk, illicit, or immoral behavior).
7. Persistent pursuit of self-destructive or high-risk sexual desire.
8. Persistent desire or efforts to limit sexual behavior.
9. Inability to stop behavior despite adverse consequences.
10. Pattern of out-of-control (compulsive) sexual behavior for two years.
11. Pattern of alternating excessive control and out-of-control behavior over five years.

12. Severe consequences due to sexual behavior.
13. Presence of a clear hierarchy of sexual acting-out behaviors.
14. Important social, occupational, or recreational activities sacrificed or reduced because of sexual behavior.
15. Presence of any three of the following associated conditions:
    —Extreme sexual shame,
    —Depression,
    —Other addictions,
    —Formerly or currently a victim of sexual abuse,
    —Formerly or currently a victim of emotional or physical abuse,
    —Secret or "double" life due to sexual behavior,
    —Sexualizing of nurturing,
    —Few or no nonsexual relationships,
    —Suicidal ideation or attempt,
    —Presence of sex-negative behavior,
    —Excessive reliance on denial,
    —Presence of co-dependent personality disorder.

Although organized in a different order than the nine elements of addiction presented earlier, there is a great deal of agreement and overlap in terms of what identifies a sexually addicted person. Again, the focus is solely on sex and does not include love addiction. There is a concurrence that powerlessness and loss of control (items 3–4, 6–12) the high (item 6), tolerance (item 6), dependence (items 2, 8, 9), obsession (item 1), compulsion (items 3–4, 6–11), secrecy (item 15), and personality change (items 5, 14, 15) all are criteria for sexual addiction. The centrality of sexuality in the addict's life and the need for the problem to have existed for at least two, and in some cases five, years also match the picture presented here.

It is obvious that we are in the process of more clearly and accurately grasping the "big picture" of any addiction, and specifically sex and love addiction. Sex and love addictions are both simple and complicated, as is the recovery process. In some ways, it simply takes a commitment to be honest and to want to change, but there are so many pitfalls and distortions in the addict's thinking, feeling, and behavior, that making it work takes a great deal of effort, support, and direction by those who understand the problem.

3

The Disease Concept of Addictions

COMPETING THEORIES OF ADDICTION

Most Americans view alcoholism as a disease. This has not always been the case and, in fact, many experts in the field of alcoholism see this change as a major improvement in terms of our attitude toward and treatment of alcoholics. There are people who object to the concept of alcoholism as a disease. They claim that the label is at best misleading, and at worst actually destructive, and an impediment to helping people get better. This is not the place for a full-fledged review of the argument, but it seems worthwhile to at least review some of the issues because it can help addicts and those who work with and care about them to have some conceptualization about what an addiction is.

The four major schools of thought about addiction are the self-medication hypothesis, the stress reduction theory, the cognitive/behavioral thesis, and the disease model. Simply put, the self-medication hypothesis states that addicts have an underlying psychological, emotional, or mental disorder that they are treating themselves with a medication that they have discovered on their own. Their underlying problems, then, are seen as the cause as well as the driving force behind the active addiction. To treat an addiction, a professional would have to help the person identify and fix the underlying problems. Once the roots of the addiction have been worked on, the addictive behavior will no longer be needed by the addict and will be discarded.

The stress reduction theory of addiction postulates that the addict uses addiction as a way of coping with the stress in his or her life. Since all of us experience stress, we have all found coping mechanisms that are more or less successful. A person's use of addiction is a poor and rather dysfunctional method of coping, and needs to be replaced with more adequate and appropriate means of coping with stress. When this new learning has been accomplished, the addict will have no more need for the addiction.

The cognitive/behavioral approach views addictions as overlearned responses. Actually, behavioral therapists have been traditionally unconcerned with the origin of the behavior, and instead have focused on changing dysfunctional behavior. The social learning school believes that behaviors are learned. Cognitive therapists believe that our thought processes direct our emotional and behavioral states. The combination of cognitive and behavioral treatment of addictions examines the thinking and subsequent emotional responses that create compulsive, overlearned behavioral reactions. They then set up new modes of thinking that are associated with new behaviors so that addictive behaviors will not be reinforced.

The disease model looks at addiction as an illness. There is a biological/medical basis to this view in that biochemistry and genetics are seen as underlying causes of addictions. The organism is considered sick and out of homeostasis. There is an etiology, a set of symptoms, a predictable course, a treatment, and a response to that treatment which can be specified for any disease, including the disease of addiction.

These four theories have competed with each other in terms of being taken as the accepted approach to the understanding and treatment of addictions. Twelve Step recovery programs like Alcoholics Anonymous, and the medical profession in general, have adopted the disease model and have had a great influence on the views of the general public, which has come to support the disease model at least for alcoholism and drug dependencies. Social scientists have opted for the stress reduction theory. Psychoanalytically trained professionals are inclined to adhere to the self-medication hypothesis. Many psychologists hold to the cognitive/behavioral thesis, and this theoretical approach has the best research base for its theory.

I think that we can learn from all the views, and that we do not yet have a comprehensive theory of addictions. My approach, and the one in which I was trained, is the disease model, which is what I will present next.

THE DISEASE MODEL OF ADDICTION

As indicated above, the disease approach stipulates that something can be considered a disease if we can identify and define the following categories:

1. Symptoms
2. Etiology
3. Course/Progression

4. Treatment

5. Response

Before we apply this paradigm to the disease of sex and love addiction, I will show how it would apply to more generally accepted diseases.

We can diagnose people as suffering from the common cold when they have the appropriate cluster of symptoms. For instance, we look for a fever, congestion, loss of energy and enthusiasm, and perhaps achy muscles, a cough, a sore throat, or even an ear ache. Sufferers do not have to have all the symptoms to warrant the diagnosis, but they need to have more than just a fever or a sore throat. With the common cold, the etiology is not known, although we do know that the person must have caught the infection from someone in the immediate environment. The treatment includes rest, drinking lots of fluids, and possibly taking some aspirin to reduce the fever, aches, and pains. The prognosis is positive, and complete recovery is expected if the proper treatment regimen is followed. If the cold is not treated properly, there is the possibility of more serious complications.

A chronic, progressive, potentially fatal illness like diabetes makes even a better comparison. With an illness like diabetes, we again can diagnose the disease based on determining whether the individual has the proper cluster of symptoms. He or she may start out with some symptoms that do not make us immediately jump to the conclusion of diabetes, such as drinking an unusual amount of water or having a strong urge to eat sugary foods. However, when the time comes that we do suspect that the person may be suffering from a chronic illness that may be debilitating and life-threatening, we do not make an effort to hide the problem because of embarrassment. The individual diabetic may experience some denial and may use other defenses to rationalize or minimize the problem, but shame and guilt are not as strong a dynamic as they are in addictive diseases.

The etiology or cause of the diabetes may differ with different people. Some people have the disease in their families and, therefore, are genetically vulnerable. This may be a primary cause in juvenile diabetes. Other people develop the disease in the middle of their lives, and it may be due to a combination of genetic and environmental factors. Still others get diabetes as a consequence of another disease process like alcoholism, so their diabetes is considered secondary. Once they have diabetes, they need to attend to both diseases, because simply treating their alcoholism will not rid them of diabetes. It is fair to say that the cause of diabetes is not known, but we do know that genetics and environment both can play a part in varying degrees depending on the individual circumstances.

We know that diabetes progresses, especially if it is left untreated. The consequences of neglect become increasingly severe with time, and include blindless and even death. Thus, it is fair to say that the course of the disease is downward, although the rate of decline varies a great deal and is determined by a wide variety of variables, including the patient's physical and mental state, motivation, level of stress and social supports, understanding of the problem and the treatment, and belief system. Some people may get the illness at a very young age, and their progress may go rapidly downhill. Other people have improvements and relapses; while still others have diabetes yet are able to manage the illness fairly well most or all their lives.

The treatment of the illness varies as well because of the wide variety of other variables involved, such as the severity of the illness, cooperation of the patient and his or her family, supports available in the local community, and other complicating stresses or diseases that the person may have. Usually, the initial elements of treatment are careful regimens of diet, exercise, and stress reduction. If this is not effective or if the illness progresses further, it may be necessary to introduce medication. The individual treatment plan follows generally accepted guidelines but is also tailored to the person and his or her lifestyle and circumstance. The doctor, family, or friends are not morally outraged if there is a relapse or a problem of some sort, even if the sick person is solely responsible for the slip. Instead, new treatments are applied or the old treatment plan is reinforced.

The prognosis for the illness is not one of cure and an end to worries. However, the outlook is generally considered good despite all the possible complications and potentially disabling, and even fatal, outcomes. Diabetes is accepted as an illness that anyone can get and that is both treatable and manageable, although slips and even relapses are both possible and likely. The patient can contribute greatly to the recovery process, or can worsen the illness by giving in to cravings for sugar, and by not changing his or her lifestyle to accommodate the potential dangers of the illness. Is addiction very different?

Diabetes is an accepted medical illness. Let us now look at a mental disorder and see if it will fit the disease model. Depression is experienced by an estimated 10 percent of our population in their lifetimes. Depressions generally fall into one of two classifications: major affective disorders and dysthymic disorders (formerly depressive neurosis). The first disorder is considered to be primarily biologically based and a chronic illness; the second is caused mainly by environmental factors, and is not necessarily recurrent. The former is at times referred to as endogenous depression (that is, due to internal factors), and the latter is called exogenous (due to external factors).

While dysthymia is more serious than the common cold, it is not considered chronic, progressive, or potentially fatal. It is more serious than "having the blues," but it is not as serious as a major depression. Still, the disease model applies. There is a clearly definable cluster of symptoms that allows us to say whether a person has the illness. Dysthymic disorder can be differentiated from "feeling down" or a chronic mood disorder. Symptoms include disturbances of eating, sleeping, concentration, energy level, and self-worth, along with feelings of hopelessness. The disorder needs to be present in adults for more than two years and to have not remitted for more than two months. The cause or etiology is related to environmental factors such as the loss of a spouse or job. The course of the illness without any form of treatment is generally one of gradually increasing severity. If it spontaneously remits in six to nine months, it is not considered to be dysthymia. The prognosis improves with treatment. Antidepressant medication is considered helpful, as is psychotherapy. The combination of the two appears to work best.

Major depression, on the other hand, is considered a chronic, progressive, and potentially fatal disease. The symptom cluster is similar to dysthymia but is more severe. There are significant problems with eating, sleep, energy, and concentration. These can go in either direction; in other words, inability to sleep or to get out of bed, no appetite or wanting to eat everything in sight. The person also experiences a profound sense of helplessness, hopelessness, and worthlessness. Suicide is a serious and common reaction to a major depressive episode. As compared to dysthymia, there also seem to be much stronger genetic and biological influences. In terms of etiology, there often are no obvious external factors but there usually is a family history of depression or alcoholism.

The course of the illness without some form of intervention is usually downhill. With major depression, there can be a rapid decline or a pattern of ups and downs, although the overall picture is more down than up. Some people with this disease have extreme mood swings and are considered to be manic/depressive, although even with this classification, the person does not necessarily experience both polarities of mania and depression. There are well-established treatment regimens for major depression. Medication usually works well with this type of disease, but as with dysthymia, the combination of drug therapy and psychotherapy works best. The prognosis for the illness is positive if the treatment plan is followed. Again, patients can improve their prognosis by being motivated, cooperative, honest, and open to making the necessary changes in their lifestyle and coping strategies. Slips and relapses are disappointing but are no cause for moral outrage or harsh, judgmental criticism. The recovery program is reexamined and revised as needed. Recovery is considered to be maintainance of a chronic condition so that the person's life can be normal in other respects.

It should be obvious at this point that there are many parallels between addiction and chronic illnesses like diabetes and depression. Nonetheless, some people strongly disagree with the disease model. The major objection seems to be that calling something a disease somehow takes away the ill individual's responsibility. We are "victims" of diseases, which place us in a powerless, helpless role. In fact, proponents of the disease model agree with this perception. The First Step of the Twelve Steps program begins, "We are powerless over [fill in the appropriate addiction]." The role of willpower is a big point of contention here. If you overdo food, love, alcohol, or sex, are you necessarily doing this against your own will? People do not choose to get diabetes or major depressions, but they do appear to volunteer for their addictions. Where is the addict's willpower? Why can't he or she choose to stop eating, loving, drinking, or having sex? Advocates of other models of addiction say that the person can stop. He or she has only to relearn new cognition strategies and behaviors, cope better with stress, or analyze the need for self-medication in order to gain control of the addictive behavior.

Professionals and recovering people who adhere to the disease model do not believe the addict can ever be in control. In fact, the idea that the addict might indeed see him-, or herself as in control scares them, as they have seen many people slip or relapse after "taking back control." After three months of abstinence, an alcoholic might say to himself:

Maybe I can be a social drinker now. Maybe those treatment people don't know what they are talking about or maybe they misdiagnosed me and I am not really an alcoholic. After all, I have been sober for three whole months. My tolerance is probably down now and I could have just one beer while I watch the football game.

This scenario is described time and again in Alcoholics Anonymous meetings as people recount the painful, up-and-down progress of accepting their disease.

Part of the initial phase of recovery in most Twelve Step programs emphasizes "surrender." Ending denial and admitting to a lack of control, manageability, and sanity are all part of the process of "surrender and conversion." The use of these terms obviously offends some people, and they misjudge participants in Twelve Step programs as overly dependent on the group, brainwashed, or acting like religious fanatics. A drug addict who recognizes that he cannot use cocaine "socially" because of the damaging effects it has had on his family, friends, work, and health, may nonetheless feel the urge to go against the advice of other people in the recovery fellowship and drink a beer. As he watches football on television, he hears the constant suggestion that "Bud Light" will make you as happy as the actors in the commercial. He tries a beer; and nothing terrible happens. He starts to change his thinking, and goes against the advice of the program that any mood-altering chemical is unsafe for an addict. He begins drinking socially with no severe pattern of such abuse as he had had with cocaine. He then decides that some marijuana might not be so bad either, so he starts to smoke pot while continuing to stay away from cocaine. By this point, he cannot tolerate going to meetings any more because he feels hypocritical and because group members are telling him that he must be drug- and alcohol-free. Therefore, he begins a less rapid and less obvious pattern of chemical dependency. Those who used the disease model would say that the addict had not "surrendered," and that his disease is continuing to progress as he keeps himself "in the driver's seat." Other approaches would view the situation differently, although almost all would agree that any drug or alcohol use is dangerous. The issues of freedom, control, and responsibility seem to be where different theorists part company.

Those who advocate the disease model do not, however, allow the addict to avoid responsibility for the illness. Just as a diabetic or depressive needs to take charge of his or her life in order to be normal, so too does the addict have to take charge of his or her recovery. "Taking charge" of recovery is a somewhat paradoxical concept, however, because it means relinquishing control and following the advice of recovering people who have proven that they can stay clean and sober. People who misunderstand the Twelve Step recovery program confuse a temporary surrender of direction with a permanent adoption of a passive, dependent role. Newly recovered people have to do numerous things while in a recovery program that require being responsible for themselves. For example, they are encouraged to go to daily meetings and to contact their sponsors on a daily basis. Readings and meditations are also suggested. The key element is that the recovering person "follow direction" and not make independent decisions without consulting someone who would have a better idea of how the choice may impact on his or her newly established sobriety.

This state of dependency does not last forever, but it is considered essential in early recovery. Part of the reasoning for this is that the addicted person's thought processes will have been distorted by the addiction. The habits of dishonesty, denial, rationalization, minimization, and projection will have become ingrained in the addicts' thinking patterns so they are likely to still think in the same way for some time (months, or even a year or two) until they have developed more healthy thought processes. Until that time, they are encouraged to follow the advice and direction of more experienced recovering people. This is seen as a positive form of dependency.

The ultimate goal, of course, is not to create rigid, mindless, dependent, and helpless robots who cannot function with any sort of autonomy, even though this seems to be the view of the critics of Twelve Step programs. Rather, the goal is to become free from dependencies of any kind. As recovery progresses, people are expected to take on increasing numbers of responsibilities in the Twelve Step program. For example, newly sober people are encouraged to take on "commitments" like making the coffee, setting up the chairs, cleaning the ash trays, or straightening out the room after the meeting is over. After the first few months, they can take on more meaningful jobs like chairing the meetings. As their sobriety grows, so do the opportunities to be responsible. Duties like speaking at meetings, being a sponsor, being a representative to the local intergroup, or being an officer for a meeting all are taken on by addicts as they grow in their recovery. In fact, the whole self-help group movement is completely voluntary, and runs better than our major corporations or institutions. Fellowships like Alcoholics Anonymous, which is international in scope, and Sex and Love Addicts Anonymous are entirely self-supporting. The entire operation is testimony to the responsibility and independence of recovering people. Meetings run like clockwork; they are rarely if ever cancelled, and occur every week as scheduled. Thus, the perception that the initial surrender leads to a simple transfer of dependencies from the addiction to the recovery group is a gross distortion and is highly uninformed.

Another aspect of the criticism of the disease model is the idea that these programs encourage addicts to forget about the past or to absolve themselves of any responsibility for it. While it is true that there is a great emphasis on living "one day at a time," this does not mean that the past is wiped clean. The "day by day" philosophy is an essential element in helping the newly recovering person cope with cravings and withdrawal. In fact, once the person has "worked" the first three steps, which may take as much as a year, there is a great deal of emphasis on self-examination and reviewing the past. Steps Four, Five, Six, and Seven have to do with making a personal inventory and sharing it, and with identifying "character defects" and accepting them. The Eighth and Ninth steps involve making a list of persons that the addict has harmed and "making amends" where appropriate. The Tenth and Eleventh steps stress daily inventories, admitting to wrongdoing, and prayer and meditation. The last step involves "carrying the message." Psychotherapy with the addict may not focus on the past initially, but the two-tiered recovery program presented later in this book makes extensive use of the addict's childhood (chapter 5) and addiction (chapter 4) to help the addicted person become less vulnerable to relapse.

Diabetics and people who suffer from major depression need to examine themselves as individuals to determine how to maintain their equilibrium. The initial emphasis is on how to manage the illness; in other words, the diabetic needs to learn to keep his or her blood sugar in a certain range, and the person with depression needs to learn to modulate his or her mood. As they become better at the control of their primary symptoms, these people can step back and take a broader look at themselves and at what might make them vulnerable to a relapse. The recovering addict needs to do the same thing with his or her illness: first get the behavior under control, and then develop a long-term strategy for preventing relapse. In order to see how this fits for the sex and love addict, we need to first review how this addiction can be viewed as a disease.

THE DISEASE OF SEX AND LOVE ADDICTION

As with the other illnesses that we have briefly reviewed, sex and love addiction needs to be seen as having a cluster of symptoms that identify the afflicted person, ideas about the etiology or cause of the problem, a conception of the course or progression of the disease process, some form of treatment, and an indication of how the sex and love addict might respond.

At this point, these criteria should be fairly clear, but a brief review seems appropriate.

In the second chapter, I identified a large number of symptoms using the nine elements of addictions: the high, tolerance, dependence, craving, withdrawal, obsession, compulsion, secrecy, and personality change. In the sections on the definition of addiction and the diagnostic criteria, I also indicated that a sense of enslavement, loss of power and control, imbalance, centrality and inability to shift focus and priorities, chronicity, progression, and potential lethality are symptomatic of sex and love addictions. Each person will vary in terms of number and severity of symptoms, but the more symptoms the addict has, the worse the addiction has become.

In the more severe cases of love and sex addiction, most of these symptoms will be fairly evident if the addict is willing to be honest. When the addict is not willing to admit the problem, or in milder cases, more effort will be needed to root out the symptoms, but in most cases many signs will appear. For example, an alcoholic priest was referred to me for an evaluation because he was unable to successfully stop drinking, and there were allegations that he was compulsively gambling and having sexual contacts with young boys. He was in a massive state of denial despite observations by the other priests, rectory staff, and parishoners that he had alcohol on his breath, purchased lottery tickets, went to the racetrack, and entertained young boys in his room, despite a clear statement by his bishop that priests were not to have any boys in their rooms under any circumstances. He clearly had all the symptoms of a sex and love addiction, although some of them were hard to verify due to his lack of openness and honesty. He obviously was multiply addicted to the highs of alcohol, gambling, and the company of young boys. He had evidence of both tolerance and dependence; in other words, he continued to indulge even after receiving treatment and being confronted with his slips. He seemed to have severe cravings although he could not admit to this and his withdrawal was hard to define since he probably was still actively involved in all three addictions. He clearly was obsessed and compelled, since he could not stop despite receiving warnings and encouragement to get help. He was highly secretive, and had become withdrawn, rigid, and dogmatic. He appeared to others to be totally lacking in free will, to be a slave to his addictions, and to be powerless and out of control even when help was available. He lost his ability to function as a priest due to church insistence that he enter long-term treatment, and his life was completely out of his hands. He was so stuck, and his addictions were so important to him, that he gave up everything else that he had lived for or stood for in his life rather than relinquish his attachment to alcohol, gambling and sex. He felt totally victimized, and projected blame onto the church authorities who wanted only to get help for him and stop his self-destruction and his victimization of others.

A milder case of sex and love addiction was observed in a woman who began acting out after she became separated from her husband. She had always had a flair for the dramatic and been somewhat narcissistic, so she managed to disguise her addiction for a period of time. However, she began to give out clues in terms of her philosophy about dating. She said that her policy about having sex with someone on the first date was: If she did not like him, she would sleep with him to find out what he was like in bed because she knew she would never see him again; and if she did like him, she would go to bed with him on the first date "to get it out of the way." In either case, she found a way to rationalize having sex, and her dating pattern involved multiple partners weekly.

She clearly liked the high, and it showed in her face when she spoke about men. She had a great tolerance for many partners and probably for various sexual activities. She was highly dependent on having relationships, and only worked to fill the time between dates. She had a voracious appetite and craving for sex and relationships both, and was quite naive and romantic at the same time. She became extremely depressed in between encounters or relationships, which was indicative of withdrawal. She was obsessed—men were all she talked about. She covered her secrecy with a pseudo-honesty that did not reveal the whole story. She became increasingly more self-centered, isolated, grandiose, and demanding as her illness progressed. She was a slave to love, and lost the power to say "no." Her life was completely out of balance and control; all she cared about was finding a "Mr. Goodbar" who would fix everything. Meanwhile, she was losing her friends, and work was unimportant to her. Her emotional life was a rollercoaster. Her thoughts revolved around sex and love, and she was constantly putting her health in danger.

The etiology or cause of sex and love addictions like the ones described above is not yet clear. As with many other diseases like cancer, arthritis, and heart disease, we know that people who have addictions in their families have a greater likelihood of themselves becoming addicted. We also know that environment plays a large part in the development of personality, and most likely in the development of addictive diseases. Consequently, we can say that there is probably a genetic predisposition that is somehow triggered by our upbringing, life experience, and individual personality. There are no germs, viruses, genetic anomilies, biological imbalances (like being "over-sexed"), familial or environmental circumstances, or personality types that we can point to as the culprit or cause of any addiction, and of sex and love addiction in particular.

We do know, however, that a large number of sex and love addicts come from addicted families, and that most of them have suffered from verbal, physical, emotional, and/or sexual abuse, and neglect. This is a correlation, not a cause. In other words, we do not really know the cause of this or any other addiction. We do know that there are certain families and environments that have more than their share of addicted people, but these factors may serve more to activate or bring out the addiction rather than being its origin or source.

The progression or course of the disease, when left untreated, is highly variable. For some addicts, when the addiction takes hold there is a steady, downward trend, as with the tennis instructor mentioned earlier: His addiction began in his late teens, and by the time he had reached his 30s, his entire life had been affected. He was unable to work or to maintain any sort of normal social relationships. His family relations, although never good, deteriorated to the point where his father and brother could not have a conversation with him without becoming enraged. His mental abilities and physical health gradually deteriorated to the point where he had to be cared for by a former girlfriend. He was more afraid of living without sex than he was of becoming destitute and unable to live or work productively, and was on the verge of becoming a "street person" due to the gradual progression of his sex and love addiction.

Other people's addictions progress quite rapidly, such as the 17-year-old boy who had already been involved with compulsive masturbation (10 to 15 times per day), affairs (he would not date a girl who refused to have sex with him), pornography (magazines, books, and videotapes), voyeurism (on our dual diagnosis unit, he drilled a peep hole into a female's room), exhibitionism (he videotaped and rated his sexual encounters with his girlfriends), and obscene phone calls (he bragged that "lots of people talked back and loved it").

Similarly, a bus driver who came to me at his daughters' request described only minimal involvement with affairs and one incidence of "wife swapping" before he became incestuously involved with his oldest daughter. He stated that he was "sexually free" with his children, and that none of them were ashamed of their bodies. They were allowed to walk from the bathroom without their clothes on, and "it was never a problem." He blamed his first wife's leaving him for a woman as the cause of his sexual relationship with his daughter: "We became very close and I felt quite needy." His first daughter eventually took him to court, but he was given only probation after admitting guilt to a lesser charge. It was during his probation that he had sex with his second daughter. He claimed that "it" only happened once with each girl, but they remembered frequent encounters. Both the older girls requested that he get treatment when they discovered the second incidence during a family argument, saying they feared for their youngest sister who was just turning 13.

Sometimes there is a pattern of acting out followed by a period of abstinence. There may be days, weeks, or even years between "binges" of addictive behavior. One client reported 30 years of celibacy (although he may have been fantasizing without acting out). Another had a period of about 5 years between incidents of making obscene phone calls (although he masturbated during this period). A love addict described "years" between a period of homosexual affairs and a period of heterosexual affairs. Sex and love addicts often report binges with pornographic bookstores, prostitutes, sadomasochistic sex scenes, massage parlors, pornographic movies, or anonymous sex in public baths or bathrooms. Masturbation, going "on the make," cruising, affairs, and "soft" pornography tend to be more regular activities. Exhibitionism, voyeurism, indecent liberties (touching), and obscene phone calls often have irregular patterns. Incest, rape, and child molesting that are addictive and not sociopathic, impulsive, and/or opportunistic are usually more ritualistic, repetitive, and consistent. It is easy to get lost looking too closely at the particular sexual incidents and to fail to see the overall progression in terms of the general debilitation of the addict as a person.

Treatment is not required to determine that something is a disease, but part of the disease concept is that when an illness interferes with the homeostasis of the organism, treatment will enable the individual to regain his or her equilibrium. Some diseases, like the dreaded acquired immunodeficiency syndrome (AIDS), do not yet have treatment that will halt the progress of the disease. There are some treatments that will ease the effects or moderate the pain, but they will not change the course. AIDS progresses onward, even when detected, with no hope for remission, not to mention a cure. For other diseases, including most chronic illnesses, we have treatment that will either arrest the progress or provide a cure. Once the person has the disease in a state of remission through treatment, he or she can live a normal life within the confines of maintaining a check on the disease. This is also true of addictions, including sex and love addictions. With proper treatment, the sex and love addict can live a normal, full, and healthy life. In fact, through the recovery process, I have observed people live better than normal lives in terms of the quality of their physical health, mental clarity, emotional growth and serenity, family and social relationships, work, and spiritual life.

What is the treatment that makes this all possible? Involvement in a Twelve Step support group like Sex and Love Addicts Anonymous is essential for initial sobriety and for long-term maintainance of recovery. Psychotherapy is necessary for defenses like denial, for personality traits that interfere with the addict becoming a part of the recovery fellowship or increase the risk of relapse, for coping skills and interpersonal relationships that have been damaged, for family issues that remain current and drain energy or impede progress, and for enhancing self-esteem that will motivate long-term recovery. As with the use of medication in conjunction with psychotherapy in treating major depressions, the combination of self-help and psychotherapy produces the best results in managing addictions. Many alcoholics and drug addicts have strongly opposed involvement in psychotherapy as both unnecessary and potentially dangerous because it stirs up issues that some have used as excuses to drink or take drugs. Psychotherapists have also earned some of this distrust by their ignorant and prejudicial attitudes toward Alcoholics

Anonymous and Narcotics Anonymous (N.A.). I had a student come to me almost in a panic because one of her patients was involved in a Twelve Step program which had helped her out of a life of prostitution, and the student's field supervisor was insisting that this woman stop attending meetings because her "dependency" on A.A. groups was interfering with the resolution of problems in her marriage. More recently, due to progress by recovering ← people in understanding the place and value of psychotherapy, and by therapists in learning the worth and need for ongoing support groups for people with addictive diseases, there has developed a more cooperative and harmonious atmosphere between professionals and recovering fellowships.

Sex and love addicts seem to me to be more open and amenable to psychotherapeutic intervention than some other groups of addicts with whom I have worked. At this point, the reasons for this are not clear to me, but it appears to be a function of the damage done by the addiction, and possibly also of the family life prior to the addiction as well as the "culture" of the addiction. What I mean by culture is that many alcoholics and drug addicts have developed a hardened, streetwise exterior that devalues the importance or role of emotions in daily living. Even though both groups of addicts (both sex and love–addicted and chemically dependent) use and manipulate people to get their needs met, the pseudo-intimacy of sexual and romantic encounters does not appear to toughen sex and love addicts the way that life on the street and in the bars seems to affect alcoholics and drug addicts. There is a macho, "tough guy," mostly male ethic among those afflicted with dependency on drugs and drink that makes them less open to and available for psychological intervention. Outpatient groups for alcohol and drug addicts typically experience a rather high rate of turnover. In our outpatient groups for sex and love addicts there has been little turnover, except for people whom we asked to leave for various clinical reasons, such as unwillingness to follow treatment suggestions.

Sex and love addictions are probably more damaging to the addict than other addictions because of the secrecy and shame involved. Our sexuality is such an important and intimate part of us that when we lose control we feel like "bad" people. The self-esteem of any addict suffers from the constant promises and failures inherent in the addictive process. The sex and love addict probably suffers most because, unlike drugs, cigarettes, drink, gambling, work, spending, or even food, sex is a part of us, both physically and psychologically. When our loving and sexual feelings, thoughts, and instincts betray us, we believe it can only be because we are deeply flawed and worthless people. Why else would our body and mind betray us? Many addicts think that they are somehow crazy or perveted. Our culture judges addicts harshly, and considers sex and love addicts the "lowest of the low." Even in jails there is a hierarchy, and so-called sex perverts are on the bottom.

Family life has also severely damaged most sex and love addicts, although many of them do not realize this early in their recovery or in the initial phases

of treatment. Patrick Carnes's (1988) research with recovering addicts indicates that three-fourths of them identify themselves as victims of physical
abuse, over 80 percent report sexual abuse, and almost universally they see
themselves as having been emotionally abused. They often come from addicted or dysfunctional families that gave them a poor foundation for further
growth. Once an addiction takes hold, normal growth and development stop.
Thus, for some, their development was arrested in adolescence or earlier.
They may have developed elaborate cover-ups and pseudo-maturity, but inside they feel like little children.

The types of treatments that are useful in the recovery process include
individual, group, and family therapies, as well as psychoeducational and
bibliotherapies. I often get clients who will agree to come for individual
sessions but are quite resistant to Twelve Step meetings, group therapy, and
family treatment. Individual therapy is appropriate for initiating the change
process, but is insufficient by itself. Individual psychotherapy is useful for
removing characterological problems that interfere with recovery; identifying
other concurrent addictions; confronting defenses; reducing the shame of
talking about sex, sexuality, and love dependence; working on emotional
difficulties unrelated to addictions (like anxiety and depressive disorders)
but threatening to recovery; and evaluating the need for medical and psychiatric supports such as medication. Group therapy offers the opportunity
to learn how to open up through practice and role modeling, to get feedback
(or "cross talk") that is not a part of normal S.L.A.A. meetings, to develop
peer relationships and learn to support others in nonaddictive ways, to have
cathartic emotional experiences, and to improve the addict's ability to experience and understand nonsexual intimacy.

Family therapy often is not appropriate, nor would it be accepted, in the
initial stages of recovery. This is due to the usually intense issues between
couples and families. However, family therapy may be a necessary and even
essential part of treatment, especially if the normal treatments are not effective.
Most addicts hide their addictions from their families and are quite fearful
of having to deal with them honestly and openly. A love addict that I treat
has never told her young adult children about her addiction, despite the fact
that they live in the house with her and observe her going out to meetings,
going to couples therapy with her husband, and reading self-help books. She
is terrified of the shame and guilt she imagines she would feel if they knew
the truth about her. She imagines they have no idea what her problems could
be even though they were present during her period of "going out with the
girls," which occasionally would bring her home in the wee hours of the
morning.

Another client is a seminarian who had to cancel fairly elaborate plans for
his ordination after the seminary director received a report of his inappropriate and possibly homosexual behavior. His parents dutifully helped him
cancel the invitations that had been sent out but never asked about the details

of the problem, and he did not volunteer the information. He is deathly afraid of the shame he would feel if his parents knew he had a problem with compulsive masturbation and had had three affairs while in the seminary. However, he might discover them to be rather supportive if informed. Not all families respond to, or benefit from, family therapy, and some families have been quite damaging to the addict offspring. However, family therapy can be a chance to break through some of the defenses, denial, and secrecy, and to build some genuine support for the recovery process.

Psychoeducational therapy, often in the form of lectures, provides recovering addicts and others with information about addictions, the disease process, the recovery process, and normal problems associated with an addiction recovery. Thus, it gives them a road map to guide them and their loved ones in the recovery process. The lecture setting provides an opportunity for learning that is not available in an S.L.A.A. meeting (at least, not in so organized a way), that is defended against in one-to-one contacts like individual therapy, or that is not clarified in the group therapy process due to lack of time or therapy style.

Bibliotherapy involves reading. In the field of chemical dependency, there is a huge array of books, pamphlets, and magazines to support the addicts and their family and friends in the recovery process. There are not yet as many resources in the area of love and sex addiction, but more are being developed. Reading can be encouraged on a daily basis, especially in times of high craving or withdrawal. Sometimes a book is the only resource available. A.A. and N.A. have developed books of daily meditation to support the recovery process. Addicts are encouraged to read them as part of their morning routine to help recommit themselves to staying sober that day. Sex and Love Addicts Anonymous has a *Big Book* that describes the recovery program and includes personal stories of recovering addicts.

Treatment options include outpatient and residential programs. The first residential endeavor was the inpatient program at Golden Valley Health Center in Golden Valley, Minnesota. There are other residential programs starting to develop around the country, but there are not yet any half-way houses, nor are there partial hospitalization programs. Residential treatment, while it is short-term—four or five weeks at a time—has a number of advantages over outpatient therapy. Being able to observe a person in a wide variety of settings and circumstances allows the treatment team to get a comprehensive picture of the addict and his or her current level of functioning. For example, addicts are assessed in terms of one-to-one interactions, functioning in group situations, how they eat, how they sleep, how and with whom they socialize, how they function at meetings, what they are like under stress, and how they use leisure time. There are also opportunities to perform a variety of medical and psychological tests. The addict interacts with a wide variety of personalities on the treatment staff and among the patient population. He or she may be given written, reading, or oral assignments that will reveal intellectual, organizational, and academic experience and abilities. A broad spectrum of disciplines and training among the staff of a residential program allows for a comprehensive assessment of the person and the addiction. The inpatient experience can be invaluable to both the client and the follow-up treatment staff since it will provide a full evaluation as well as giving the patient a "running start" in recovery.

Clearly there are a number of treatments available that should change the course of a sex and love addiction. This brings us to the last aspect of the disease concept, the recovery. Essentially what is hoped for in this part, according to the disease theory, is that some improvement in the addiction will be observable when some form of treatment is applied. Certainly this is the case with sex and love addictions. Recovering sex and love addicts founded the S.L.A.A. program in 1977, and it has been growing like wildfire ever since. In 1984 in Philadelphia, four people started the first S.L.A.A. meeting. In 1989, there were over 50 such meetings in Philadelphia's Delaware Valley. The base of experienced and trained therapists is growing as well. Professionals and Twelve Step fellowships together are helping many people who would have been doomed to lead a life of shame, deceit, depression, despair, and jails and institutions, to recover from the insanity of their sex and love addictions.

A man who was thrown out of the Society of Jesus for his alcoholism and sex and love addiction has reclaimed his life as a teacher and local coordinator of S.L.A.A. A doctor, who was desperately suicidal after his recovery from drug and alcohol addiction only drove him deeper into his sex and love addiction, is now sober and looking forward to a new life. A mother and housewife has returned to school to study social work after her sex and love addiction put her in the hospital with back problems and sexually transmitted diseases. A priest plagued with a compulsion to make obscene phone calls that frightened and embarrassed his family has freed himself from his impulsive behaviors and become an intergroup representative for S.L.A.A. All these and many more stories are testimony to the dramatic and complete turnarounds that recovery can bring. Not only are these addictions in check, these addicts are becoming happier, healthier people with renewed vigor, direction, and spirituality.

Recovery is, then, clearly possible for people who are sex and love addicts. The best treatment is a combination of a Twelve Step program like S.L.A.A. with professional help. These interventions produce dramatic changes in the life of an addict, and have the potential to make him or her an even stronger person than before recovery. It is much like the broken arm that is stronger when it knits back together or the "wounded healer" who is more sensitive and compassionate to the suffering of others. People who have an active recovery program in their lives constantly are aware and have opportunities to challenge themselves and to be open to help from others.

Using the criteria of symptomatology, etiology, progression, treatment, and outcome, sex and love addiction can be considered a disease. The purpose of the conceptualization is not to exempt the addict of responsibility or to whitewash the past. Viewing sex and love addiction as an illness that has destroyed the person's equilibrium rather than a deliberate act of will, a bad habit, or overlearning, will help to offset the shame and stigma currently attached to those who suffer from this disease.

PHYSICAL, MENTAL, EMOTIONAL, SOCIAL, AND SPIRITUAL ASPECTS OF SEX AND LOVE ADDICTION

The Alcoholics Anonymous program has developed a great deal of wisdom over the years, and that has been passed on, both within the A.A. program and to other Twelve Step programs like S.L.A.A., through their sayings and slogans. One of the most often-repeated sayings is that alcoholism is a "physical, mental, emotional, and spiritual disease." In other words, the illness is not just physical, even though there may be many physical problems. It is also mental (the obsession), and damages a person emotionally and spiritually, too. If we stop to think about it, this is true of almost any illness, not just alcoholism. When you have a cold, you feel physically bad, but in addition you are less mentally alert, less emotionally stable (irritability or depression), and less spiritually content (asking God, "Why did you do this to me?"). A cold is only a temporary thing; now imagine that you have a chronic, progressive, and potentially fatal disease like diabetes. Certainly you would be affected physically, mentally, emotionally, and spiritually. Imagine if you had a sex and love addiction. How would you cope? Would you have physical, mental, emotional, and spiritual struggles? You would. Moreover, it would affect you socially as well. What they say in the program is that this illness influences a person's entire life. Sex and love addiction, then, affects—to varying degrees—the whole person, and it therefore must be viewed wholistically. We cannot simply treat the physical problem—for example, reducing the craving with medication—and ignore the rest of the person. The treatment and recovery programs outlined in the following two chapters, (on short- and long-term treatment and recovery,) are based on a wholistic approach to therapy and recovery. Before we look at how to work on the addiction, we need to look more closely at its effects on the whole person.

Physical

Sex and love addictions have a variety of physical affects on the addict. First, the pursuit of highs makes the addict's body expect excitement and "run on overdrive." When sex and love addicts are on a binge, they may drive themselves to the point of physical exhaustion. An addict came to see me after one of these "runs," reporting that he had been up all night going to topless bars and pornographic bookstores, and masturbating to the point where he could not go to work the next day. Other addicts have described days of acting out followed by days of collapse and being unable to get out of bed. Many sex and love addicts are not this extreme in their acting out but nonetheless struggle with a constant sense of fatigue and lack of energy.

A more serious physical complication of sex and love addictions is the exposure to sexually transmitted diseases. Herpes, fungal infections, venereal warts, chancroids, gonorrhea, nongonococcal urethritis, granuloma inguinale, lymphogranuloma venereum, syphilis, and HIV infections all can be transmitted through sexual contact. Many physicians, nurses, healthcare workers, and public health personnel treat sex and love addicts for these diseases— sometimes frequently—without ever seeing the real cause, namely, the addict's out-of-control behavior. Addicts themselves often know the cause better than the doctor or healthcare person whom they are consulting, but because of their shame and fear, they do not ask for help. In fact, many of them will continue to infect others because they have no hope for help for themselves, or are so lost in their addictions that they have stopped caring. One love addict that I treat had a relatively brief affair with a Vietnam veteran who infected her with a number of sexually transmitted diseases. It is not clear if he was a sex addict, but he obviously did not care about infecting others. Her sexually transmitted diseases were both physically painful and medically difficult to treat. They cost her a great deal of money, and her self-worth was severely damaged by having to be registered with the Centers for Disease Control in Atlanta. She may never be free from these illnesses. Another addict, a housewife who is sex and love-addicted, felt terrible shame and guilt when she had to tell her husband about her sexually transmitted disease.

Another physical threat that exists for some sex and love addicts is that of self-inflicted harm. Some addicts harm themselves in the pursuit of their sexual or romantic high, such as individuals who masturbate to the point of self-injury or who use "sex toys" that harm them, such as a soda bottle inserted in the vagina. Others may hurt themselves by accident through having sex in an unusual place or position. A sex and love addict will frequently suffer from chronic back problems and may need surgery for actions such as having had sex on a tile floor.

Love and sex addictions are also life-threatening. The risk of contracting HIV continues to grow unchecked. A sex and love addict recently told me that he had been thrilled to hear on the news that morning that a vaccine for HIV had been discovered (actually, the report said a possible vaccine had been identified for research purposes) because it meant he would not have to give up his addiction. Many accidents and accidental deaths are related to either acting out or the suicidal depression that follows compulsive behavior. One patient was admitted to a psychiatric hospital with burns on his legs due to the use of cattle prods in one of his sadomasochistic scenes, but the physician who examined him never questioned the cause of the injury. The patient had also been driving at over a hundred miles an hour in hopes of a fatal crash.

Mental

As has been indicated before, there are profound effects on mental processes caused by sex and love addictions. Mental alertness and acuity as well as concentration are affected. The intrusion of unwanted thoughts and fantasies can prevent addicts from working or even concentrating on a normal conversation. At times they appear distracted or as if they were not paying attention, but often they will have trained themselves to appear alert even when they are not; for example, they may prepare to ask a question in a meeting, class, or interview just to throw off suspicion that they are "not really present."

Even worse than the disruption of attention are the distortions in thinking that occur as the results of addiction. Lying, denial, rationalizing, minimizing, and projecting become a way of thought that continues even after the acting-out behavior stops. For example, a recovering addict wanted to blame his wife's criticism and lack of warmth for their inability to relate to each other sexually without taking into account how he had pushed her away and made her feel unattractive, especially while he was acting out. Another individual was furious with his employer for what he saw as unfair treatment but was unable to admit that his own father might have been unfair with him in any way. He insisted on his rationality in projecting blame onto a superior who was trying to help him, and at the same time avoided acknowledging that his father's perfectionism had helped make him a harsh critic. Often addicts are not at all aware of their distortions in thinking because they have become ingrained and habitual. Thus, addicts need frequent redirection to examine their own logic and to separate their thoughts and feelings.

The thinking patterns that take place during the period of preoccupation, fantasy, and ritual can be so distorted as to be delusional. The addict, lost in his or her own addictive world, has lost touch with reality. For example, the adoptive father who thinks that his incestuous relationships are advances in the "sexual revolution" is not just distorted in his thinking, he is delusional. I originally disliked the word "delusion" because of my formal training and the association of delusions with psychotic illnesses like schizophrenia. However, the more I have learned about addiction, the more I see exactly this sort of irrational thought process. Delusions are considered to be rather fixed, irrational ideas like "I am Jesus Christ" or "I am Joan of Arc." The addict actually thinks this way. Sex and love addicts convince themselves that they are someone they are not. For instance, a pedophile came to see me because he was convinced he was being victimized by the legal system, which was prosecuting him for his sexual activity with boys when he swore that he would stop and had been in therapy (with an untrained therapist) for six months. The reality is that he was the victimizer in this case despite having been victimized himself when he was a boy. He had turned reality inside out. He thought he was someone that he was not; that is, he thought he was a safe person to allow near children when instead, without proper treatment, he would most likely become a repeat offender.

Delusional thinking, seeing the world as the opposite of what it really is, is commonplace among addicts. They may think they are "killing the pain" when they go to the bars, bordellos, bookstores, and massage parlors, but in fact they are creating more pain which will persist in an endless cycle of pain/shame/guilt/fix. The addict thinks he or she is "not hurting anyone but myself," despite the damage to relationships, marriages, friendships, and children. An addict with whom I worked saw himself as victimized by his profession when the bar took away his license to practice law for stealing from a client to feed his addiction while at the same time physically and emotionally abusing his wife and children. Sex and love addicts often become paranoid in their thinking. They view the world as being "out to get them" and may have paranoid delusions. For instance, a seminarian was so convinced that his superiors would throw him out of seminary if they discovered his sex addiction that he could not ask them for help. He was afraid to tell them that he was seeing me for psychotherapy because I had "a reputation for treating sex and love addicts." He was convinced that his history of alcoholism would be used against him, despite the fact that his superiors knew all about his other addiction. He so tied his own and my hands with his paranoid, delusional thinking that treatment became impossible.

Another thinking problem from which most addicts suffer is pessimism or hopelessness. Usually by the time they finally get to treatment, they have experienced so many personal failures (such as attempts to stop or promises they failed to keep) that they have very little confidence left in themselves or in anyone else. They have been putting up a front of optimism and false bravado for so long that when it collapses, they are afraid to be positive or to look forward to any success in recovery. A sex and love addict who had nine months of recovery with only two slips was not able to see this as an accomplishment. He was correct in realizing that ultimately he needed to be sober without any slips, but he could not give himself any credit for what had been a big change in his pattern of acting out. The year before, despite being in therapy for depression, he had acted out "regularly" with constant masturbation as well as visits to bookstores and anonymous sex in bathrooms. He was afraid to hope, on the one hand, but he also secretly thought that if only he could get his job back, "every thing would be O.K." His parents' religious outlook fostered a belief in miracles and, in fact, his parents were planning a trip to a holy place in Europe and wanted him to come along. He wanted to be more positive, but was afraid because he had always failed in the past and could not yet stop beating himself up for acting out. As with other sex and love addicts, it would take time to change his distorted thought processes.

Emotional

Addictions have a profound impact on the emotional life of a sex and love addict. Feelings are usually "stuffed" or repressed, and the addict becomes numb, unfeeling and uncaring. The lack of a real emotional life leaves the addict like a boat without a rudder. Addicts' lives are not directed by their feelings about themselves or other people about whom they care, but instead are driven by an addiction that is never satisfied. They grow to hate themselves for their loss of control and lack of feelings, and can be quite defensive and irritable when others remind them of how they come across. Most people who care about an addicted person are struck by their apparent lack of real feelings. They often think to themselves, or even say out loud to the addict, "If you really cared about me, you wouldn't treat me like this." The truth is that the addict does not care about him- or herself, so how could he or she be capable of really caring about others? He or she may have periods of caring or may be able to act caring, but when the choice comes down to the addiction or other people, the addiction wins. Addicts talk of walking out on their children to go act out even though they know their families need them at home. A sex and love addict who would normally never think of doing anything to hurt his family (and would even fiercely come to their defense) was able to numb his feelings enough in a fit of obscene phone calling to call his nephew. For some addicts, this habit of emotional numbness takes a long time to give up, while others feel like a "raw nerve" in their withdrawal. Even this emotional experience is self-centered, and they cannot experience deep feelings for others.

Another emotional affect of an addiction is that the emotional growth that would normally be taking place is blocked. Because addicts are in a quick-fix mentality, they do not have to develop the emotional maturity to delay gratification and be patient. Often they come across as emotionally immature. They may be childish, impatient, or demanding. One sex and love addict with whom I worked would even adopt a high-pitched, childish tone of voice, and would start to whine and complain. I had to remind him that he was acting like a child and that if he wanted to be related to as an adult, he would have to act like one. My client could shift gears in response to this intervention, which indicated that he was quite unaware of his behavior. He could see it when it was pointed out to him, but he could not catch himself in the act of being childish and manipulative. Addicts also program themselves to expect instant gratification, thus enabling themselves to regress to more immature levels of development.

Some addicts are quite adept at covering up their immaturity and childish attitudes. They can act grown-up when they need to, but in the privacy of their acting-out sessions, they are surprisingly childlike. For example, a pedophile would wrestle with young boys in order to initiate some physical contact and to see how the boys would respond if he "accidentally" touched their genitals. If the boys acted surprised or upset, he would pretend it was a mistake, but if the boys allowed him to touch them or acted interested, he would pursue the "game" under the pretense of childlike play. This same man could be quite proper and adult-like in the company of other adults. When queried about how he could take advantage of a child, he indicated that for him, "it was like two children together, not an adult and a child." With grown-ups, however, he was able to act as if he felt grown-up as well. It is not uncommon for high-powered executives to want to play a very childlike and dependent role with the call girls that they hire. They may want baby talk or motherly attention, which they may be afraid to ask for from partners who are not paid to do exactly as they are told. Before and after these regressive encounters, the executives will act decisive, dominant, aggressive, and in charge.

Irritability, depression, emotional instability, passivity, hopelessness, and suicidal thoughts and attempts are other emotional outcomes of sex and love addictions. Even for a person who has no family history or personal tendency toward depression, an addiction will create dysphoria, much as it creates pessimistic, negative thinking. The two are, of course, related, as cognitive therapists have clearly shown us. In other words, it is hard to feel happy when you are thinking "down" thoughts. Conversely, it is difficult to maintain a feeling of hopelessness when you are thinking pleasant and hopeful thoughts. Sex and love addicts, then, think and feel negatively. They have little energy and motivation to change, an act that seems like such a monumental task that it is never even attempted. Getting to meetings, calling sponsors, and reading—all activities that are encouraged in early recovery especially—all seem like "too much work." The addict emotionally wants to be "fixed" just as he or she was in their active addiction. Addicts do not feel like doing the hard work of recovery. They have forgotten the lesson that things that come easily are not worth much to us, do not build self-esteem, and are not valued highly. When a person climbs Mt. Everest, he or she is literally and figuratively "on top of the world." Doing difficult things makes us feel good and enhances our self-worth. Easy things like indulging in addictive acting out destroy self-esteem and create despair and desperation when they involve us in degrading, detached, and embarrassing actions.

A sex and love addict recently came to me in tears because he felt that he "just could not do it" (stay sober), and added that "it" was just "too hard." He had become so accustomed to using his addiction as the "easy way out" that he had totally lost the sense that he could do anything that felt difficult to him. He was having suicidal thoughts, and wondered if he should be hospitalized. While residential treatment is quite useful, it is not a place to hide when recovery is too difficult. That is a set-up for the person and the program, because then if the addicts go home and have trouble, as they will if they are running from their addiction, they will blame both treatment and themselves. The young man in question had lost sight of his capacity to accomplish difficult things. He had earned a graduate degree and worked his way up to running an outpatient therapy program, both of which were not easy tasks. Since he was feeling so depressed and worthless, he of course minimized the effort involved with either of these accomplishments, and lied to me that they were "easy." Due to the depressing effects of his addiction, he lacked the ability at that time to support himself and to boost his own mood. He was able to respond to encouragement, fortunately, and more intensive interventions were unnecessary. When sex and love addicts are too depressed or too suicidal, medication or hospitalization may be required. The hospital needs to be chosen with care, since many hospital staffs are untrained in treating sex and love addictions and may give inappropriate messages like, "Masturbation is O.K."

Addictions, as mentioned previously, do great damage to self-worth. Good self-esteem is an essential ingredient for a healthy and balanced emotional life. Without this foundation of positive self-worth, sex and love addicts are vulnerable to mood swings, being overly or underly emotional, and feeling insecure. Any of these problems can trigger a slip and relapse. One sex and love addict whom I treat is extremely sensitive. He was a sensitive child, and was labeled a "sissy" by his physically and emotionally abusive father. His mother apparently would throw up her hands in frustration and exclaim, "What are we going to do with you?" when he would cry and fail to act tough like his father and older brother. He ended up hating his own sensitivity and himself. In recovery, he is struggling to achieve sobriety. He has received much support from S.L.A.A. and A.A. friends, from his therapy group, and from me; however, it seems to do little good in helping him build his self-worth to the point where he feels he is "worth getting sober for." He "beats himself up" for his failures, and sets up others to do the same, even though he knows it is a replay of his family life, when his father and older brother beat him. He knows that neither he nor his group can beat his sensitivity out of him, because his father "tried and couldn't." Thus, he is in an impossible position; neither positive nor negative feedback can improve his self-esteem. His only real choice, other than continuing his addiction, is to get sober. In other words, by doing something that is hard to do, he will start to build self-worth. Then, and only then, will he begin to believe he is what others see—a good person. Only he can make that choice, and no matter how much we want him to do it, it is up to only him.

Another sex and love addict who suffers terribly with low self-esteem developed his addiction feeling he was worth less than other people because he had an obvious birth defect. He was teased as a child for his cleft palate, and had difficulty with speech. His parents assured him that "someday" things would be better and told him not to feel badly about himself, but it did not help. He believes that this was partly because he was not allowed to express his feelings of sadness, hurt, and rejection that were due to being "different."

When he grew up and had achieved some status in life, his problem with self-worth became severely complicated by his addiction. When people would give him compliments or acknowledge him for doing something positive, he—like most addicts—would think to himself, "If you only knew, you wouldn't say that." He negated any positive feedback or chances to improve his self-esteem by thinking about his addiction. This terrible secret colored his life and made it impossible for him to feel good about himself.

For this man, the "hard thing to do" in recovery was to feel good about himself. He was still haunting himself with his past. Instead of using his memories of addiction to motivate his sobriety, he still was "wishing it didn't happen," and beat himself with images of past abuses. His habit of maintaining his low self-esteem, which he did despite some success in recovery, had been established in childhood, reinforced by his addiction, and, unfortunately, underscored by a therapist who would say about his addictive activities, "How could you do that to children?" His therapist should have known that addicts act like addicts. In their addictions, addicts do lots of abusive things to themselves and to others because they are emotionally numb. Recovery for this sex and love addict means finding a way to build self-worth and discontinue his bad habit of feeling like a "bad person."

Social

While not in the original litany of areas affected by addictions—physical, mental, emotional, and spiritual—the social aspect of the addict's life is profoundly affected by addiction. When I refer to the social area of a sex and love addict's life, I am speaking of family, friends, acquaintances, and work life; in other words, all the arenas where there are opportunities for human interaction. First, the family life of an addict is usually the most damaged by an addiction. The spouse and children live with the addict at closer quarters than do friends or coworkers. At the very least, sex and love addicts neglect and detach from their families, and in the worst cases, they abuse and harm them emotionally, physically, and sexually.

Our family is supposed to be the place where it is safest to be our real self. In the work world or in social situations it is normal to be somewhat guarded, and many people feel the need to be phony to impress others, at least to some degree. At home, however, there are not the same pressures to look good or achieve things. Instead, there is the expectation that we will "let our hair down" and act as we really are. For the sex and love addict, this expectation of openness and honesty, no matter how small, is an impossible demand. To be truthful would require revealing the addiction and risking rejection or an expectation of change. Most addicts do not risk this. Some try to appear open by telling part of the truth, but they also remain in control but not being completely truthful. A sex and love addict recently bragged to me that he had told his wife "at least 50 percent" of the truth about his addiction to affairs with other women. He had himself convinced that he was being truthful, when in fact he was being quite deceitful and manipulative by only providing censored information.

Sex and love addicts steal time, attention, affection, and money from their families, and share their ill-gotten gains with their addictive acquaintances. They often will try to convince themselves that they are being attentive and loving with parents, spouses, and children. However, in their delusional way of thinking, they are ignoring the reality of their self-centeredness, greed, and inability to genuinely love or care for anyone. They manipulate everyone to get what they want. Sometimes they will be tyrants who rant and rave and are so demanding that everyone is afraid to tell the truth. Others act like needy, helpless, passive victims who need everyone to take care of them because they obviously cannot take care of themselves. In any case, pseudo-intimacy or "living seperate lives," which is the compromise many couples achieve, does not change reality, which is that the sex and love addict is taking from and not giving to the family.

Some sex and love addicts also become overtly destructive with their families, although the effects of subtle abuse can be as bad or worse than those of overt abuse. At least when the abuser is observably out of control, as when beating or sexually abusing a spouse or child, there is a clear victimizer. Someone can be identified as causing the pain that the family feels. However, unlike alcoholics or drug addicts, many sex and love addicts are more subtly abusive with their families. Take, for example, the sex and love addict who relocates many times in order to "start over." This "geo-graphic cure," as it is known in the S.L.A.A. program, is doomed to fail because the addict "brings himself along" on the relocation. The addict's family members, moreover, are forced to pull up roots and reestablish new relationships at each stop along the road. Their security and social lives are damaged, and they are usually lied to about the reasons for moving. Children may grow up unable to establish good social relationships, insecure, isolated, guarded, suspicious, pessimistic, and detached, without any obvious reasons why they feel this way because the truth is a "family secret."

Because so many addicts feel like victims (and, in reality, are victims of the disease of addiction), they have great difficulty seeing how they have victimized others whom they love. Even well into recovery, there may be much denial and defensiveness with regard to the effects of the addiction on others. In the S.L.A.A. program, looking at this issue is saved until the Eighth and Ninth steps, by which time, hopefully, the recovering addict will have developed the habit of honesty and openness. Families can collude with the addict to ignore the damage being done. We call this co-dependency, or "being addicted to keeping the addict addicted." Still, the pain of the family may be the key to getting a sex and love addict into treatment. I have seen addicts only admit the truth when confronted by their children. Others have come for treatment because a spouse has said that he or she can "take no more" or that "something has to be done." Parents can get addict children to accept treatment when they stop protecting, rescuing, and covering up, and instead say that treatment is necessary. These ultimatums do not always work—and the addict will inevitably test the strength of the family's conviction—but many times they are the key element in the start of recovery.

Friendships suffer greatly from sex and love addictions. One addict sadly complained that many of his sexual encounters had started out as friendships, but for some reason unknown to him, when sex was introduced into the relationship, the friendship would always end. He had a great longing for closeness, but his sexual preoccupation intruded into his social life and left him more lonely after a sexual escapade than before. Since he was in the habit of sexualizing people—when he looked at someone, he did not see a person but instead a potential sexual object—he inevitably would sexualize his friends. Once he began thinking of them in sexual terms, some sort of sexual exploration (for example, ascertaining whether they would respond to a touch, a look, or a hug) was unavoidable. Usually these sexual encounters were short-lived and the relationship would then die. The addict would feel hurt and rejected, which of course would fuel the need for further acting out.

Many sex and love addicts are very lonely people. Some can maintain the appearance of having friends, but they are really just acquaintances. Others are extremely isolated and have few or no friends. A love dependent patient whom I saw for years had curtailed her social network to zero at one point, despite encouragement to socialize from her family and her therapist. Another sex and love addict seemed a warm and friendly person in his administrative position at work, but he lived alone and never went out with friends. His social contacts were confined to pornographic bookstores and movie theaters.

Other sex and love addicts are quite the opposite of the "loners" described above. They are extremely social and have a large network of friends. Socializing may represent an opportunity for "cruising" or a chance to "score." In general, their relationships are shallow and manipulative. They are "users," as are all addicts. They do not feel good from being open and sharing with others, even though some of them can put on an act of pseudo-intimacy. Their interest in relationships is in terms of what they can get for themselves. Giving may be necessary to get; but, for them, there is no giving without some sort of payback. A sex and love addict consulted me recently because she found she was not able to let go of abusive relationships. She was not being beaten by the men that she chose, but she always ended up feeling "used." She tried to work this problem out in analytic therapy and knew that she made bad choices of partners, but she felt she could do no differently. She felt doomed to put her life at risk with men that she did not really know or trust, and had become quite depressed and overweight. She was afraid of contracting AIDS, but at the same time, she knew that during a "fit of passion" she would not protect herself with a condom. She could be quite social and had no problem establishing social contacts, but her addiction was driving her to the depths of despair and hopelessness.

A person's work life is also greatly affected by a sex and love addiction. In chemical dependency treatment, employers often initiate the treatment process because they have become aware of the addict's chemical dependency through lateness, large numbers of days off, inability to come to work after weekends or holidays, difficulties with concentration, lowered production, and even use of drugs or alcohol on the job. Sex and love addicts can have all these same symptoms yet their addiction may be overlooked or misdiagnosed. One of my patients described a late-night binge that left him so tired and disgusted that he did not report to work on Monday. He did not call his employer, and when he went to work on Tuesday, his supervisor told him that he could be terminated for not calling and saying he would be out. He had been late for work every day the past week due to his acting out. He was angry about being confronted on Tuesday, so he childishly called in sick on Wednesday. His work had not been done well and he was having difficulty concentrating, so his production was slipping. He was getting close to being fired, which had happened to him on his last job. Obviously, he did not have time to both work and continue actively in his sex and love addiction. This is usually what has happened to chemically dependent employees at the point when they get referred for treatment.

Sex and love addictions can be costly to both employer and employee. Lost time and lowered production is costly to businesses. Lost careers and squandered career opportunities cost workers. As with drug and alcohol addiction, many sex and love addicts prefer jobs with little direct supervision and lots of contact with people, such as sales, teaching, therapy, or ministry, as the best opportunities to act out. Salesmen often can control their schedules so that they have fairly large amounts of time to conduct affairs, visit prostitutes, or go to pornographic bookstores. Teachers, especially college professors, may seduce students, manipulating them with grades or outright blackmail for sexual favors. Psychotherapists can use or abuse patients sexually. The biggest single cause for dramatic increases in the cost of malpractice insurance for psychologists is sex with clients. It is already unethical, and it is now becoming illegal in some states. For addicts, all this time and energy spent in sexual and romantic pursuits takes time and energy away from more productive professional activity.

Many sex and love addicts have lost or damaged their careers because of their sex and love addictions. One minister had to take time off because he needed to get his addiction under control. A doctor lost his license to his medical ethics board (the Pennsylvania Psychiatric Association) for having sex with patients. A college president had to resign due to taking indecent liberties, e.g., rubbing a female colleague's knee in a meeting. A lawyer had to resign a new position at which he was well liked because he had to surrender his license to practice law to the bar. One politician had to drop out of his race because of the adverse publicity he received when he entertained a single woman overnight. The list goes on, and is almost constantly in the daily news. We overlook the problem because we do not know the signs of sex and love addiction. While our eyes are closed, however, sex and love addicts are seeing their work lives damaged or destroyed by their addictions.

The economic cost of sex and love addictions has not yet been estimated. It is most likely that it will equal or surpass the cost of alcohol and drug addictions, which are currently estimated to cost billions of dollars each year in lost time and productivity. Certainly, one obvious cost is the great expense of pornography and prostitution. One client estimated that he spent over a thousand dollars a month on pornographic magazines, books, and movies. This did not include the cost of prostitutes or cruising at bars. An employee assistance counselor told me the story of a man who came to him for financial assistance because he had charged all his credit cards to the limit. The counselor did not recognize the sexual addiction even though many of these charges were for massage parlors and bookstores. A seminary rector told the story of a student who came to tell him that he had to drop out to pay off his debts, which were from his sex and love addiction. Feeling sorry for the young man, the rector paid the debts. When the student returned in the fall, however, he had run up even more. Likewise, expense accounts can be a wonderful hiding place for the cost of a sex and love addiction. "Entertainment" takes many forms, and the addict may rationalize that his or her acting out is "necessary" for the sale. The actual cost to addicts, their families, and the public is probably staggering, despite at this point being almost unnoticed.

Spiritual

Spirituality is one of the first things to go and one of the last things to return for a sex and love addict. By spirituality, I am not speaking of any type of formal or organized religion, but rather the experience of one's own life force. It can be as simple as feeling glad to get up in the morning or as profound as feeling serene and whole while observing a sunset at the beach. In the Twelve Step tradition, Sex and Love Addicts Anonymous encourages the belief in a "higher power" or a "power greater than ourselves." This is an important aspect of the surrender process that opens a person up to help from others. As people come to feel their own spirit, their will to live, and their own life force, they usually come to believe that it is in some way connected with a larger force, which some call "God."

Concepts of God and religion are damaged and often destroyed by an addiction. Addicts, many of whom have had formal religious training as children, become disenchanted with God and religion because they have failed to help the addicts avoid the slide into their addiction. Many addicts will pray (only, of course, when they are in a tight spot), "God, if you will only get me out of this, I will never do it again and I will go to church every Sunday." Usually these childlike prayers are seen as unanswered, and the sex and love addict will become increasingly angry with God. Many have looked to religion for relief from their suffering. They attended church, said prayers, confessed, sang in the choir, got involved in church activities, or contributed money, all with the secret hope that miraculously, the burden of their addiction would be lifted. Some were clergy or vowed religious themselves, and felt especially betrayed by their church and God. "Why me?" they would ask themselves, and would turn their backs on their spiritual lives.

Addictive living fosters the indulgence of the body—giving in to impulses, greed, hedonism, and self-centeredness as temptations of the flesh—all things that religion and God oppose. The addict feels increasingly hypocritical, dirty, and sinful as the addiction progresses, and will eventually find it difficult to be in the presence of people who are trying to work on their spirituality, concern for others, patience, generosity, faith, and compassion.

It is fairly common for sex and love addicts to embrace religion as a solution to their addiction. Incestuous fathers and rapists, especially while in jail, are known for their religious conversions. An exhibitionist with whom I worked was "born again" while in jail for the second time, and expected God to save him from continuing to act out. He put a great deal of emphasis on his prayer group, which, I believe was made up of good and caring people who know nothing about addictions, and he neglected to work on his S.L.A.A. program. He is back in jail today because of continued offenses. Similarly, an incestuous father talked to me about a half dozen times, but showed much more faith in a Salvation Army group to help him control his sexual compulsions. I am not trying to infer that God, religion, or faith cannot help recovery. Clearly, they can. Some people say they find Twelve Step meetings more spiritual than their church. However, what I want to emphasize is that involvement with a spiritual or religious group is not a substitute for the work that must be done to recover from a sex and love addiction.

As people recover, so does their spirituality. In fact, this is one of the indicators that I look for in terms of progress in recovery. Many recovering addicts return to organized religion (usually the religion of their childhood), but this is not necessarily the point or concern. What is important is that the person begin to feel alive, experience a joy in living, feel a reverence for his or her own life, and begin to feel gratitude for the gift of living. Addicts have lived their lives in fear and shame, burdened with terrible secrets and profound embarrassment. They cannot even accept a compliment, let alone feel grateful for living. Life is filled with pitfalls, temptations, dangers, and rejections. In recovery, all this changes—although not overnight, like the instant gratification the addict prefers—and life begins to give rewards that eventually go beyond one's wildest dreams.

A former priest who lost his vocation to alcoholism and sexual addiction now finds joy in riding the bus; teaching children; sharing in the fellowship of S.L.A.A.; working in his local parish; driving people to church; daily prayer and meditation; and the ability to see God in his everyday life. He advocates spiritual direction as part of the recovery process. A recovering sex and love addict feels excited about being his "old self" again, and is learning to love himself for the first time in his life. Another love and sex addict now finds serenity, peace, and centeredness within herself and the world as she sits alone in the early morning with her coffee and her writings. A teacher finds his teaching is more "alive" and real as he grows in recovery. Now he can talk to his students without having to defend or explain everything. These are all spiritual experiences that indicate the kinds of changes that people undergo as they recover. Often the first year or so is focused on the compulsive behaviors and the obsessive thoughts, so progress in the spiritual realm is not readily available until the third year and after. That is not to say that there are no spiritual changes even in the beginning, because there are. For example, a priest who had had years of professional training in religion and spirituality came to realize in his first year of recovery that he has always had a very limited and childlike relationship with God. His prayer life essentially consisted of asking God for things, like taking away his addiction, and then being angry and disappointed because he did not get exactly what he had prayed for. He went through the motions of his ministry but always felt like a phony and a hypocrite. His preaching and other occupational activities reflected his spiritual barrenness. In recovery, he felt both scared and excited about the opportunity to examine his ministry and his spiritual life.

SEVERITY OF SEX AND LOVE ADDICTIONS

Determining the severity of a sex and love addiction, while important, is also frought with difficulties. An assessment of severity can help with prognosis and treatment planning. It can also be used as an excuse to avoid or minimize the necessity of intervention. Nonaddicts react to the information that a sex and love addiction is mild or moderate rather than severe with relief and feelings of hope and encouragement. An addict, however, will have the opposite reaction. The sex and love addict who is told that the addiction is mild or even moderately severe will think, "Great! Now I don't have to do anything about it until it gets to be severe," "Hey, this means I can continue to act out because it is not as bad as I thought," or "I might be able to get away with masturbation because my addiction is not as bad as others." In other words, the addict will twist the truth in a delusional way of thinking in order to find a way to continue with the addiction. The nonaddicted person, on the other hand, would be delighted to have a milder case on the grounds that the prognosis for recovery is improved and the amount of effort necessary to change will be less. Thus, the question of measuring severity of a sex and love addiction is a double-edged sword.

Chemical dependency specialists used to be afraid to mention the idea of slips and relapses to addicts because they knew all too well that many addicts would distort the teaching on the subject and use it as an excuse to get drunk or high once more. Addicts frequently interpret the message that roughly two-thirds of chemically dependent people pick up a drink or a drug again not as a warning about the severity of the disease and the difficulty of recovery but rather as permission to use drugs or alcohol "at least once more." They are not thinking rationally. They are thinking as addicts think; "There must be some way to use chemicals again, even if it is only for one last time." Knowing that addicts think this way, it is with fear and trepidation that we therapists discuss things like severity, because we are afraid that the addict will not hear what is really being said, but instead will use it to manipulate and to find an excuse to act out again.

In any case, sex and love addictions vary in terms of their severity, just as do arthritis, diabetes, heart disease, depression, or schizophrenia. Some cases are worse than others. However, there are no clearly distinguishable categories yet. This is partly due to the fact that, at this stage of the game, we are still trying to convince people that sex and love addictions exist. We also have not yet clearly established the proper criteria for diagnosis. It seems reasonable, however, to estimate that sex and love addicts will fall into one of three categories: mild, moderate, or severe.

The next question is obvious: How do we determine to which category the sex and love addict belongs? The four criteria that I consider when trying to make a determination of severity are: (1) the rapidity of onset, (2) the severity of consequences, (3) the length of the addiction, and (4) the amount of risk-taking behavior in the addiction.

Before we look at each of these criteria, a word about why a determination of severity is useful seems appropriate. Basically, a severity assessment can be helpful in treatment planning and in prognosis. If we determine early in treatment that a sex and love addiction is quite severe, then we will plan a more intensive treatment. If it is less severe, we can have more time for planning, trial and error, and mistake making; in other words, for the addict, this may mean having slips.

A couple of examples may illuminate this point. One client consulted me after being referred by church authorities for reportedly kissing and hugging a man in his early 20s. My client had been engaged in these behaviors about half a dozen times, according to him, and was also involved in compulsive masturbation, mutual masturbation, and visiting pornographic bookstores. His problem had gradually worsened over the past 10 years. Before this he had had a period of 30 years of comfortable celibacy, according to him. In terms of the criteria, I estimated his sex and love addiction as mild, due to the slow onset, periods of abstinence, lack of severe consequences, relatively short duration, and lack of life-threatening behaviors. In short, it could have been a lot worse. He could have created a public scandal that would have had great shame attached to it. He could have acted out more frequently. He could have had oral sex and risked AIDS.

In comparison, another cleric, who came to me on his own initiative, had a long history of transvestite behaviors. He was not able to continue in his seminary training, and was risking jail and death by stealing from the parish and visiting prostitutes. He had been addicted almost all his life with few periods of abstinence. He was also a recovering alcoholic. His sex and love addiction was quite severe, in my estimation.

Consequently, the treatment process for these two middle-aged men was quite different. The mildly addicted man was superficially cooperative but made very slow progress. He was quickly able to establish his bottom lines and maintain sobriety, but he became lax after this and only slowly began to work on the second level of sobriety, which is necessary for long-term recovery (see chapter 5). The severely addicted men was still employing a great deal of denial, and could not cooperate with treatment in a meaningful way. He viewed himself as having a mild addiction, and minimized the amount of risk taking in which he was involved. Eventually this difference of opinion provoked a crisis. In an effort to get him to surrender, and in the hopes that he would acknowledge the extent of his loss of control (and his need for pseudo-control in terms of defining how severe his addiction was), he was confronted and told that he had to do treatment "our way": He had to follow his therapists' advice on such things as number of meetings to attend, or else withdraw. Unfortunately, he chose to withdraw.

This is a good example of how an addict will use the concept of severity in a negative way. The crucial diagnostic and personal decision is whether the person is an addict. If you have the disease, you need to change. If you do not, then you are free to choose whether to change. Severity has nothing to do with the decision about whether change is needed; it is only relevant to the question of what to change and how much.

In the second example above, the sex and love addict made the struggle out in terms of how badly he was doing. That is, he would not do certain things asked of him, like going to S.L.A.A. meetings more frequently, because he did not see himself as very sick. He thought he could still handle things his way. He feared being discovered by his religious order and losing the opportunity to pursue his studies, but he did not realistically judge how his sex and love addiction would ruin his chances to achieve his goal. He also underestimated the amount of work needed on his part to obtain sobriety, so he saw our expectations as unreasonable, insensitive, and more risky than doing things his way. He manipulated the idea that he was "not that bad" to mean that he probably was not even an addict and did not need to do what the other addicts were doing. He was operating under the delusion that he could manage his compulsive behavior and still keep the secret from his order. His delusional thinking made it possible for him to think that he could be a good priest when he was filled with dishonesty and deceit.

Recovery begins with the statement, "I am a sex and love addict." Other people may make this decision before the addict comes to this conclusion, and their realization of the existence of an addiction may help the addict see the truth. Recovery does not start with the evaluation of how severe the addiction is. All addictions need treatment, just as all other types of diseases do. The nature, extent, intensity, and focus of treatment vary with the severity of the disease, with more intense interventions required for more severe addictions. In the two cases described above, the former could be treated with a minimum of rigidity and confrontation, while the latter needed immediate change. The first addict may require a slip in order to accept that he is truly addicted, while the latter is in danger of getting into high-risk situations every day that could lead to "jail, institutions, or death," as they say in the S.L.A.A. program.

Rapidity of Onset

The initial criteria for determining severity is the speed of onset of the addiction. The quicker the addiction takes hold, the more severe it is. This is due to the fact that an addiction with a rapid onset will most likely have a rapid progression once a relapse occurs. For example, an addict with whom I was working did not get "into" his sadomasochistic sex scenes until about six years prior to treatment. His progression was rapid, and could almost be traced on a map with concentric circles that were getting closer and closer to home. When he was younger, he was involved with self-flagulation to enhance the erotic excitment in masturbation, but his addiction did not really take hold until his middle 40s. In recovery, he has a "photographic" memory of the phone number of a person with whom he acted out, and while under stress, he has called the number only to hang up when the person answers. It would not take much, perhaps only a few words, to get him back into not only some form of sexual activity but also the behavior that led him to suicidal thoughts and actions. The devastation of losing all that he had gained would probably be enough to push him "over the edge." Thus, the rapidity of onset of his sex and love addiction, shown by his rapid progress into S&M, is a clear indicator of its severity. The speed at which his mind goes to the phone number is also a good clue to the level of severity.

Another factor in rapid onset is the person's chronological age. The younger the person, the more severe the addiction. In the field of chemical dependency, there is an almost bell-shaped curve representing the age of the addict population. Adolescent chemical dependency represents about 5–10 percent of the total population of drug and alcohol addicts, yet adolescent addicts have the worse prognosis for recovery and the hardest time admitting and accepting the need for treatment. The same scenario is probably true for adolescent sex and love addicts, but the data is not yet available to confirm this hypothesis. Adolescent addictions interfere with normal growth and development at a crucial time, so adolescent addicts have more impaired social, emotional, and intellectual skills. Adolescent alcoholics and drug addicts in our program average two full years academically behind the average adolescent. There is a higher percentage of children with learning disabilities in the adolescent chemical dependency arena. Adolescent drug and alcohol addicts lack emotional control and social competence, both of which make them highly vulnerable to relapse due to their inability to relate to a new, straight peer group and to handle their age group's emotional lability. Adolescent sex and love addicts are most likely more damaged by their sex and love addictions, since sex and love are such an important part of adolescent life. The onset of a sex and love addiction at an early age calls for the same poor prognosis as in an addiction with a rapid onset.

Severity of Consequences

The severity of consequences of the sex and love addiction is another criterion for determining the overall severity of the addiction. Consequences like medical problems, AIDS, jail, legal difficulties, loss of a job or reputation, suicidal thoughts or attempts, and divorce or separation are all indicators that the disease has progressed to the point where it is quite severe. When consequences like these occur, they suggest the need for a highly intensive and broad-based treatment approach.

For instance, a pedophile came to me recently to ask for an evaluation to be used in his forthcoming court hearings. He had lost his job and was facing jail due to his compulsion to be sexual with young boys. I judged his addiction to be quite severe due to the severity of the consequences to him and to his victims. He was attending Homosexuals Anonymous and therapy with a therapist who was untrained in the field of sex and love addictions. I determined that he was not safe based on the disastrous damage done to him and the children and on the minimal effort he was putting into change. Rather than surrender to my opinion and recommendations, he tried to get me to change my evaluation. His delusional thinking and resultant poor judgment had turned reality on its head so that he believed I was the one who should change, not he.

In general, it would be safe to say that male sex and love addicts have more legal and employment-related consequences, whereas females tend to have more difficulties with relationship and mood disorders. Both sexes have medical consequences of undetermined frequency. One love addict who had not been particularly concerned with the lack of sex in her marriage during her addiction became more interested in rekindling the passion in her relationship only to find out that her husband had thrown himself into his work and no longer placed much value on sex. She was faced with the prospect of living a celebate life in her marriage or getting a divorce and finding a partner who wanted a full relationship including sex. Neither of these alternatives was acceptable to her. Thus, her addiction cost her a great deal, although it did not go so far as to cause a divorce. This is a mitigating factor in her situation, and would cause her addiction to be judged less severe. A love and sex addict who, by the time she was 21, had attempted suicide three times, been psychiatrically hospitalized, and burned her boyfriend with a curling iron in a rage induced by the paranoia of her addiction, would be diagnosed with a severe sex and love addiction.

Some sex and love addicts do not try to kill themselves, are not thrown in jail or institutions, and do not lose jobs or relationships, but their addictions instead cost them their reputations. For someone like a professional, a clergy person, or a politician, this can be an overwhelming loss. Reputations take a lifetime to develop. A physician who is accused of sexual involvement with his patients, a minister who cannot leave his flock alone sexually, or a politician who insists on "womanizing" while under scrutiny by the press all stand to lose something irreplaceable. This sort of consequence, although not exactly like going to jail or contracting AIDS, can be equally deadly for the addict. The addict who willingly follows his or her addiction despite consequences like those outlined above is more severely addicted than the addict who still is fearful of such severe consequences, and therefore is less numb emotionally, less intellectually delusional, and more spiritual. The less these and the social and physical factors are present, the less severe the sex and love addict.

Length of Addiction

The number of years that the sex and love addict has been active in the addiction is also an indicator of severity. This is because the years of repetition will produce a "groove" or "rut" that the addict will find hard to change. The habit pattern and conditioning are so strong that even a highly motivated client can have trouble getting a significant recovery program going, especially if we are talking about a person who began to use sex and love as an emotional fix at age five, six, seven, or eight. When thinking is still quite concrete and emotions are close to the surface, experiences can contribute to deeply rooted psychological structures. For a person who did not get into the addictive cycle of behavior and did not have sex and love as the basic fix in his or her psychological organization until the 20s, 30s, 40s, or even later, there will not be the same level of rigidity and rootedness in the ruts or habit patterns.

Since there are a wide variety of addictive patterns, this is another factor that needs to be considered when determining the length of the addiction. In other words, if a person has been able to achieve periods of sobriety, this can be indicative of a less severe form of the addiction. On the other hand, it can make treatment more difficult because the person may see less need for active involvement in the recovery process. Other diseases can have periods of remission where the disease is still present but the acute symptomatology is not shown. This is also true with sex and love addictions, in which there can be long periods of remission of the acting-out patterns. Sex and love addicts can also reach plateaus of behavior and stay there for a fairly long time. An example of a remission would be the priest who was celibate and refrained from masturbation for over 30 years. He then started going to pornographic bookstores and participating in mutual masturbation. "Plateau" would also describe the state of the sex and love addict who had 37 affairs in the 13 years of his marriage, but in the 18 months of his separation from his wife had a steady girlfriend with only 2 incidents of sex outside his primary relationship. He considered his behavior to be normal during his separation, despite the fact that he was unfaithful to his new girlfriend.

Most addictions have periods of greater and lesser intensity. This is partly due to the fact that when the addiction is intensified, the addict cannot sustain this high level of activity for long because of the strain it puts on him or her physically, mentally, emotionally, in other relationships, financially, and in relation to work. Binge-type behavior, where there is a great deal of acting out, takes a great deal of energy and requires much deception, scheming, and manipulating. It can be costly, and is highly distracting to the other responsibilities of a person's life. It is actually surprising that most addicts can find the time, energy, resources, and support of unwitting friends, family, and coworkers to do as much acting out as they actually do. They need plateaus, remissions, and periods of abstinence and quiescence in order to regroup and keep their lives from going out of control completely.

Risk-Taking Behaviors

A fourth area that should be considered in terms of estimating the severity of a sex and love addiction is the amount and type of risk-taking behaviors with which the addict is involved, such as unsafe sex, risking accidents or harm, or toying with suicidal thoughts or behaviors. The more risk-taking behaviors are present, the more severe the addiction. Activities like anonymous sex, sex with partners who are not well known, use of prostitutes, failure to use contraceptive protection, use of devices to inflict pain or heighten orgasm, going to dangerous areas, having sex in unusual places or positions, or acting out despite feeling depressed and disgusted with oneself, are all risk-taking situations that may prove lethal. The ability to take potentially fatal risks while not caring about the possible outcome is indicative of a severe form of sex and love addiction even without the presence of risk to others.

Some addictive behaviors are dangerous or harmful to others, and therefore are more severe. These behaviors include exhibiting oneself, voyeurism, indecent liberties or touching, obscene phone calls, sexual abuse of children, incest, and compulsive rape.

The risks involved with AIDS and other sexually transmitted diseases, and even with dangerous neighborhoods, are fairly obvious, as are the risks inflicted on other people by the invasion of their privacy, personal space, and bodies. One area that is not always as clear is the risk taking involved with thoughts or behaviors that toy with suicide. As I was writing this book, I got a letter in the mail from a sex and love addict who had read one of my articles on the subject. He reported having struggled with a sex and love addiction for years despite psychotherapy, and included this poem:

Shotgun Pellets

Have you ever lived with a shadow,
A shadow looking larger than dreams?
Have you ever cringed in the mirror
When sight reveals scar tissue and pleas?

Have you ever loaded your shotgun,
Hoping birdshot pellets would destroy
What is surely not worthy of creation,
What you wish most sincerely no more?

When last did you cock the hair trigger,
Being careful as to keep from the jerk,
A jerk that would send the lead bullet
Spiralling headlong first into dirt?

Have you ever run from your shadows
'Till you had nowhere else left to run?
Tell me, when will you blow your fool head off?
Tell me, how far can a headless man run?

The risk level for this addict is obviously high; often, addicts will not tell people how suicidal they really feel for fear that someone will try to stop them. I had another client who told her friend that she had almost bought a large number of pills at the drug store, but during her session with me she said nothing about this. Fortunately, her friend alerted me to the situation. Even when I confronted my client with the fact that she had withheld information from me, it took a long time for her to finally tell me the truth.

Other sex and love addicts take risks such as driving recklessly and hoping to have an "accident." Their suicidal impulses put them at risk because they are not always able to control the outcome, as in the case of accidental asphyxiation when sexual pleasure enhancers do not work as planned.

The presence of other addictions can add to the risk involved in various activities. Drug and alcohol addictions can impair judgment, increase impulsivity, and decrease inhibitions so that dangers become less apparent or frightening. Chemicals can enhance the addict's numbness and "don't-care" attitude. This makes risk taking easier and even challenging. Addicts get excitement from "living on the edge." They need to add to the power of the fix as their addiction progresses and tolerance increases. Taking chances with the potential for disease or injury actually enhances their arousal and the intensity of their experience. If they are sedated with depressant drugs or alcohol, they will need a bigger fix or "charge" in order to "get off." If they feel hyper from stimulant drugs or "mellow" from marijuana, they may need to take more risks in order to feel any sexual stimulation or arousal at all.

Assessing the severity of a sex and love addiction using criteria like rapidity of onset, severity of consequences, length of addiction, and risk-taking behaviors can create problems for both the clinician and the client. At this point, the best we can do is make a gross judgment that lacks precision or the ability to predict future behaviors. We can "guestimate" that a sex and love addict has a mild, moderate, or severe form of the addiction, but there are many other factors that interfere with the prognostic ability of such a judgment. Motivation, for example, is a critical factor that can improve the prognosis for a person with a more severe form of sex and love addiction and decrease the success of an addict whose addiction is only mild. Addicts will distort the meaning of the severity level, for example, and tell themselves (although they often will not tell you) that they can take their time, that the addiction is not so bad, or that they may "grow out of it." They will resist more intensive therapeutic intervention, often because their addiction is not as bad as others they hear or read about. They lose motivation for long-term maintainance of the addiction because they see it as a less severe case. They think, "I'll wait until it gets worse before I do anything." They lose sight of the fact that the crucial element in needing treatment is the presence of the illness, not the severity of the case. Severity relates to the types and amount of treatment needed, not to the need for treatment. When an addiction is present with any level of severity, treatment is necessary so that more damage will not be done to either the addict or those people around him or her.

MULTIPLE ADDICTIONS

Our awareness of addictive behaviors is bringing us to see the presence of multiple addictions in clients. As with sex and love addictions, many of these multiply addicted people stand right in front of our eyes, yet we do not see their many addictions. For instance, it has long been customary for coffee to be served at meetings of Alcoholics Anonymous and for cigarette smoking to be tolerated. No one viewed caffeinism or smoking as addictions. They were merely bad habits, while chemical dependency was considered a "real" addiction. When we consider the question of severity—caffeine is a chemical to which millions of people are mildly addicted, and nicotine injuries and kills nonsmokers as well as smokers—it is obvious that many alcoholics are, in fact, multiply addicted to alcohol, nicotine, and caffeine, although some of their addictions are worse than others. Still, the pattern of depending on something outside one's own internal resources to improve one's mood, calm down, or relieve stress or tension is strikingly similar. The habit patterns are very much the same although the chemicals are used differently and have differing effects and potency.

It should not be too surprising, although it may be rather annoying—especially to the addict—to see that anyone who has become addicted to anything is vulnerable to becoming multiply addicted. Addictions are rooted in both genetic and psychological habit patterns that have formed deep grooves or ruts. They are difficult to escape, and easy to fall back into. The Augustine Fellowship of Sex and Love Addicts Anonymous was founded by someone who found that recovery from chemical dependency did not solve his sexual acting out problems as he had expected it would. Another addiction was present that had to be dealt with before he could achieve the serenity and order in life that other recovering people had found and that he had heard so much about in A.A. meetings.

As with addictions in general, multiple addictions have both a physiological and a biological base. The genetic and physiological bases of multiple addictions are unclear. Little has been done in this area, although it will be explored in great depth in the future as the science of addictionology gains more recognition and acceptance. The best genetic research has been done in families of alcoholics, and has indicated that there is a clear pattern of alcoholism running in families such that individuals with a family history of alcoholism are at a two-and-a-half-times greater risk for developing the disease themselves than someone with no family history of alcoholism. This means that the odds are 1 in 10 that anyone might become alcoholic, but they are 1 in 4 for someone with an alcoholic in the family.

Studies of the genetic susceptibility for alcoholism have been difficult to conduct due to factors such as the lack of records, families that move or cannot be located, family secrecy, and disagreement over the diagnostic criteria for alcoholism. The traditional estimate for clients entering treatment for alcoholism was that 50 percent had alcoholism present in their families. However, further research showed that when you asked about grandparents as well as parents, the average shot up to 75 percent. It is quite likely, therefore, that there is a stronger genetic factor in alcoholism than had previously been believed.

Researchers in chemical dependency have not had much success in getting information as accurate as that of researchers in other disease areas. This is partly because of the social stigma attached to chemical dependencies and related family secrets. Information on family histories of sex and love addiction will no doubt be even more difficult to obtain due to the shame and embarrassment associated with sexuality in general, and out-of-control sexuality in particular. It has been my experience that far fewer clients come to me with information about other sex and love addicts in their family trees than about other addictions. Many of them do not recognize the existence of more obvious addictions like workaholism, nicotine addiction, and over-eating, so sex and love addictions, which may have been hidden from the children, will be less well known.

One recovering alcoholic who came for help with his sex and love addiction described a mother who was alcoholic and a "man chaser." Another had a father who had a reputation for womanizing. An acquaintance reported his family as having moved a number of times due to efforts to start over and break the cycle of repeated affairs. Another acquaintance told me of her grandmother's history of affairs, and the shame and scandal experienced by the family due to this woman's "self-indulgence" and "lack of willpower." These may all be examples of sex and love addictions, but without the concept and the diagnostic criteria, it is impossible to get an accurate picture of the percentage of sex and love addictions in the families of sex and love addicts currently in treatment or recovery. It is also extremely difficult to estimate the number of multiply addicted relatives of a multiply addicted person. A good guess, however, is that there are more addicts and multiply addicted people than have been identified as yet. If this is found true, it will increase the power of the genetic factor in all addictions, including sex and love addictions.

The psychological factors in sex and love addiction are a bit easier to define. First, people who become addicted develop obsessive/compulsive patterns of behavior. They form strong habits. They become attached to repetition and ritual, and seek comfort and predictability in their routines. Many people find it hard to understand how this can be; to outsiders, the addict's behavior appears so painful to him- or herself and to others, and so lacking in rewards and successful outcomes, that they cannot see why the person remains so dependent and attached to negative behaviors. In chapter 2, we reviewed the power of the high to hook a person; thus, part of the reason for continuing multiple addictions is the reinforcing power of the addiction. The other part of the dependency is the inertia and resistance that we all must overcome at some time.

This contentment with the status quo and fear of trying things differently was borne out to me by a family of multiply addicted people who had their 12-year-old daughter in inpatient treatment for drug addiction. The mother was addicted to prescription medications and nicotine. Her 18-year-old daughter, 14-year-old son, and the 12-year-old in treatment were likewise all addicted to drugs and nicotine. The mother's boyfriend had the same two addictions. I suspect that all three women in the family may have been sex and love addicts. The mother was extremely dependent on her boyfriend, and had a history of being sexually abused. The oldest daughter had a child by her 40-year-old school teacher (a secret that did not come out to family and therapists until she was hospitalized with a suicidal depression). The 12-year-old was seductive, dressed to appear older, and could not stay away from the boys on the unit. Dishonesty riddled this family. Despite two months of intensive treatment that included family therapy, the mother, boyfriend, and 12-year-old colluded to hide from treatment staff the fact that the patient did not attend an A.A. meeting as required on any of her three passes home. At the end of the girl's stay, when the family was confronted with their habit of lying, the mother could only say, "We are doing the best that we can." Multiple addictions and their concurrent requisite of dishonesty were a way of life for them, a deep groove from which they could not yet find their way out.

Psychologically speaking, there are a number of facets to the addiction groove. First, there is the pattern of seeking a high. The instant-gratification, quick-fix habit has been repeatedly ingrained in the addicted person. Addicts "want what they want, when they want it," as they say in the S.L.A.A. program. They are accustomed to predictable, fast, comfortable outcomes. They do not like to have to work for something, to wait, or to be bored or uncomfortable. They resent having to be patient or making an effort when there is "an easier, softer way." For example, a female sex and love addict complained about the large number of men at the meeting that she attended, but later admitted that "laziness" kept her from going to the women's meeting that I had recommended because it was farther from her home. Another sex and love addict was annoyed that his confession of multiple affairs did not bring him immediate relief or fix his marriage. He was ignoring the fact that he had kept this secret through months of marital therapy brought about due to his lack of sexual interest in his recovering sex and love addict wife.

Second, the habit of dependency is a hard habit to break. The addict has become acclimatized to coping with increasing tolerance, growing dependencies, expanding cravings, and an avoidance of withdrawal. He or she knows how to operate, how to function in this world. A world without dependencies and their related cravings, withdrawals, and tolerance may seem dull, lifeless, and empty. Reality is turned inside out, so the real emptiness of cruising is seen as "really living," and the richness of peace and commitment is sloughed off as worthless and foolish. The true dependency of the addiction is hidden behind a smoke screen of lies to oneself and others. The addict tells him- or herself that there are real friends and support in his or her addict world when the truth is that the only thing that holds the group together is mutual addictive behavior. I frequently see this in the hurt and disappointment addicts experience when they are hospitalized and none of their addicted friends call, write, or visit. What the addicts have deluded themselves into thinking were "true blue" bonds of friendship proved instead to be superficial user relationships, without commitment or loyalty. However, when addicts leave the hospital, whom do they seek out? Old habits are hard to break. Therefore, addicts return to their old dependencies rather than trying to find friends who will be as dependable in foul weather as they are in fine.

Third, the routine of obsessions and compulsions is difficult to stop. The habit of thinking or fantasizing and then having to compulsively act out is like the binge/purge cycle of the bulemic. As thoughts fill the addict with excitement, anticipation, and energy, he or she feels closer and closer to losing control. When the rush into action takes place, it consumes the person with the passion of the moment, and all reason and rationality are lost in the explosion. What a "rush!" What a release! What an orgasm! The guilt, shame, and remorse come later. For the time being, the addict feels fulfilled. The pattern of riding the wave of sexual and romantic excitement to the crash on the beach is worth the ride and is difficult to give up. Ordinary life pales in comparison to the highs and lows of the obsession/compulsion routine. A sex and love addict cannot imagine living any other way. He sees regularity as void of life and commitment as enslavement. However, some addicts find that they can use this habit pattern to strengthen their recovery process by obsessing about their recovery program and feeling compelled to make meetings and talk to sponsors. A recovering addict with whom I worked faithfully kept a daily journal, kept every therapy appointment (while obsessively keeping count) and asked for more when needed, and reportedly drove over five hundred miles a week for therapy and S.L.A.A. meetings in a car that did not always function properly during his early stages of recovery. Any direction he was given was obsessively and compulsively followed. Thus, a bad habit was put to good use.

Fourth, the pattern of secrecy and living a double life is hard to give up, especially in the early stages when the addict feels vulnerable. The addict believes that if he or she decides to drop all pretense and be completely open and honest, he or she will be hurt, rejected, or abused, just as happened in the past. Moreover, "getting away with" things is fun. One teenage sex and love addict lit up when he started telling me that people actually would listen to him during his obscene phone calls. "I couldn't believe that they would listen to that crap," he exclaimed with obvious delight. He was thrilled by the clandestine nature of anonymous calling, and the fact that "half of them would actually listen and some even talked back" added to the kick. Another sex and love addict had the best of both worlds. He was an undercover federal agent, which made for easy excuses to his wife for not coming home, so he was able to be sneaky at work and at play. He could not imagine life without some sort of intrigue, and he was not satisfied with having it only at work.

Addictions wear grooves. Multiple addictions wear deeper grooves. Releasing and getting out of these patterns, habits, and ruts is hard work. Add to this the genetic programming that may make an addict vulnerable to developing these grooves or may even have preprogrammed them, and you have a big problem. Recovery means getting out of the old ruts and making new, positive ones. For the multiply addicted person, it means falling back in the addiction hole more than once and more than once having to climb out again. Fortunately, a positive aspect of this phenomenon is that if the person does have an initial recovery experience, relapse can be handled somewhat more easily because the new grooves of recovery have begun to be established.

Combinations of Addictions

In his research with recovering sex addicts, Patrick Carnes (1988) has been able to provide some initial data on the types and percentages of multiply addicted sex addicts. He found that about half the sex addicts in his study reported also being chemically dependent, a third indicated an addiction to food, roughly a quarter saw themselves as workaholics, and only about 5 percent said they were addicted to gambling. He did not have figures for other addictions like nicotine, caffeine, sugar, exercise, religion, spending, or power. Put in tabular form, the rough data looks like this:

Rough Estimates of Cross-Addictions for Sex Addicts

Chemicals	half
Food	one third
Work	one quarter
Gambling	5 percent
Nicotine	?
Caffeine	?
Sugar	?
Exercise	?
Religion	?
Spending	?
Power	?

Some addicts for whom we have initial data fall in more than one category, so a person could be chemically dependent, nicotine-addicted, an overeater, an overspender, a religious fanatic, a sex and love addict, an exercise fanatic, a workaholic, a gambler, and a coffee lover with a sweet tooth. Some recovering people that I know groan every time they hear of another thing on which a person can get hooked because they know that either they already are hooked or it will be only a matter of time before they contract that particular addiction. They are only half joking when they say, "Oh, no, not another addiction!" I worked with one client whose addictive patterns with chemicals, sex, food, religion, spending, and work were identified in the therapy process. I expect that he will continue to discover more patterns of his "addictiveness," as he called it, as he continues to evaluate the past and the present.

Patterns of Multiple Addictions

While defining specific patterns of multiple addictions is quite risky and is based primarily on clinical experience rather than scientific data, there is some experiential evidence to suggest two broad types: consecutive addictions and coexisting addictions. In consecutive addictions, as one addiction is brought under control, another develops. In coexisting addictions, two or more addictions are active at the same time. An example of a consecutive pattern of addictions would be a drug addiction followed by a food addiction and then workaholism. It would look like this:

A coexisting pattern of multiple addictions might be the combination of sex and work or the twosome of sex and food. It would look something like this:

There are all sorts of possible combinations and permutations that could be imagined, but the important point is that the addict and those who care about him or her must be aware of the existence of more than one addiction and the possibility that more addictions may develop later.

An illustration of consecutive addictions would be the schoolteacher who recovered from alcoholism only to discover that he had a sex and love addiction. After he tackled this problem, he began to find himself totally devoted to his students. He began to come in early, leave late, take on additional assignments that no one else would do, and create an elaborate system of rewards for his pupils. He refused to stay home sick or to consider taking time off from work for any reason at all. His life became his work. When he was finally able to get his work life back into a manageable framework, he started to binge on food. He was embarrassed by his program of starvation and its follow-up, a public binge that brought on comments about his excessive appetite. When he went to work on his food addiction, he then began to want to overspend. He felt like everywhere he turned he encountered another addiction. His addictive self would migrate from addiction to addiction, and never appeared to be satisfied. He found that he was always seeking some sort of good feeling outside himself to heal his deep wounds of neglect and abuse. He could not imagine ever being able to make himself feel all right by himself or that he could have friends and supporters who would affirm him just as he was.

Coexisting addictions seem to stack one on top of the other in order to improve the intensity of the high. A physician, who was well known, successful, and well-off, needed to combine the gratification of power with sex in order to get off. A young cocaine addict found that the numbing power of the cocaine allowed him to combine his sex and love addiction with his drug high. He could delay orgasm longer when he was using cocaine, so he could have "the best of both worlds"—drugs and sex. One addiction seemed to fuel the other. After a six-month period of abstinence due to a relationship, he started using drugs again. He eventually found that he needed cocaine to be the lover he wanted to be, and that he needed sex to maximize his drug high.

Another addict had a pattern of consecutive addictions, followed by co-existing addictions, and then consecutive addictions again. He began his sex and love addiction, as is often the case, during his adolescence, and did not begin to drink and use drugs until later. He had a well-established pattern of compulsive masturbation as well as an obsession with young men by the time he began his addiction to drugs and alcohol. The two types of addiction coexisted for a while until he achieved sobriety from chemicals. As addicts usually do, he believed his sex and love addiction would go away once he got rid of the chemicals that reduced his inhibitions and allowed him to act out sexually. This was not the case, and he suffered for more years as a sober alcoholic and an active sex and love addict. Finally he was able to achieve sobriety from both chemicals and his sex and love addiction.

The Drive and Cycle of Multiple Addictions

While we are not able to say exactly what causes an addiction, we are able to identify some of the driving forces behind addictive behaviors. Even though there may be more than one addiction, the dynamics behind all addictions seem fairly similar. A major factor is low self-esteem and feelings of being worthless, useless, and empty. Addictions take a terrible toll on a person's self-worth. The constant repetition of loss of control, broken promises, and weakness in the face of temptation will create a lack of self-esteem even in those who felt some self-worth to begin with. For those who were damaged before addiction, self-esteem will be buried even deeper.

Patrick Carnes (1983, 120) has identified what he calls four "Core Beliefs" that sex addicts hold:

1. "I am basically a bad, unworthy person."
2. "No one would love me as I am."
3. "My needs are never going to be met if I have to depend on others."
4. "Sex is my most important need."

These beliefs drive the addiction on its progressive and destructive course. On a basic and primitive level, the sex and love addict lacks a sense of value and worth. His or her existence is not and has never been celebrated by anyone. This feeling of essential unworthiness creates an intense need in the addict. He or she craves to be valued, to be worthwhile, and to be of importance to someone else. Sexual or romantic attraction and attractiveness can simulate this core value. Lovers say, "I cannot live without you." This is the fix that the sex and love addict is seeking for his or her gnawing emptiness and lack of self-esteem. To be chased, pursued, desired, needed, and demanded hits at the core deficits of the addicted person. In a sexual or romantic encounter, suddenly they become "someone." They count for something. The addiction high feeds the sex and love addict's empty core. Nothing and no one else are needed.

As sex and love addicts become hooked on their "goodness" (their value and worth in the sexual and romantic arena), they begin to create the illusion of being loved. Their feelings of unlovableness fade as their passion grows, and they begin to create the grand delusion that will rule their life. "Maybe," they think, "someone will love me after all." Addicts have reservations, however, that their needs are so great and so consuming (like their passion) that they will never be realistically met by another person or by any sort of activity. The addiction, at least temporarily, makes this fear diminish as well. There are periods of satisfaction. There is a sense of fulfillment. There is, again, the illusion of contentment. Alas, however, it never lasts, so the addiction drives the addict further down the never-ending road. Satisfaction seems close at times, and yet so far. Perhaps it will come the next time if I have the right partner, or maybe the right sexual stimulus. Driven farther and farther from reality, the delusional thinking of the addiction takes over the addict's mind and reinforces the power of these core beliefs.

Carnes (1983, 15) outlined this process in what he calls the "Addiction Cycle." The cycle begins with the core beliefs that create impaired thinking. Impaired thoughts beget preoccupation. Then, rituals take over, followed by acting out. After the compulsive behavior, there is a period of despair that leads back to the need for a fix. More sex and love preoccupation is the easy answer. The cycle creates unmanageability in the addict's life, which reinforces his or her core beliefs. (See figure on facing page.)

An example of how this cycle works for the sex and love addict would be the gradual sexualizing of the counseling relationship of a professional who has been consulting with me. This man, in his early 60s, grew up in a "good," working class, religious family. His father was a salesman and his mother cared for the children. His mother was the more organized and dominant partner. His father was passive and somewhat detached, but was a reliable provider without any obvious character defects. There were never any verbal or physical expressions of love or affection in the home, and the children were expected to behave. A cat-o'-nine-tails was available to enforce discipline, but this was seen as normal for the time and locale. There were no overt signs of neglect or abuse, but this sex and love addict grew up feeling vaguely

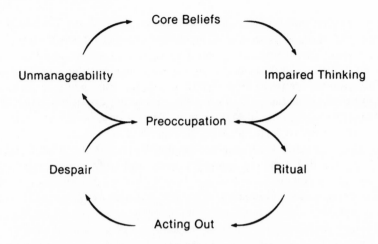

Source: Carnes, Patrick, *Out of the Shadows: Understanding Sexual Addiction.* Minneapolis, MN: CompCare Publications, 1983, p. 15, "The Addictive System." Reprinted with permission.

bad and unworthy. He did not feel loved by those who were supposed to love him. He had a sense that his needs would not be met, even though he was not clear what they were. Sex was an important early need, although it was kept quite secret and never discussed, which may have reinforced the power of sex to fix his emptiness and unworthiness. Compulsive masturbation was a problem into his 30s.

This sex and love addict grew up with an unspoken set of core beliefs that made him vulnerable to the fixing power of sex and love addiction. These beliefs began to distort his thinking. He had been taught in his professional training not to touch or have physical contact with those who came to him for counseling. He also was taught not to allow himself to stare at, ogle, or fantasize about others, because this might feed into sexual and romantic desires and might result in his acting on these feelings and urges. His low self-esteem and need for recognition and affirmation, however, began to undermine these teachings, and he started to think that touching clients might be all right. He used the current climate in counseling that was exploring boundaries and sexuality to begin to build a rationale for hugging. He ignored the physical turn-on he felt when he hugged good-looking young men. Soon he developed impaired thinking that allowed him to hug and kiss his clients. The addiction began to take hold. He became more preoccupied with contact with attractive young men, and started to develop rituals that would make sexual contact possible. Hugging and kissing developed into mutual masturbation, and eventually he ended up frequenting pornographic bookstores. Despair followed acting out, and his self-worth eroded even more. The cycle was now in full swing. He became so unmanageable that he was eventually reported, and thus he was able to get the help for which he could not bring himself to ask because of his system of core beliefs and impaired thinking.

This pattern seems obvious from a distance, but when an addict is deeply involved in the cycle, he or she cannot get enough perspective to see what is really going on in their lives. The rut or groove that addicts are in seems normal to them most of the time, and "not that bad" when it is really out of control. Most of us are similarly unaware of the habit patterns and routines that rule our everyday lives, and only notice them when something happens to disrupt them. The other day I noticed I was feeling somewhat nervous and anxious when I stopped at work on my day off. I was out of my usual pattern and time schedule, and had a brief flurry of uncertainty because I did not have my usual set of guidelines and expectations for my time, activities, and behaviors. Vacations can cause similar disruptions in routines and patterns that we take for granted, and may leave us temporarily feeling lost or out-of-sorts, saying "I don't know what to do with myself."

Addictions, driven by core beliefs such as unworthiness, create these cycles of thinking, feeling, and behavior. Sex and love are powerful reinforcers. Multiple addictions can cause deeper cycles and be even more reinforcing. The pattern of reinforcement is not constant, but this is the most powerful type of reinforcement. In psychology, we have defined differing types of reinforcement. There is positive reinforcement, which means giving a person a positive reward for producing the desired behavior. If we want a child to be quiet, when they comply, we reward them with a kind word—"You are being so good"—or a token of appreciation like a piece of candy. Negative or aversive reinforcement works the same way: An undesired behavior is ignored, criticized—"Don't do that"—or followed by consequences like losing a toy or confinement to one's room. Both positive and negative reinforcers will gradually be taken for granted and will become less effective if they are routine and expected. For example, the weekly paycheck is a reward for working, but it loses its reinforcing power since it comes routinely. Likewise, a physically abused child becomes used to being hit, and the blows lose their effectiveness. The most powerful reinforcement is intermittent reinforcement. The unexpected word of praise and the unanticipated reward have the most impact. An unexpected compliment by your boss, for instance, will make more of an impression than your regular paycheck, even though you can do more with the money. Addictions have both routine and intermittent reinforcing powers. Sex and love addicts can count on their high, and use it routinely to make themselves feel good. They also can find unexpected and exciting new highs in new activities, new partners, new scenes, and new acting-out behaviors. Multiple addictions can multiply the reinforcing possibilities for addicts.

Order of Treatment

When considering multiple addictions, one of the most important questions is which addiction to tackle first. The answer will vary with the individual, but there are some fairly clear guidelines that professionals and recovering people can follow. The first rule of thumb is that if there is a chemical dependency, it must be addressed first. The addict must be free of alcohol and drugs before any other problems can be attended to in treatment. The obvious reason for this is that an actively using drug addict or alcoholic has chemicals in his or her brain that will interfere with thinking, feeling, and the ability to control behavior and impulses. Therefore, being drug- and alcohol-free is basic and essential for beginning any recovery process.

The second rule of thumb is to address the addiction that is most dangerous to the person or to others. Some addictions are potentially more immediately lethal than others. A sex and love addiction, especially if there is acting out that might expose the person to AIDS, places the addict at more imminent risk than smoking, gambling, or overeating, although the latter clearly have the potential to damage the person physically and psychologically. We know that nicotine addiction can kill, but lethality is possible only after years of abuse, whereas drugs can kill at any time via an overdose, and sex and love addiction can kill with a single sexual encounter that includes unsafe sexual activity.

The third rule of thumb is to treat the addiction that has the highest potential for relapse or that may be the cause of relapse into other addictions. Sex and love addictions are frequently the cause of relapse in drug and alcohol addictions. The recovery programs of A.A. and N.A., in fact, recommend that new members refrain from involvement in new "relationships" for at least a year. They are referring to falling in love, not making new friends. A love relationship has a high potential for making a chemically dependent person vulnerable to relapse. If the relationship fails, the person may reach for a drink or a drug to "drown their sorrows" and numb the pain of hurt and rejection. If the relationship works, it may pull the recovering person away from the program in terms of the time, energy, and thinking that the love affair takes. The new love may also use drugs or alcohol or have friends who do, which will put the recovering addict or alcoholic in the face of temptation. If recovering addicts and alcoholics need to be careful of new relationships, sex and love addicts need to be twice as cautious because of their increased vulnerability. Whatever makes a person more at risk for relapse needs to be treated.

These three rules—removing chemicals, lethality, and relapse producers—seem to dictate a strategy that would treat chemical dependency first, sex and love addiction second, and other addictions (like food, work, gambling, spending, nicotine, or religion) next. There are benefits to the recovering person from such a program. First, it would probably be much too confusing to try to deal with all the problems at once. The likelihood of relapse in one area would be high, and the person might feel either overwhelmed or like a failure. Second, the experience of recovery from addiction in one area will provide the person with a model for recovery, a groove that could make the second recovery a bit easier. Third, most sex and love addicts who are also chemically dependent say that recovery from sex and love addiction is harder, so some strength, hope, and experience from another recovery will aid in the struggle to overcome sex and love addiction. Fourth, sex and love addictions usually have their roots earlier in childhood than other addictions like gambling or chemical abuse, and the letting-go process will be harder for the behavior that has been around longer and has more primitive roots.

There may be circumstances that require the concurrent treatment of multiple addictions rather than the consecutive treatment outlined above. One alcoholic who also had pedophilia and gambling problems could not stay sober due to the interaction of his three addictions. Moreover, his sexual acting out with minors was both damaging to the children and illegal, and could not be tolerated while he was getting sober from alcohol. His gambling was less a danger to others, but could not be ignored once it was uncovered, as it would be a double message to treat the alcohol and sex and love addictions while ignoring compulsive gambling. His habits of impaired thinking would distort the intention of focusing on the more destructive addictions and see it as permission to continue to use other addictive behaviors to solve problems or cope with feelings. Most of the time, however, it is possible to take one addiction at a time in the recovery process. As addicts discover their own tendencies to become addicted, they will be on the lookout for new fixes and new things on which they might become dependent, like food, work, spending, power, or religion.

4

Short-Term Treatment and Recovery

The last two chapters describe short- and long-term treatment and recovery. The idea that recovery from an addictive disease involves two major phases is not new. Ernie Larsen has written about the two stages of recovery from chemical dependency in *Stage II Recovery—Life beyond Addiction*. He defined the first stage as obtaining abstinence and the second stage as putting one's life back together. Much the same concept will be described in the next two chapters. Short-term treatment and recovery focuses on achieving sobriety from sex and love addiction. Long-term treatment and recovery looks at how to sustain sobriety over the long haul.

Initially, the sex and love addict needs to stop his or her addiction. Usually this is the primary focus of attention and energy in the first year of the recovery process. The recovering person needs to learn that he or she has an addiction to love and/or sex, and what to do to change the addictive cycle that has been ruling his or her life. This involves discovering that there is help, support, and hope; that there are Twelve Step programs and professionals who know what to do; and that he or she must commit to a program of recovery. Addicts learn that they need to identify "bottom-line" behaviors and "triggers." They find that they need to change their habit of lying to cover their addiction. They surrender to the wisdom of other recovering people, and find solace in the fellowship of a Twelve Step program. They start to deal with their feelings of shame and guilt.

As recovery progresses, they begin to have answers to their own questions like "Why me?" or "What did I do to deserve this?" They become able to live without so many defenses, and they start to eliminate their practice of denial, minimization, rationalization, and projection. They learn helpful slogans, say-ings, and prayers with which to help themselves when they are really strug-gling with their addictive impulses and ruminations—like "One day at a time" or "H.A.L.T." (*H*ungry, *A*ngry, *L*onely, *T*ired). They start the process of relin-quishing their victimhood, and come to see the reality of both their victim-ization and their victimizing. They go through a process of grief and mourning. They begin to grasp a sense of spirituality and joy in living, and they learn the dangers of slips and relapses.

Once sobriety has been established for at least six months, the recovering person can begin to look at the bigger picture. He or she can start to consider what long-term ("the rest of my life") treatment and recovery involves. Addicts begin to discover the overall ecology of the recovery process and how the various components work together in their lives. They continue to reinforce the things that they have found to "work for them" in terms of day-to-day sobriety and, at the same time, they start to build an outer layer of self-protection by furthering their own understanding of themselves and what might make them vulnerable to returning to their sex and love addiction. They may experience some Post-Traumatic Stress Disorder (P.T.S.D.) symp-toms either from their addiction or from prior stresses that were never processed due to the addiction's primacy. They may have delayed or ongoing medical problems or symptoms that they need to understand and put into perspective, or they may need to come to grips with the reality of the risks they took while they were in their active addiction. They need to connect with the addict and the child within them, and be able to identify which is which and how to help each part. They need to be able to affirm themselves and see themselves as persons of worth and value.

During long-term recovery, addicts must take a look at their family of origin and see how both environmental and genetic factors are active in the disease process. They need to discover what healthy intimacy is and how it relates to sex and love. They should be able to look at their support system and evaluate how strong and effective it really is. They need to identify how to be responsible and assertive on their own behalf. These ideas are presented as aspects of long-term recovery and treatment, since they are not the focus of the first 6 to 12 months of recovery, and are better examined once some initial sobriety has been established.

These two dimensions of treatment and recovery can be conceptualized in terms of the addiction cycle outlined by Patrick Carnes in his book *Out of the Shadows*. Recovery in some ways turns the cycle upside down. If we look at the cycle that Carnes suggested and start at the "bottom," we can identify where to begin short-term treatment and recovery. As we progress, the second circle shows us what is involved in long-term recovery and treat-ment (Carnes, 1983, 15). (See figure on facing page.)

The initial focus of treatment and recovery is on stopping the acting-out behaviors in order to establish some mental clarity and stability in the re-

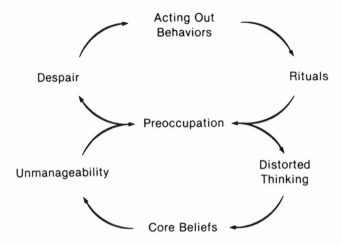

covering addict's life. Soon thereafter, issues like the despair, depression, and pain of the addiction and withdrawal become important. At the same time, rituals connected with the sex and love addiction are addressed with concerns like "people, places, and things." Then, the mental obsession and preoccupation are tackled as the recovery process is solidified.

Later on, as the addict establishes some sort of sobriety and control over his or her life, the larger issues are approached. The addict begins to come to terms with the unmanageability of his or her life, and starts to think about his or her "stinking thinking," which inevitably leads him or her back into addiction. Finally, the sex and love addict will address core beliefs related to self-worth, lovability, needs, and the role of love and sex in his or her normal life. These are long-term issues with which we all struggle in some form. The sex and love addict cannot afford to take his or her time or to ignore these important issues because they are the essence of the outer layer of defense against relapse and remission of a chronic disease. Relapse is a common aspect of chronic disease, so sex and love addicts need to develop strategies of living that will protect them not only from immediate impulse or temptation but also from the more subtle "set-up" to act out sexually or romantically that will characterize sober life after the first year of abstinence.

Human beings have a tendency to forget their pain. We are better at remembering the joys and highs than we are at recalling the hurts and sorrows. For example, I can only vaguely remember getting up in the middle of the night to feed and care for my infant son, who is now eight. At the time, I seem to recall, it was a stressful, almost torturous, experience, but now, with the glow of fond memories, it does not seem so bad. Addicts go through the same sort of forgetting process. At first their addiction is a horrid thought that some can barely allow themselves to remember. It is painful to talk about and brings on intense feelings of shame, embarrassment, and humiliation. As sobriety grows, however, it becomes easier to recall and speak about the "living hell" of an active sex and love addiction. Unfortunately, after still more time, the painful memories fade and the recollections may become more favorable. This is a danger sign, a warning of imminent relapse. Addicts in Twelve Step programs make it a point to regularly attend two, three, or four meetings a week to "keep it green"; in other words, to keep the memory of the reality of the pain, suffering, and degradation fresh in their minds and uncluttered by thoughts like "Maybe, it wasn't so bad." This is an essential part of the long-term recovery program.

In their haste to recover, some addicts jump from a short-term program into long-term recovery issues. Often, this effort to speed up the recovery process fails disastrously. The basic foundation for recovery has not been firmly established, so it is easily abandoned after some initial success. The usual result is relapse, feelings of hopelessness, and shame. The second go-round can be harder than the first, so it is better for all concerned to do it right the first time. "Doing it right" involves a short-term recovery program focused on establishing and reinforcing sobriety. It means learning the "tricks of the trade"—the tools of recovery like the Twelve Steps, S.L.A.A. meetings, sponsors, readings, prayer, and meditation. When these have been firmly established, the sex and love addict can then move into long-term recovery issues like self-worth, families of origin, and healthy intimacy and sexual relations.

TWELVE STEP PROGRAMS: H.O.W.

The most effective and reliable means of recovering from an addiction to date has been to use a Twelve Step program of recovery. The Twelve Steps originated with Alcoholics Anonymous over 50 years ago. Since then, over two hundred self-help groups have adopted the Twelve Steps as their guide to recovery from obsessive and compulsive thoughts, feelings, and behaviors. The Twelve Steps seem to be particularly effective with addictions. Over 90 percent of those who have attended A.A. for five years or more have been able to stay sober. Many sex and love addicts came to their fellowships after having become sober from alcohol and/or drugs through A.A. and/or Narcotics Anonymous.

Currently, there are three Twelve Steps fellowships for sex and love addicts. Sex and Love Addicts Anonymous (S.L.A.A.) is found mostly on the East Coast. Sex Addicts Anonymous (S.A.A.) can be most readily found in the middle states. S.A., or Sexaholics Anonymous, is primarily established on the West Coast. The groups' headquarters are Boston, Minneapolis, and Simi Valley, California, respectively. As of 1988, they represent over one thousand local meetings. There are many commonalities, including the basic criteria for membership: "a desire to stop." There are differences, most obviously the inclusion of love addiction in S.L.A.A., but these appear to be minor compared to the broad similarities between the three programs. The approach in this book is compatible with the Augustine Fellowship, Sex and Love Addicts Anonymous.

Step One
We Admitted We Were Powerless over Sex and Love
Addiction—That Our Lives Had Become Unmanageable

This is the beginning of the recovery process. It is a surprisingly simple, and yet complex, step, as is the entire recovery process. On one hand, it is quite simple—stop! On the other hand, it is the one thing that a sex and love addict finds the most difficult to do in his or her life. Nonaddicted people often find the addict's struggle perplexing, confusing, frustrating, and un-necessary. They feel the solution is so obvious. Why can't the addicts see it, or if they see it, why can't they do it? Nonaddicted people often assume that the addict lacks willpower, morality, motivation, insight, caring, or intelli-gence. None of these stereotypes are true. The sex and love addict has a chronic, progressive, potentially fatal disease that affects him or her spiritually, mentally, emotionally, socially, financially, and physically. The awareness, acceptance, and management of this disease is a complicated and difficult ordeal, but it has great rewards and restorative powers if undertaken with sincerity and dedication. It requires the willingness to be open and honest, to follow direction, and to ask for help, and the courage to risk depending on the wisdom and insight of a fellowship rather than the guile and manip-ulations of the active addict.

The first word of the first step, "we," is significant. None of the other steps start with this word. "We" symbolizes the fellowship of recovering people. Recovery is not an "I" program. It is a "we" program that requires involvement and contact with other people, and not just any people, but other people who are suffering and recovering from the same disease. This program cannot be undertaken in isolation. The sex and love addict's addiction was filled with loneliness and isolation—despite attempts at pseudo-intimacy—so the reversal of this process, recovery, requires that he or she make contact with other people who have the same problem and who are struggling with the same difficulties.

Some love addicts can fool themselves into thinking that they have rela-tionships ("I had 37 affairs! You can count them!"), while most sex addicts are painfully aware of their inability to connect with people ("I can only have anonymous sex in parks, bookstores, and bathrooms.") Addicts, especially sex and love addicts, are users of other people. They do not really feel for or care about any one, least of all themselves, or they would not make themselves and others suffer the degradation and humiliation inherent in sex- and love-addiction–related behaviors.

The second word, "admitted," is also of vital importance in the recovery process. Addicts use many defenses to avoid dealing with the reality of their lives: They deny, rationalize, minimize, and project. The step of admission is crucial to any treatment and recovery process. Without the addicts' admission to themselves that they not only have a problem with sex and love but actually are addicted to them, no progress is possible. Many addicts have gone into treatment or started attending meetings for other reasons than the admission of the problem. For example, sex and love addicts will pretend to admit to their addiction in order to save their relationships, marriage, job, status, friends, and even their image. Eventually, this inauthentic and unfelt profession of addiction fails, and the person relapses because of a failure to really believe that he or she was addicted in the first place. The decision that one has an addiction to sex and love is a very personal and life-changing event. It cannot be taken lightly by the addict who is starting a recovery program.

The admission of an addiction to sex and love is the first part of the surrender process that is involved in the first three steps. People who recover from an addictive disease need to go through a change process that is often referred to in addiction circles as "surrender and conversion." Many people are offended, turned off, alienated, angered, and put off by the idea that a person has to go through something called "surrender and conversion." They may get images of a religious ceremony, brainwashing, intimidation, coercion, loss of freedom, lack of responsibility, or mind control. The transformation that is reflected in the idea of admitting to the disease of sex and love addiction, and then surrendering to the recovery program and the wisdom of the fellowship to convert from dependence on sex and love to a healthier and more balanced way of life, has no resemblance to the totalitarian state implied in the images of submission conveyed by phrases like brainwashing. In fact, the S.L.A.A. program is a program of "attraction," not coercion. The people who have been able to achieve sobriety from their sex and love addictions know that the addicted person has to want to change and that they cannot force anyone to adopt a new lifestyle. What they can do is offer hope, direction, and support, which is more than nonaddicted people can give. When the sex and love addict is in enough pain, he or she will ask for help and surrender to the change process.

People who care about sex and love addicts can have a good deal of trouble with this concept that the addicted person needs to want to change. A wife of a sex and love addict who had had multiple affairs came to see me, and was angry and frustrated that her husband was not getting better fast enough. She wanted to get involved in his recovery program and tell him how to do it. She was hurt, and felt left out when he turned to others for help. She needed to understand that her role was to tell him that he needed to change or she and their son would not be part of his life. After this, she had to let go and let others help him. She could not be objective, and tended to over-react. He would then respond with anger and defensiveness. She could not understand why he did not think she had good ideas and was trying to be supportive. He experienced her as critical, intrusive, and faultfinding, much like his parents were. Even though the addict had begun an intensive out-patient program, his wife did not feel safe because he had not followed her recommendation of inpatient treatment. She could not acknowledge the things that he was accomplishing because she did not trust his motives. She should have been creating pain for him in the area of his addiction; namely, by telling him that she and his son would not live with him if he continued in active addiction. Instead, she was making recovery painful with her anxiety, anger, suspicion, and lack of encouragement. Surrender and conversion come from the first kind of pain, not the latter.

The next important word in the First Step is "powerless." Sex and love addicts have tried to control their addictions in many ways before coming into treatment and recovery. They have repeatedly experienced failure in terms of their ability to have power over their sexual or romantic thoughts, feelings, and behaviors. Periods of abstinence are a good example of this loss of control. Most addicts can stop for periods of time, but the problem is that they cannot "stay stopped." One sex and love addict went five years between obsene phone calls but continued to masturbate during this time. Such pe-riods of "good behavior" lull addicts into thinking, "It won't happen again," or "I'm cured," while the addiction creeps back into their lives.

Powerlessness is a difficult concept for us to accept. As Americans, we are socialized to believe that success comes from "rugged individualism." The model we are taught to follow is that of the poor, underprivileged man who overcomes all odds and "pulls himself up by his bootstraps" to become an unqualified success. Men are also taught to be tough and to need no help in conquering their problems. All people have a strong urge to appear as capable as the next person and to hide their frailties and shortcomings. We are reticent to admit that something has gotten the best of us. We do not want to feel out of control, inadequate, incapable, or "weak." We do this with all diseases. We do not want arthritis to get the best of us. We do not want diabetes to get us down. We do not want heart disease to cripple us. We do not want cancer to slow us down. Certainly, we do not want to have a problem with sex or love that could do all these things. What a blow to our ego! How could something so natural, so much a part of us, as sexuality or love go out of control and render us powerless over our sex and love addiction? We all have a great resistance to seeing ourselves as powerless over anything, even though in reality most of us are powerless over many things in our lives—like the weather, our neighbors, or the economy.

Powerlessness can be a blessing rather than a curse. The whole concept of surrendering and admitting powerlessness leads to an increase in control of one's life, and not the opposite. Critics point to the use of the term "powerlessness" to mean that addicts are not to be held accountable for their actions or that they are to be forgiven without having to express remorse or guilt. This is far from the truth. In fact, sex and love addicts will be called on the carpet and held accountable more strenuously by other recovering people than by nonaddicts. It is a misconception to believe that the term "powerless" in any way absolves the sex and love addict of responsibility for either the past or the future. Admitting powerlessness is paradoxical. By giving up control, you get it. By letting go, you gain control. By admitting powerlessness, you get the capacity to send your life on another course.

Examples of powerlessness center on instances where the sex and love addict has created the illusion of control whereas the truth of the matter was that he or she was completely out of control. For instance, a sex and love addict who wishes to start over may move his family thousands of miles from the area where he or she had many affairs. Thinking that a geographic cure may be the solution, he or she will disrupt the whole family in order to try to stop having affairs. However, despite the addict's good intentions, in the new location he or she may still end up having another affair due to a basic inability to control his or her behavior.

The other important idea in the First Step is the concept of "unmanageability." Powerlessness refers to the person's inability to predict or control behavior in the future—the inability to keep promises and commitments to themselves or to others. Unmanageability refers to the consequences of powerlessness. The life of a sex and love addict is not normal. It is not balanced or managed with any sense of appropriateness or health. Examples of unmanageability include difficulties with families, relationships, work, social life, studies, finances, spirituality, emotions, and even physical health. During one of my lectures, an employee assistance person was finally able to identify the cause of his client's financial instability: The client would run his credit cards up to their limits at massage parlors and pornographic book stores and, even after financial counseling and refinancing, the problem persisted. One sex and love addict, who has a master's degree and is the youngest team leader in his mental health agency, was afraid to pursue graduate studies until he had $100,000 in the bank so he could "live off the interest." He had a totally false sense that money would provide him with security when what he really needed was to regain control of his life, develop some self-esteem, and learn to depend on himself and his recovery program rather than the illusion of sex and love as the ultimate security blanket. He was not managing his life. His apartment was unkempt. He did not pay his bills on time or in any regular fashion. He was behind with his paperwork at the office. He was neglecting his clients and, at times, abusing them for their addictive behaviors with overly aggressive confrontations stemming from his guilt at not being in control of his own life. He had no relationship with his family. He had no friends. He had no leisure activities or interests besides sex and gambling. Money in the bank would not fix all the things that needed fixing, but recovery would.

Powerlessness is inside the person. Unmanageability is outside. Lack of control—powerlessness—has to do with thoughts, feelings, impulses, needs, and wants. Manageability has to do with actions, social and coping skills, relating to the environment, and the external world of the sex and love addict. Powerlessness, then, can be harder to see than unmanageability because it concerns the inner world of the addict. Unmanageability is easier to spot, but most of us excuse it due to our own problems handling our lives.

In recovery, many sex and love addicts write down examples of powerlessness and unmanageability caused by their addictions in order to more clearly see for themselves the truth involved in "doing" the First Step. Some even keep these accounts in their wallets or pocketbooks to help them remember why they chose to resist an impulse to follow a sexual or romantic desire.

Step Two
Came to Believe That a Power Greater Than Ourselves
Could Restore Us to Sanity

After the sex and love addict has been able to admit to him- or herself that he or she is out of control and that the addictive behavior is affecting his or her life; he or she will come to the next step. Addicts need to find out what to do. The S.L.A.A. program suggests they look for guidance outside themselves. All the person's efforts to establish control, power, and manageability over the sex and love addiction have proven worthless. Someone or something else must have the answer. For the addict, this is a major obstacle because for years, he or she has only relied on him- or herself. For example, no one else, in the addict's life knows the real truth or the whole story. Everyone has been lied to, misinformed, or uninformed. The addict may have even appeared to seek out and depend on the guidance of others, but in his or her heart of hearts, the addict has always believed that he or she knew what was best. This is the narcissism and grandiosity that were mentioned earlier. Many addicts are good at deceiving, and basically think they have the answers. As one recovering sex and love addict recently put it, "I have to find God and remember that I am not Him."

Thus, the next task is to find help. Twelve Step recovery programs generally agree that help means changing one's belief system and acknowledging that some "Power" other than one's self may have the solution to this terrible problem of obsession and compulsion in the area of sex and love. Changings beliefs is difficult for anyone. For sex and love addicts, it means letting go of their dependency on sexual or romantic activities for their high or fix—their feeling of meaning, peace, worth, or serenity. This would be easy if they could have a guarantee that this other thing, program, or "Higher Power" would be as dependable, satisfying, and exciting as their addiction. However, it will not be. In fact, the Second Step calls addicts to make the "leap of faith" and trust that someone or something can make them healthy and whole again, with no guarantee. The recovery program makes the long-term promise of rewards "beyond your wildest dreams," but it requires belief, faith, trust, and steady, hard work—qualitites that the addict knows he or she has only in short supply. However, the program also knows that the addict has only so much to give, and therefore only asks for a full commitment "one day at a time." With time and an honest effort to follow the Twelve Steps as they are laid out, the rewards of sobriety, serenity, self-worth, and self-confidence will come to the sex and love addict. In order to start on this journey, sex and love addicts need to relinquish the false belief that they have the answers, and "come to believe" in someone or something else.

The second part of the belief step looks at what it is that the sex and love addict should believe in. This is a place where many people stumble because they misunderstand or misinterpret and meaning of the step. It is in no way a form of religion or a requirement to believe in God. Some people choose to give it that meaning, but it does not have to be seen in that light. Most people in Sex and Love Addicts Anonymous would say it is not important what form the Higher Power takes as long as it is not the addict him- or herself. Many addicts have lost their faith in God or the religion of their upbringing, and some are quite angry with their Higher Power for inflicting a horrible addiction on them. They do not need to go back to church or develop some sort of formal theological thought, but they do need to see the need for guidance and direction from some power other than themselves. This Power can be the S.L.A.A. program, their sponsor, or their therapist. What is essential is that it be outside themselves. They can no longer afford to give themselves counsel. They need to find some external source of direction for their lives, be it a therapist, an S.L.A.A. group, or a program sponsor.

Third, addicts need to see this Higher Power as being able to "restore them to sanity." This means they need to see that they have been crazy. Their sex and love addiction has so profoundly affected them and their lives that they no longer function reasonably, with balance or control, or with direction or purpose. Insanity is a very difficult concept for some sex and love addicts to accept. They will admit to some problems, but to have to say that they have gone so far off the beaten track as to be "crazy" is scary, humiliating, and uncomfortable. They often want to bargain at this point—"Maybe it wasn't so bad"—and lapse back into rationalizing and minimizing. Accepting that they have truly become insane can help them commit themselves more fully to the recovery process.

Step Three
Made a Decision to Turn Our Will and Our Lives over to the Care of God as We Understood God

The Third Step calls the sex and love addict to go beyond belief and take action. A decision must be made. It may have seemed implicit in the Second Step that if we believe in something we will automatically follow its direction. However, the sex and love addict needs to make this a conscious, overt step. He or she has often gotten in trouble in the addiction by taking things for granted. Recovery is different. It needs to be thought about, and requires that specific actions be taken to ensure change. The sex and love addict needs to "make a decision" to go along with the "leap of faith" in Step Two. Addicts get in the habit of avoiding responsibility and blaming others, so they need to make a clear, rational choice to begin to do things differently in their lives. They cannot afford to assume that just because they believe in it they will automatically go along with the program.

The Third Step is another part of the "surrender" process that makes up the first three steps. The sex and love addict must decide to "turn it over." This is another part of letting go, of transferring dependency on sex and love to the Higher Power. Since the addict feels badly about him- or herself, the idea of trusting someone or something else is terrifying and unsettling. Addicts basically feel that their needs will not be met if they surrender control. The program tells them, "Get out of the driver's seat." Turning over the controls makes addicts feel vulnerable and childlike. They anticipate neglect, abuse, and abandonment—all of which they have probably already experienced in the past. They cannot imagine that some Higher Power will care for them, guide them, love them, and never let them down. Addicts may have had childhood experiences with formal religion or parents who were poor role models, could not be trusted, and let them down when their children trusted them, so this "decision step" becomes a major issue.

One sex and love addict who consulted me reported that at age six or seven he was extremely independent. He had distant, neglectful parents who looked to him to take care of his younger siblings. He was intelligent and resourceful, so he made the best of his situation and developed a life completely independent of his parents. As an adolescent, which was when his sex and love addiction became firmly rooted, he was almost never at home. He joined a religious community with some hopes of finding a family and people to parent him, but he essentially carried on his family experience, especially since he now had something to hide, namely, his addictions. For him, despite the pseudo-surrender of his religious life, the idea of surrendering control was terrifying. He had no model for it. If anything, he saw his life as a series of confirmations that you cannot trust anyone or anything other than yourself, and that if you do, you will inevitably get hurt, neglected, abused, and rejected. Consequently, how could he agree to "turn his will and his life over?"

Other sex and love addicts find this step relatively easy and readily turn over control in the beginning. However, after things start to improve in their lives, they quickly seize it back. Their surrender process involves a series of moves of letting go, taking back, and then having to let go again because their way does not work. This taking back of control can be a fairly subtle thing, especially to the untrained eye, but the return of addictive ways of thinking, feeling, and behaving eventually become obvious to all, because there inevitably will be a slip or full-blown relapse. An example comes to mind of a sex and love addict who had had a daily program of prayer and meditation and regular contact with his sponsors. As he progressed in his recovery, he became more involved in helping others and getting the message out that sex and love addicts do recover. He neglected his own program, lost his sponsors, did not attend as many meetings, failed to take time to center himself through prayer and meditation, and eventually had a relapse. He had taken back control slowly and in small ways until the end result proved the point.

The Third Step clearly states that the sex and love addict must turn over his or her "will." In fact, the will is turned over before turning over one's life. Sex and love addicts, whether or not they were this way before becoming addicted, become very willful individuals. They resemble people who have a narcissistic personality disorder: They are self-centered, grandiose, controlling, demanding, childish, impatient, impulsive, egotistical, self-serving, selfish, envious, unreasonable, and unempathetic. They may do a good job of covering over these traits, but down deep the flaws are there. Addicts have to become manipulative and devious in order to appear different on the outside, so they become good at seduction and at making others think that they care about them and recognize their needs. For some sex and love addicts, in fact, this game—the chase, the pursuit, the cruising, the intrigue— is the most intoxicating and addictive aspect of their problem. They may need to let go of this to get better, but they definitely do not want to let go of it. They want the power, the control, the sense of authority, the feeling of their will winning out. The idea of turning over their will, that "Thy will, not mine, [will] be done," scares them to death.

The Third Step requires, however, not only the release of personal will, but also the surrender of the person's whole life. This refers not only to the day-to-day control of the person's activities, but to his or her whole life plan as well. Addicts often spend a good deal of time in fantasy. They frequently have the fantasy of some particular person coming into their lives and making everything better. Turning over your life means abandoning plans and fantasies like these and allowing yourself to be ignorant about what will come next or how things will improve.

A highly intelligent and successful physician shared with his group the fact that he had had a fantasy since he was young that some handsome, young, virile man would come along and love him, and that this would "fix everything." He was starting to realize after almost a year of sobriety that this is a delusion, although relinquishing his fantasy would seem to invite despair, disillusionment, and hopelessness to descend on him. He had suffered from suicidal depressions and feared their return. He was angry with God for giving him so much pain throughout his life. Giving up his fantasy of a "Prince Charming" and turning his "life over to God as he understood him" seemed to him like asking to die. At best, it meant continuing to live a life barren of joy, happiness, love, and contentment. His fantasy had promised all these and more during most of his life. Now he was starting to see the insanity of this belief, and yet he was scared that if he let go, he would have nothing.

The last part of the Third Step uses the word "God" instead of "Power greater than ourselves," but the addition of the words "as we understood God" is intended to make this as open-ended as the Higher Power of the Second Step. Some people see the use of this word as forcing religion or Christianity on the recovering addict. However, the S.L.A.A. program in no way intends to force anything on anyone. It is a program of "attraction," and others who suffer from the addiction to sex and love have found that when they become more spiritual, it helps them recover. The fact that many treatment programs use the Twelve Steps may add to the addict's feeling of being obligated to adopt religious or spiritual beliefs with which he or she is uncomfortable. One alcoholic veteran sued the U.S. government for making him participate in a religious program in his addiction treatment (A.A.), and won. However, most addicted people find the spiritual aspect of the program uplifting and comforting, even though they may initially be put off by the use of concepts like God or Higher Power. The idea of the Third Step is that someone or something—"God as we understand God"—is in charge of our lives, and that whatever happens is up to this Higher Power rather than us. It is a step that teaches humility, not humiliation. It emphasizes letting go and not being in control. It encourages addicts to see the destructive role of will in their active addiction and the constructive role of surrender in their recovery. It is a decision step that puts belief into action.

Many recovering people and professionals see the first three of the Twelve Steps as the basic building blocks of recovery. In fact, many people recommend that sex and love addicts concentrate only on working the first three steps during their first year of recovery. If the addict has gone through the first three steps before the year is up, then he or she should go through them again rather than forging onward—like a typical addict in a hurry to get it done—and risking overconfidence or an inadequate integration of the true meaning of these essential steps to recovery: admit, believe, and decide. Acknowledge powerlessness and unmanageability, come to believe in a Higher Power, and make a decision to turn over your will and life. Repeat this process over and over. Develop a rut, make it a habit, and use it as a way of coping with life. This is what is emphasized early in recovery. The addict's addiction was essentially on oft-repeated pattern. Recovery works the same way. The first three steps make up the foundation for all that is to come later. If the foundation is poorly made, all the rest of recovery may crumble under later stresses and strains. If the foundation is strong, it will withstand the inevitable tests that the recovering sex and love addict will face as he or she moves through this new phase of life.

Step Four
Made a Searching and Fearless Moral Inventory of Ourselves

Only after sex and love addicts have established a solid recovery program can they take a deeper look at themselves. There is a good reason why this is not the first or even the third step. Most addicts, while active in their addiction, have beaten themselves unmercifully with their judgments about themselves. They tell themselves everything that anyone else has ever said in a critical moment, and more. They hate themselves. They hate their inability to set things straight. They are furious with their impulses and their "weakness"; their lack of control over their desires. They desperately want to be normal. They constantly pretend to the rest of the world that they are all right, knowing all the while that they are not. If they were to do an inventory in the early stages of recovery, it would be terribly distorted and negative. The time for an honest look at oneself is not during withdrawal or the high stress of starting a program of sobriety. Once being sexually and romantically sober is not quite so much work, the sex and love addict will then be ready to take a closer and more truthful look at him- or herself.

The Fourth Step involves making an "inventory." Many people are unclear about what this means. I often use the comparison to taking an inventory of the merchandise in a supermarket. When a store owner does an inventory, he or she wants to check all the shelves and see what is there, what is not there, and how much of each item there is. An inventory of one's self seeks to do the same thing. The person wants to identify what personal characteristics he or she does have, what amount of each particular trait there is, and what the deficits are; in other words, what are the "holes" in his or her personality?

There are two important factors to note here. The first is that the inventory is neither positive nor negative. In fact, it should include both; that is, the "good" and "bad" qualities. The point, however, is not to be judgmental and skim over the healthy traits while dwelling on the unhealthy parts of one's character. The inventory is supposed to be an objective, comprehensive, and honest overview of the personality. The second point that needs to be made is that the person doing the inventory needs to have a full view of the various possibilities as far as character traits are concerned and therefore needs a complete checklist of potential personality characteristics. This is especially important in terms of taking a new look at oneself. It involves seeing things that have been overlooked as well as seeing what should be there but is missing. Often, recovering people who are working on the Fourth Step utilize workbooks or lists of potential character traits in order to help themselves see the big picture.

A recovering sex and love addict with whom I worked asked for some feedback on his Fourth Step. His first list overemphasized the negative. He was accustomed to beating himself up, so when he went to do his inventory, he only thought of his character defects and the things that he thought should be changed or corrected. His second attempt was somewhat better. He had two columns—positive and negative—and they were neatly balanced in his usual compulsive fashion. He was thinking that an honest, balanced look at himself would look like just that—balanced or even on both sides. This was an improvement, but it was hardly an accurate picture of him. Even a person who is suffering from an addiction should be expected to have more good than bad qualities. Most people have lots of positive, healthy traits as well as some missing, negative, or unhealthy characteristics. In some cases, the negative and unhealthy aspects of a person so dominate his or her character and actions that this is all we see, but the truth is that even in this extreme, there will still be positive and healthy traits as well. In the case of an addiction, because the person has lost control, his or her negative and unhealthy traits are the major focus in his or her mind, and often in the minds of others. The negative and unhealthy side of the person has come to overshadow the many positive and healthy characteristics. Eventually, this particular addict and I were able to develop a better list which had many positive qualities and a few areas that needed improvement.

The use of the descriptors "searching," "fearless," and "moral" before the word "inventory" in the Fourth Step are intended to encourage the sex and love addict to do a comprehensive and honest job. While active in their addictions, sex and love addicts avoid looking at themselves. Defenses like denial, rationalization, minimization, and projection help them avoid the truth about themselves and their lives. They get in the habit of covering up reality rather than searching for it. They learn to lie–first to themselves, and then to the rest of the world. They become experts at covering up, at hiding the truth. They develop a quick-fix mentality that lacks the time or energy to search for the truth. A glib lie, a quick cover-up, and a clever excuse have become their stock-in-trade, so taking an accurate inventory will require an entirely different approach; namely, taking their time, searching for answers, and being patient with the process rather than pushing for the product.

Fear is something with which the sex and love addict lives everyday. As the disease progresses, the fear grows. Addicts are afraid they will be found out. They are afraid they are "really crazy." They are afraid they will be humiliated. They are afraid they will get a sexually transmitted disease or, worse, AIDS. They fear that their parents, spouses, friends, employers, or children will discover what they are doing. They fear public scandal or shame.

They fear losing respect, their families, their lives. They also worry that someday they may have to stop, and they cannot imagine a life without their sexual
or romantic fantasies and activities. Becoming fearless is, for them, a tall
order. Of course, the dictum to make a fearless inventory does not come at
the beginning of recovery. The sex and love addict who has established some
sobriety will have already begun to rebuild his or her self-esteem, and will
have been exposed to other recovering addicts who are models of fearlessness
and honesty.

Likewise, sex and love addicts lose their sense of morality along the way.
Just as a sex and love addiction corrodes the addict's self-worth, an active
sex and love addiction errodes the addict's moral values. For many, this is a
slow process, involving a series of gradual reductions in moral standards.
For example, one sex and love addict first allowed herself to go to bars or
singles clubs "just to dance and have a good time." She had her own personal
morality that included rules like: "No sex on the first date" and "No dating
married men." As her love addiction progressed, she no longer went to bars
and clubs for fun but rather spent her time cruising or on the make. Sex on
the first date became not just a possibility but a reality, and she wondered
what was wrong when it failed to happen. As she became sicker, married
men became less of a threat, and even began to offer some appeal because
they were not really available. She could have sex with them and feel less
guilty and degraded because they were "at her level." As her moral standards
crumbled, she learned to laugh at her own values and to regard them as
"childish," "prudish," and "unsophisticated." Part of her recovery will involve
reestablishing her values and learning to feel all right about being moral and
having moral values and standards. She will come to see taking a moral
inventory as a step toward feeling better about herself. Finally, this addict
will begin to discover that having moral values can protect her and boost
her self-esteem, not in a snobbish way but in a way that gives her a solid
footing and a sense of being grounded.

This sort of self-discovery is the essence of the Fourth Step. Continued
personal inventories are a part of the Tenth Step, so learning how to discover
who you really are—both the healthy and unhealthy parts—is part of the
ongoing recovery process. It is important in terms of developing an awareness
of vulnerabilities and potential triggers for addictive thinking or acting out,
and for developing long-term strategies for protecting against relapse.

Step Five
Admitted to God, to Ourselves, and to Another Human Being the Exact Nature of Our Wrongs

After the sex and love addict has been able to take "a searching and fearless
moral inventory" of him- or herself, then he or she will be ready to learn to
be more open and honest, not only about him- or herself, but also about the

addiction. The regeneration of self-worth accomplished in the Fourth Step is a necessary foundation for being able to be completely open about the addiction. There is a great deal of shame, embarrassment, and guilt for any recovering addict, and especially for someone addicted to sex and love. In order to be prepared to cope with these feelings, the sex and love addict first must build up his or her self-confidence through the Fourth Step inventory.

The Fifth Step presents the sex and love addict with the progressive challenge of opening up "to God, to [oneself], and to another human being." The sex and love addict has a life of secrecy of which he or she may be quite proud, taking a "junkie pride" in being able to keep a secret and to fool others. It is this false pride that needs to be eliminated, and in its place the sex and love addict must develop a sense of pride in honesty and openness. This represents a dramatic change in the way the addict thinks, feels, and behaves. The habit of secrecy needs to be replaced with the habit of honesty. It involves learning to take risks and to be humble, both things that sex and love addicts avoid—although they may have told themselves that they are risk takers and humble people.

Since the sex and love addict has learned to relinquish control, to "take the back seat," and to rely on his or her "Higher Power" for direction in the Third Step, sharing "the exact nature of our wrongs" with God "as we understood Him" comes before sharing with ourselves. The sex and love addict's "I" is so strong that it needs constant reminders to stay in its place. After the ego building of the Fourth Step, there is the danger that the unhealthy, narcissistic, addict ego will regain control and displace the still-growing, healthy ego. Consequently, God comes first. The addict still needs to learn the difference between being humble and being humiliated. During the addiction, there were numerous, if not constant, experiences of humiliation. Being humiliated means being made to feel inferior, less than, lower than, or worse than others. It is being "put down," shamed, or degraded, or being made to feel worthless. It is being insulted or called names like "whore," "homo," or "pervert." On the other hand being humble is being equal, the same as, or as good as others. It is being accepted, affirmed, and made to feel worthwhile. It does not require praise, status, or a need to be better than others. Sharing with your God is an exercise in developing humility. It is a recognition that you are not God, as many addicts may have believed during their active addictions. The addict's "Higher Power" is in a position to offer comfort and acceptance, of which the recovering addict will be in great need, despite his or her progress in the first four steps.

The sex and love addict must also learn to be completely honest with him- or herself about the nature and extent of the addiction. After sharing with God, this part should be a little easier. Most addicts have been most dishonest with themselves. This "honesty step" requires that the sex and love addict take a truthful and in-depth ("exact") look at what he or she has really been up to as far as sex and love are concerned. The pretense needs to be erased. The cons need to be dropped, the lies need to be eliminated, and the distortions need to be straightened out. This may take some time depending on the length and extent of the addict's departure from truth and reality.

Finally, when he or she has been able to be honest and open with God and with him- or herself, the sex and love addict needs to share the truth "with another human being." This is an essential step in breaking down the secrecy, shame, and isolation of the addicted person. Recovery cannot happen alone. It cannot happen only between the addict and God (most addicts have already tried that many times,—"God, if only you will get me out of this one, I promise to. . . . "). Recovery requires other people. It necessitates learning how to talk to other people about what is going on with you sexually and romantically. If the addict can learn to talk about his or her fantasies, thoughts, impulses, and feelings, he or she will not have to act on them. On the other hand, when thoughts, feelings, fantasies, and impulses are bottled up, they come out in actions. The Fifth Step teaches the sex and love addict to be completely open and honest with another human being and to realize that he or she will still be accepted, loved, and affirmed.

It is important that the sex and love addict think carefully about whom they choose for their Fifth Step. Usually recovering people pick their S.L.A.A. sponsor or someone else in the program whose recovery they admire. Some people do their Fifth Step with a clergy person or a therapist. Not surprisingly, I learned a great deal about a recovering alcoholic who did her Fifth Step with me after two years of individual psychotherapy. However, the addict should not choose someone with whom there is a need to make amends. That comes later. In the Fifth Step, the person needs to feel he or she can say "everything and anything" without any censorship or holding back. Therefore, the person the sex and love addict picks must be "safe" and nonjudgmental. The purpose of the step is to learn to be open and honest, and not to fix things or be forgiven. The person should not be someone with whom the addict wants to build a relationship, especially in terms of sexual or romantic interests, because this will lead to intrigue and dishonesty.

It is also important that the sex and love addict not start telling "war stories." "X-rated" accounts of the past that tend to glorify the addiction are destructive rather than constructive. Anything that would distort the truth in order to enhance the memories, improve the image, or soften the blow should be avoided. Stories that make the addiction seem better, less painful, or more fun than it really was will start to trigger the addictive process rather than stopping it, which is the intention of the Fifth Step.

Honesty can be abused. Stories that are too graphic can be a subtle attempt to turn the listener on. There is a significant difference between saying, "I had oral sex" and saying, "I sucked cock." Simply reporting that "I acted out" is not sufficient, but saying that "we had great sex" is not the truth either, because it leaves out the pain. Honesty can be used sadistically. For example, addicts can use specific facts to hurt someone else or themselves. A sex and love addict who gives too many details of his affairs to his spouse may be subtly getting back at her for what he perceive, as neglect, abandonment, or abuse. An addict who shares too much may also be secretly trying to shock the other person. The "brutal truth" may, in fact, be an act of sadism rather than a sharing intended to clear the air. The sex and love addict can use the Fifth Step in a masochistic way as well. That is, the sordid details can be exposed in order to confirm the addict's feelings of worthlessness and perversion. It is almost like a challenge to the listener to "see how bad I really am." Rather than improving things, which honesty and openness will do, sadistic or masochistic honesty creates more problems and allows the addict to begin to doubt the recovery process. However, when done with care and proper intentions, the Fifth Step can enable the sex and love addict to become even more open and honest in all areas of life. Step Ten again uses this foundation in the ongoing principle, "When we were wrong, promptly admitted it."

Step Six
Were Entirely Ready to Have God Remove All These Defects of Character

Steps Six and Seven are often misunderstood, skipped over, breezed through, or underestimated. On the surface they appear to be easier than any previous steps. Why wouldn't we be eager to have our character defects removed, especially after becoming so aware of them in Steps Four and Five? However, what is really called for in these steps is a dramatic transformation from victim to partner, from an underdog to an equal, from a person with thousands of excuses to someone with none. After our defects of character are removed, we have nothing to hide behind and no one else to blame. We have to become ourselves, to grow up and be responsible. This is a very frightening thing for a sex and love addict. Without defects, he or she will lose all self-pity, self-loathing, and self-hatred, and will have to care for, respect, and love him- or herself, and addicts are not used to this.

In order to slow the sex and love addict down long enough to help him or her realize what is in store, the Sixth Step begins with the suggestion that the addict become "entirely ready." Merely being ready is not enough. The sex and love addict must be "entirely" ready. What does this mean? It means the addict has to stop and think about what is to come. It means the addict must be prepared to accept the consequences of this action. It means the addict must make an internal assessment of his or her current state (sort of like an inventory). An addict is not accustomed to thinking before acting, accepting consequences, or being aware of his or her inner self.

The Sixth Step is another exercise in humility. The sex and love addict is called to ask, "Am I entirely ready?" The corollary question also comes to mind, "If I were to become without defects, what will I be?" Some see this as an invitation to gradiosity and perfectionism. What is a person without defects—a "saint?" The answer is no, a person without defects is a person without excuses. For years, sex and love addicts have fueled their addictions with self pity ("I can't help myself"), excuses ("I tried to stop"), self-indulgence ("I'm just a bad person"), and self-hatred ("I'm not worth helping"). They are used to feeling bad about themselves, and need these feelings to justify continuing to act out sexually and romantically. Without the pain to which they have grown accustomed, they will feel uncomfortable, awkward, vulnerable, and disoriented. Rather than seeing that an absence of defects will allow them to be human, they will go to the opposite extreme—as addicts tend to do—and require themselves to have to be perfect and without sin. The Sixth Step does not ask God to "make me perfect." It simply asks that our defects of character—those parts of ourselves with which we beat ourselves—be removed.

Another aspect of this lesson in humility is that we ask our "Higher Power" to take the action, not ourselves. The Sixth Step is not to "try like heck to make myself perfect" but rather is a reminder that, once again, "I am not God." The paradox of this sort of approach to change is confusing for some people. They misinterpret the step to mean that they do not have to do anything, that the job of reforming themselves and their lives is up to God, and that they can relax. This is typical addictive thinking, but it is completely the opposite of the truth. Becoming "entirely ready" is a great deal of work. Moreover, "turning it over" and trusting God is another big job for most addicts. They would rather do the character fixing themselves, and let God run the universe. Trusting that God can or will do something to help is difficult. The Second and Third steps have paved the way for the Sixth Step, but in between there was much opportunity for the addict to do the work—making inventories and sharing wrongs. Here again, in the Sixth Step, the sex and love addict is being asked to step back and let God do the work of removing character defects. Getting out of God's way can be difficult, especially without trust and faith.

However, being able to take the Sixth Step is necessary for spiritual growth and for developing the capacity for intimacy. Hanging on to defects keeps God and people at a distance. If the addict becomes human instead of defective, than he or she can allow him- or herself to be loved by God and by other human beings. Defects create a sense of distance and a fear of being known. Being without defects of character makes contact and closeness possible as there is no longer anything to hide. Shame and self-hatred can be replaced with pride and self-love. When the sex and love addict can love him- or herself, then he or she can admit the love of God and others, which had been there all along but had been blocked by the defects.

Step Seven
Humbly Asked God to Remove Our Shortcomings

The Seventh Step is the action step, and again we begin with the word "humbly." Ongoing humility is especially important to the recovering sex and love addict. With some success at managing what before had been unmanageable, and some self-confidence having been developed in steps Four, Five, and Six, the sex and love addict will be quite vulnerable to becoming overconfident or to the return of "unbridled will run rampant." Humility, not humiliation, will keep the addict's ego from becoming overinflated. The road of recovery is strewn with lives wrecked by the sex and love addict's lack of ongoing surrender.

After the preparation in Step Six of becoming "entirely ready," the sex and love addict now has to act, and the action again is talking. The addict has to "ask" for something. He or she cannot just get ready and sit back expecting that God will take the next step. The addict must ask. This is taking responsibility. This is working together with God and the recovery program. This is using your Higher Power appropriately, rather than the myriads of inappropriate, childish requests made during the active addiction.

On the surface, the Seventh Step appears quite simple. It is the shortest of the steps. It should take about five seconds to do, then, the addict just has to wait for the results. Unlike getting high in an addiction, asking God "to remove our shortcomings" takes time. It is a step that teaches patience and persistence as well as humility. It needs to be done daily. Over time, the experience of asking God brings out the idea that recovery is a process, not a product, and that progress, not perfection, is the goal.

In the first place, asking to have shortcomings taken from us brings to mind the question of what they are. Perhaps the sex and love addict is asking to have temper, impatience, or pride removed. Usually the addict does not experience a cloud of smoke, flash of lightning, or other supernatural response; moreover, the shortcoming remains. This allows the addict to question what he or she truly needs from the Higher Power. Perhaps the addict is only asking God to solve all his or her problems and to fix everything without any effort on the addict's part. These sorts of childish requests will go unanswered, much like the requests for God to somehow rescue the person during active addiction. Are temper, patience, and pride something that addicts could work on themselves without divine intervention? Most sex and love addicts discover that much of what they ask for is not really what they need from God or their Higher Power. What they really need is a sense of God's love and direction in their lives. As they begin to relinquish their petty shortcomings, they become more open to seeing the real shortcomings in their past lives: shortcomings in meaning, love, and spirituality. When recovering addicts begin to ask for these shortcomings to be removed, they miraculously discover that they have begun the program of recovery.

The discovery of love, spirituality, and meaning in their lives—usually present but unnoticed—helps sex and love addicts appreciate the progress they have made in recovery, and fosters a sense of gratitude. As the "attitude of gratitude" grows, addicts can accept progress and relinquish perfection. They start to see more clearly that it is the journey that matters, not the goal. The shortcomings that they expected to have removed remain, and the real emptiness in their lives is gone instead. Many addicts, for example, want their addictions removed. They still desperately want to be normal—free of their disease. What God actually removes is this shortcoming—the need to escape the addiction—and they find peace and acceptance while keeping their sex and love addiction. Addicts come to see the addiction as a wonderful road to growth and fulfillment "beyond their wildest dreams." Their lives contain real friendships, loves, and usefulness that was totally lacking before. They can experience a partnership with God and a serenity born of accepting the things that they cannot change and changing the things that they can.

Step Eight
Made a List of All Persons We Had Harmed, and Became Willing to Make Amends to Them All

The Eighth Step is one of the most frequently noticed steps. Many guilt-ridden addicts want to do this step first, or at least early on in recovery, so they no longer have to feel like a bad person. On the other hand, many self-centered addicts never want to do this step because they do not want to consider how their behaviors have affected others. While many people never reach or understand the Sixth and Seventh steps, most sex and love addicts know exactly what is meant by making amends, even if they have no intention of ever doing so.

The Eighth Step is placed in that order for very good reasons that the newly recovering sex and love addict cannot really appreciate. The amends that are made after a significant period of time in sobriety are quite different from the often self-serving amends that a person new in the program would make. Early in recovery, the addict is not in a position to accurately assess the impact of the addiction on others. In fact, most sex and love addicts have a great deal of trouble seeing the effects of their addictions on themselves, let alone on other people. Objectivity comes with surrender, self-discovery, humility, and acceptance—all of which are developed in the first Seven Steps.

Step Eight is not an action step either. Again, a period of meditation and reflection is essential to the process. The Eighth Step asks the sex and love addict to make a list and to "become willing." In the years of their sex and love addiction, addicts have accumulated a great deal of garbage that needs to be cleaned out. The Fourth and Fifth steps allow for some internal house-cleaning, but the Eighth and Ninth steps provide sex and love addicts with the opportunity to set things straight with the rest of the world as well as with themselves. They are steps that require a great deal of humility, self-acceptance, and concern for others.

Most sex and love addicts have a great deal of difficulty seeing themselves as victimizers, and are much more in touch with their own victimhood. In fact, most sex and love addicts have been both victims and victimizers. They have been users and have been used. They have been abusers and have been abused. They have been top dogs and they have been underdogs. They tend to see and experience themselves as victims who have been used and abused by many people in their lives. A sex and love addict who came to see me for help with legal charges for pedophilia could not attend to society's need to know that he was a safe person, and redirected the discussion to his own history of sexual and emotional abuse. He also felt abused by the legal system, by his employer (a school bus company that fired him after he seduced boys on his bus), and by me when I would not support his use of Homosexuals Anonymous rather than Sex and Love Addicts Anonymous as the basis of his recovery program. His homosexuality was not the issue. His legal difficulties were directly the result of his sexual addiction and acting out with minors.

Many sex and love addicts see their partners as willing participants rather than victims of their manipulations, deceit, and dishonesty. Addicts who use pornography, prostitutes, and anonymous sex delude themselves that there are no victims in their acting out. Who makes the pornographic pictures, movies, and magazines if not victims of addictions or abusive relationships? Who are the prostitutes if not sex or drug addicts or else victims of incest or abusive relationships with pimps? Sex and love addicts tend to want to overlook the destruction that their addictions do to others, but the Eighth Step calls them to be honest and truthful with themselves about the effects of their addiction on others and the need to make amends.

Step Eight also involves developing or furthering the sex and love addict's ability to forgive. In order to compose the list of people who have been harmed, the sex and love addict needs to accept the addiction and forgive him- or herself for the inevitable acting out associated with any addictive process. Acceptance has been a recurrent theme throughout the steps, and forgiveness is there as well. The Eighth Step allows the sex and love addict to make this self-acceptance and self-forgiveness more concrete. It brings it down into the reality of the particular people who were hurt. It requires a full evaluation of the history of the person's addiction. It specifies a list, and it involves learning willingness to fix as much as possible of the damage that was done.

In addition to forgiveness, the Eighth Step continues the addict's growing sense of humility and responsibility. Many sex and love addicts would not find it possible to make amends early in the recovery process without feeling a great deal of humiliation. Most of them have kept their addictions fairly secret over the years, and just the idea of making amends is overwhelming and produces feelings of shame and guilt. This is one reason why this step comes late in the recovery process. Earlier on, it could be a trigger for acting out or relapse should the addict experience too much shame and guilt. Done with humility, making a list and becoming willing is an uplifting experience. With humiliation, it is a strong temptation to dive back into the illusion of security promised by the active addiction. Preparing for the action Step Nine makes the sex and love addict take more responsibility for his or her actions during the addictive phase. This will strengthen the ability to take responsibility in ongoing recovery. At this point in the process, the sex and love addict is more independent and is preparing for the maintenance steps, so more responsibility is healthy provided it is taken on with humility and acceptance.

Step Nine
Made Direct Amends to Such People Wherever Possible, Except When to Do So Would Injure Them or Others

After the period of meditation and reflection that is inherent in the Eighth Step, the Ninth Step offers the recovering sex and love addict an opportunity to complete the task of putting the past back where it belongs. Many sex and love addicts live with great reservoirs of guilt and shame that they cannot seem to surrender, even after fairly long periods of sobriety. Step Nine is a chance to close the book on many of the past actions and errors that were an inevitable part of a sex and love addiction. Resolving these feelings of guilt and shame requires more than good thoughts or intentions. Recovering addicts are well aware of the difference between good intentions and healthy actions because in their addictions they often had the right intentions but were frequently unable to follow through on them due to the "call" of their addiction. They felt badly about their inability to do what they had intended, and hated themselves for their shortcomings. The act of fixing the past by finally being able to follow through on good intentions will reverse this process and make the addicts feel good about themselves and confident in their ability to do what they plan to do.

As with all other aspects of the Sex and Love Addicts Anonymous program, making amends requires courage, honesty, and willingness to "check out" intentions and plans with other sober S.L.A.A. members. This can be a dangerous step for the addict and for others, since it may involve some form of contact with people from the addict's past, most of whom will have been absent from the addict's life for some time.

The process of making amends often involves setting the record straight with someone. This could be a person that has been kept "on the hook" in some way, or it could be someone who feels responsible for the failure of a relationship and was unaware of the addiction. The sex and love addict may just need to write a letter to the person, check it out with an S.L.A.A. member, and send it without a return address. Making amends might involve talking to a person whose friendship was dropped without explanation or who was pushed away in a manner that made him or her feel worthless or ashamed. In correcting these harms, sex and love addicts should get objective help in seeing what will be appropriate and helpful. Even with some sobriety, the addict will be vulnerable to a return of intrigue, seductive behaviors, and romantic fantasies. In other words, the good intentions risk going awry again without some healthy direction from sponsors, therapists, and other people in the addict's support system, such as S.L.A.A. members.

Another potential problem is that the sex and love addict may unintentionally use the opportunity to correct past harms as a chance to get even. There may be strong feelings of anger, hurt, rejection, or abandonment that may creep into the process of releasing the past. One of the defenses that sex and love addicts frequently use to cover their guilt and shame is anger and irritability. Contact with people from the past may allow these feelings to resurface, especially if the addict is unaware of their existence. Again, checking out the feelings, intentions, and process will help keep the addict safe from unintentional anger and defensiveness.

Sometimes the most difficult part of the amends steps involves resolving issues with spouses, partners, children, and families. Some of these people may not know of the sex and love addict's problem or may not want to know more about how they themselves were hurt or deceived. This is where the concept of potential injury to others comes into play. While addicts may feel better confronting past neglects and abuses, the other party may feel worse; this process does have the potential to damage the self-esteem, confidence, and reputation of others. The Ninth Step is not just a confession of the past to others in order to "dump" it. It is a process of repairing and making better what the sex and love addict damaged or destroyed during the active addiction.

A fairly clear example of a potentially harmful amends making is the recovering sex and love addict who, while in his active addiction, had sexually abused young boys. During recovery he wanted to teach young children about healthy relationships. This was a bad idea: For one thing, it takes an addict a long time to learn to develop healthy relationships, even with adults. A recovering sex addict may never be in a position to have close contact with children in any capacity. The sex and love addict needs to abandon his need to be close to children as part of his recovery. Children are the "people" of the "people, places, and things" that he should avoid in sobriety. Another sex and love addict who had acted out sexually with children decided to make a donation to a program that helps runaway children, who are often victims of sexual abuse, rather than having any direct contact with children himself. This was a more proper amend.

The act—more than just the thought—of making right what the sex and love addict has done wrong to others allows him or her to finally put the past where it belongs—in the past. Letting go is somewhat frightening because many sex and love addicts have used guilt and shame about past behaviors as a way of keeping themselves in line. If they relinquish their bad feelings about what they have done and who they have been, they fear they will let themselves slip back into the addiction. This is where the next three steps come into play: Steps Ten, Eleven, and Twelve are the means to maintaining lifelong recovery.

Step Ten
Continued to Take Personal Inventory and When We Were Wrong, Promptly Admitted It

Once the past has been dealt with in a healthy way, their shortcomings have been surrendered, and their inventory has been taken and shared, sex and love addicts are ready to form an ongoing recovery program that will help them continue to maintain sobriety in the future. This is a difficult task since so many sex and love addicts slip and relapse, but the path is outlined in the last three steps: continued inventory, admitting to wrongs, prayer and meditation, carrying the message, and practicing these principles in every aspect of life.

The beginning—Step Ten—reminds us of the Fourth Step because a "continued ... personal inventory" is required. Personal awareness, self-reflection, sensitivity to our inner world of thoughts and feelings, and self-assessment and diagnosis are the key to ongoing health. Formerly, the sex and love addict avoided all self-knowledge and instead turned to romance or sex to fix any problems, conflicts, anxieties, inadequacies, boredom, and needs for excitement. The Fourth Step inventory was intended to improve honesty, develop self-awareness, and start the process of balanced self-appraisal. In the Tenth Step, the sex and love addict is taught to use self-awareness as a basis for action, as an internal rudder for balance and direction.

The reflection on oneself involved in this step also provides a constant correction for the addict's tendency to "take the inventory" of others. Sex and love addicts have sensitive antennae and are quite adept at perceiving other people. They have developed and used this skill in cruising for romantic or sexual partners or in finding excuses that worked for activities involving pornography or pornographic bookstores. They often are hypercritical of others, just as they are hypo- or under-critical of themselves. Step Ten mitigates against this tendency to be overly critical of the rest of the world by directing the attention of the addict to personal inventories rather than inventories of others.

In addiction to this corrective device, the sex and love addict is directed to "promptly admit" when he or she is wrong. This advice is geared to prevent the buildup of unexpressed feelings, especially shame and guilt for wrong doing, which can be potentially so dangerous to the addict's ongoing sobriety. Self-hatred, self-pity, feelings of worthlessness, and depression, as well as shame and guilt, can grow from hidden wrongdoings on the part of the addict. Keeping secrets leads to great pain. In the S.L.A.A. meetings, time is given for people to "get current" with the same intention as the Tenth Step: to keep the sex and love addict's conscience clean and prevent the buildup of bad feelings about oneself.

As sex and love addicts grow in their recovery process, they learn that they have little power to control or change other people or outside events. However, the addict does have some control over him- or herself. This is the focus of the Tenth Step. Developing self-control and the willingness to share and admit to wrongdoing will strengthen the addict's recovery process. The "white-knuckle" self-control of early sobriety, where sex and love addicts try intense willpower to control their thoughts and urges, needs to be replaced with the control of openness, honesty, and the willingness to admit to being imperfect, to making mistakes, and to "doing wrong." An admission of the addict's limitations opens him or her to direction from their Higher Power, which is what the Eleventh Step is all about.

Step Eleven
Sought Through Prayer and Meditation to Improve Our Conscious Contact with a Power Greater Than Ourselves, Praying Only for Knowledge of God's Will for Us and the Power to Carry That Out

The Eleventh Step suggests a program of "prayer and meditation" for the recovering sex and love addict. Many addicts may have already incorporated daily prayer and meditation as a regular part of their routine. It is a frequent suggestion to newcomers or to people struggling with slips or relapses. Daily prayer and meditation, usually done in the morning soon after rising, can help the sex and love addict focus his or her thoughts and energies to deal with the stresses to come during the day. Certainly, the activity of prayer and meditation is antithetical to the fantasy and mental preoccupation so present during the active addiction. While acting out, the mental energy spent anticipating romantic and sexual activities was like a prayer to a god of sex and love, a fulfiller of all needs and anxieties. Obsessing was like a meditation on the illusions of satisfaction and peace that acting out sexually or romantically would bring to the suffering addict. By the time sex and love addicts reach the Eleventh Step, this sort of addictive thinking should be fairly well behind them, but they then must replace this void with a positive, healthy form of spiritual development.

During the active phase of the addiction, the sex and love addict doubtless experienced a constant striving, searching, and yearning, which he or she saw as a sexual or romantic quest; "If only I could find the right guy, . . . " "If only I could reach the ultimate orgasm, . . . " or "If only I could lose myself in the oblivion of sexual release, . . . " Sex and love addicts seek something to provide a sense of peace, acceptance, and caring. In reality, however, this is a spiritual quest, not a worldly search. The addict is looking for love in all the wrong places. The Eleventh Step seeks to redirect sex and love addicts to grow in the direction of "conscious contact" with their Higher Power.

Spiritual growth and recovery are both based on surrender. The focus of prayer and meditation is "only for" the "knowledge of God's will for us." The addict is not encouraged to ask for special favors, rescue from difficult circumstances, or exceptions to the rules—all of which he or she sought fervently during his or her addiction. Self-will, egotism, and self-direction all present a great danger to the recovering sex and love addict. Taking back control, getting into the driver's seat, becoming overconfident, and being unwilling to follow direction are indicators that the addict is on the edge of a return to addictive thinking and behavior. The Eleventh Step attempts to build in a regular course corrector that will remind the addict who is in charge and where he or she must look for direction and comfort.

Actually, most sex and love addicts will have already begun to do this, and thus find the philosophy of the Eleventh Step both obvious and reassuring. In recovery they have begun to experience, in ways they never believed possible, God's grace. The goal of their often frantic sexual and romantic activities—acceptance, nurturing, and love—has not been met by throwing themselves entirely into worldly, carnal pursuits, but rather is being fulfilled by "conscious contact" with their Higher Power. They have discovered that what they considered their "burdens—for example, spouses, children, work, and obligations—are in reality their blessings. By giving up the degrading, humiliating chase for sex and love, by surrendering and accepting power-lessness and unmanageability over their addictions, and by believing in and turning their will and lives over to their Higher Power their lives have been turned inside out. They can get what they want—love and acceptance—by letting go and allowing God rather than by grabbing tightly to erotic or romantic pleasures. Step Eleven builds this awareness into a regular routine to balance the addicts' lives in recovery.

Step Twelve
Having Had a Spiritual Awakening as a Result of These Steps, We Tried to Carry This Message to Sex and Love Addicts and to Practice These Principles in All Areas of Our Lives

The last step speaks directly of the spiritual renewal in the Eleventh as well as the other steps, and outlines the final suggestions for ongoing recovery:

service and maintaining the principles[Most recovering people who reach the Twelfth Step have no question about the existence of "a spiritual awakening," and are often eager to tell others how profound this change has been both within themselves and in their lives. It is almost impossible to go through all these steps and not experience a huge change of heart and perspectives on life and love.]

Quote

The sex and love addict comes into the program quite selfish and self-centered. In the Twelfth Step, the transformation from "His (or Her) Majesty the Baby" into a caring, concerned, and sober person is completed. The addict is called to stay sober by "carrying the message" to addicts who are still suffering from this painful addiction. Again, the idea is paradoxical: "You keep it by giving it away." The founders of A.A., Bill W. and Dr. Bob, found this to be true over 50 years ago. Bill was able to stay sober by finding another "drunk" to talk to, Dr. Bob. These men were selfish in their unselfishness, and they helped themselves by helping others.

None of the Twelve Step fellowships around the world would function were it not for this essential aspect of the recovery process. All are entirely voluntary organizations that depend solely on their membership for all they need to operate. The entire purpose of the organizations is to keep their membership sober by "carrying the message." They run marvelously well, in fact. This is due to the truth of the idea that the only way to "keep it green" and to remember "how bad it was" is to keep in touch with the newcomers. As people with some sobriety help console and advise addicts who are just coming into the S.L.A.A. program, they need to recall their own struggles and the pain and suffering of their own active addiction and early recovery. This helps guard against the inevitable fading away of the painful memories and constant reminders of their active sex and love addiction.

As well as service, the sex and love addict is directed "to practice these principles" in all his or her dealings. Honesty, openness, willingness, and responsibility are the basic principles of a good recovery process from a sex and love addiction. In order to maintain and continue the personal growth that has been achieved by working the Twelve Steps, sex and love addicts need to continue to operate their lives using what they have learned will change things into a healthy, balanced, positive approach to living. Some people may argue that this is not possible in one context or another, such as the business world. However, whether everyone operates their businesses honestly or ethically is not the point. The point is rather that for the sex and love addict, the bad habits of secrecy, dishonesty, lying, deception, and living a double life are deep grooves that would be easy to slide back into. If the recovering sex and love addict can separate his or her business life from recovery, then, he or she is already beginning to be a split person and lead a double life. It is only a matter of time and opportunity before they will be faced with the question of renewing their addictive lifestyle. If they are not "practicing the principles" in their day-to-day life, it will be much easier for them to again justify double standards and secrecy. At that point, a return to acting out, will be only a matter of time.

With all the steps in place, the sex and love addict can put love and sex in their proper perspective in his or her life. The recovering addict will be able to see that sex is an expression of love, and that love and sex are part of true intimacy between partners. Sex and love are a part of life—hopefully, a special part—but they are not life itself. A life that is consumed by an addiction is not a life that is truly being lived. Compulsive sexuality and obsessive love affairs actually restrict addicts' freedom to express themselves in loving and sexual ways through a relationship characterized by openness, mutuality, honesty, trust, caring, and responsibility. True intimacy requires that partners be wholly present, without secrets and reservations. With recovery, the sex and love addict can learn to experience this grace from his or her Higher Power.

BOTTOM LINES AND TRIGGERS

Sex and love addicts in the recovery process have identified two key areas in establishing and maintaining sobriety: bottom-line behaviors and triggers. Bottom-line behaviors are self-selected actions that constitute "addictive behaviors." They need to be stopped completely. Triggers are thoughts, feelings, events, things, or persons that make the sex and love addict want to initiate or return to the bottom-line behaviors.

The pamphlet by the Augustine Fellowship of Sex and Love Addicts Anonymous, *Suggestions for Newcomers,* defines bottom-line behavior as "any sexual or emotional act, no matter what its initial impulse may be, which leads to loss of control over rate, frequency, or duration of its occurrence or recurrence, resulting in spiritual, mental, physical, emotional, and moral destruction of oneself and others." While this is a somewhat complex and cumbersome definition, it conveys the message that bottom-line behavior is the beginning of the addiction, and leads to damage in all areas of the addict's life. The other important part of this definition is that it involves loss of control, or powerlessness. It may not lead to a constant, or even regular, set of behaviors, but the disease has been set back in motion for the individual's unique pattern of acting out. The sex and love addict will fall back into the progression of his or her addiction, and things will only get worse.

In a lecture at our intensive outpatient treatment program for sex and love addicts, many of the participants shared their ideas of what for them was bottom-line behavior. They mentioned:

A. "Doing or giving in to some sexual activity either mentally or physically that I do not want to do; repeating different acts for hopefully the same purpose."

B. "Any specific self-destructive actions which an individual defines as caused by or related to his or her addiction and which one had decided to quit or avoid in order to achieve sobriety."

C. "The acting out resulting from an addiction sexual or otherwise; this behavior may manifest itself in various ways, is compulsive, and also can be a number of inter-related addictions."

D. "Behaviors that are self-medicating and habitual and isolating, for relief of stress, anxiety, loneliness, sadness, and other feelings that an individual has not developed healthy and non-destructive coping mechanisms for."

E. "Behaviors that cannot be controlled or managed through willpower; they are incessant, and take away spiritual and personal growth; they are behaviors that take away my feeling [of being] well and whole."

F. "An act or actions which begin the sex and love addict's cycle; behavior that is considered acting out or precipitates acting out."

G. "Behavior resorted to to alleviate pain, loneliness, self-hatred, shame, self-loathing, ranging from fantasy, masturbation, and pornography, to anonymous sex; behavior that is progressive and self-destructive."

H. "That activity over which I can exercise no control which leads me to act out sexually, and/or the acting out itself, in order to alter mood."

I. "Acting out sexually, and/or romantic intrigue involving obsessive romantic and/or emotional dependence on one or more people; when my life is in such a state of mind that my other self is in total control."

J. "Any behavior you have no control over; it possesses you; it keeps coming back; it fills a void."

K. "Not necessarily negative behavior; trying to do something good, but we get so involved that it leads to something bad."

L. "Feeling of giving something away that I didn't want to, loss of choice."

M. "Any sexual activity, fantasy, action that we are powerless over; distracts us from our primary purpose."

N. "Something done compulsively to fulfill a need not being fulfilled; I was always looking for something[:] . . . for acceptance, for being loved."

O. "That activity, social, emotional or physical, fantasy or real, which causes discomfort and is harmful to physical or emotional states, causing shame and/or guilt; it is or can be obsessive, compulsive, and can occur in binges, repetitively, or in isolated incidents, and persists despite all consequences; it is a very short relief presenting long-term consequences."

In these personal and informal definitions of bottom-line behaviors, sex and love addicts have repeated a number of common theses about the sexual or romantic thoughts, feelings, and behaviors that lead them back into the active phase of their addictive disease. Some of the common elements are:

1. The addict's powerlessness, loss of control, loss of choice, inability to desist, or to quit or avoid the behavior.

2. The repetitive, compulsive, habitual, incessant, and persistent nature of the behaviors.

3. The self-destructive, unhealthy, uncomfortable, harmful, isolating, and damaging side of bottom-line behaviors.

4. The self-medicating, stress-reducing, short term relieving, pain-relieving, mood-altering, void-filling, isolation-fixing, and need-fulfilling quality of sexual or romantic acting out.

5. The addict's poor coping mechanisms for stress, anxiety, sadness, anger, loneliness, pain, dysphoria, discomfort, tension, insecurity, and lack of acceptance.

6. The loss of personal and spiritual growth and of feelings of wellness and wholeness during the acting-out periods.

7. The inclusion of fantasy as well as actual behaviors.

8. The effect of bottom-line behaviors on the body, mind, emotions, spirit, and social life of the addict.

9. The idea that participating in bottom-line behavior starts the addiction cycle again.

10. The progression of the disease.

11. The dependency problems of the addict.

Together, these elements give a powerful picture of the importance of bottom-line behaviors in the addiction and recovery process. To put these parts together into a definition, bottom-line behaviors are the thoughts (fantasies) or behaviors over which the sex and love addict is powerless, and that are compulsive, self-destructive, self-medicating, and mood-altering. They also help the person find short-term relief, yet produce long-term negative consequences like starting the addictive cycle and progression, stopping personal and spiritual growth, increasing dependency, and producing guilt and shame. Again, the definition is long and awkward in some ways, but it must be comprehensive to convey the full meaning of bottom-line behaviors for sex and love addicts.

The following series of questions may help clarify what must be included in a recovering sex and love addict's concept of bottom-line behaviors:

1. Am I unable to stop?

2. Do I feel depressed afterwards?

3. Am I compulsively doing it to maintain or to continue sexual energy?

4. Does doing it deaden or reduce my capacity to love?

5. Is it intoxicating or mind-altering?

6. Is it dangerous, abusive, or distasteful?

7. Am I desperate to do this?

8. Has this made me miserable many times before?

9. Do I avoid calling someone in S.L.A.A. first?

10. Am I secretive or ashamed about it?

11. Do I think I can control it?
12. Am I using it to avoid or create painful feelings?
13. Am I out of contact with my Higher Power now?
14. Do I feel I may never have sex again if I don't do this?
15. Is this only second best or only better than none at all?

If the thoughts, fantasies, actions, and behaviors that the sex and love addict are considering get an affirmative response to some of the above questions, then they are most likely candidates for the person's list of bottom-line behaviors.

In order to make the definition and questions more concrete, I will give some examples of bottom-line behaviors that have lead addicts into the recovery program as well as examples of how these addicts' bottom lines then changed. The basic question that these sex and love addicts were answering was; What renders you powerless, both in the past and as you go along in the S.L.A.A. program?

A. Masturbation, pornography, acting out with peers, acting out with adults, anonymous sex, sex with teenagers, bookstores, sex in restrooms and gay areas, and "cruising" brought me into S.L.A.A.

As time went on, my bottom lines included fantasy, intrigue, food, anything that took me away from dealing with feelings, sexualizing people, anger, and self-pity, and I continue to come up with different ones as I go along.

B. My initial bottom lines were gambling, love addiction, and pornography.

Later, my bottom lines included masturbation and anonymous sex. Masturbation was not listed first, but later I included it because of what it would lead to in terms of my intrigue and fantasies.

C. Initially, my bottom line was anonymous sex in adult bookstores.

Then, my bottom-line behaviors expanded to include masturbation to relieve stress and loneliness, cruising, anonymous sex, sexual fantasies at work and in bed at night, angry ruminations and obsessions at work and after work, feeling powerless and inadequate, and conflict that leads to a need for a fix.

D. Initial behaviors that brought others into the S.L.A.A. program were anonymous sex, masturbation, obsession, emotional dependence on people, sadomasochism, falling in love, latching on and never letting go, seeking out pain (with others or self-inflicted), cross-dressing, fantasy, swinging parties, and compulsive and exotic masturbation.

After being in the S.L.A.A. program, these people now included in their bottom lines anything done around sex that separates one from feelings, substituting one addiction for another like food for sex (it is still acting out because it feels good [until] the pain from overeating hits, as in the addiction cycle), and emotional yearning for a person.

These people found that they were able to be honest with themselves, and that this brought on new discoveries; changes in attitudes, feelings, and stereotypes, and a readiness to deal with feelings.

This is certainly not an all-inclusive list of bottom-line behaviors and how they change over the course of the recovery process, but giving some concrete and real instances of behaviors that brought sex and love addicts to a state of powerlessness and willingness to begin the S.L.A.A. program should nonetheless help illustrate the complex definitions reviewed above.

Obviously, knowing what a bottom-line behavior is and doing something about it are two different things. In the rooms of Sex and Love Addicts Anonymous meetings, as well as in consulting and therapy rooms, there is an ever-growing wealth of knowledge about bottom-line behaviors and how to stop them. Our ability to help those who suffer from this difficult and painful illness is increasing rapidly with better ideas of what addicts can do to stop and how they can "stay stopped."

The following is a long list of ideas that the sex addict can do to stop or avoid starting the bottom-line behaviors that he or she has defined as initiating his or her addictive process. The ideas are not put in any particular order, because what is most effective for one person may be less helpful for the next. Each of these suggestions comes out of the real, practical experience of sex and love addicts themselves. The suggestions can be seen as a set of skills or tools that the recovering sex and love addict must master in order to recover. As with any set of tools, some work better than others, and much depends on the particular circumstances and people involved. As with any skill, the more they are practiced, the easier they will be to use and the more effective they will prove. Therefore, each of these many suggestions should be considered and tried, preferably more than once, before being discarded as not helpful or irrelevant to the recovery of any particular sex and love addict.

Ideas for avoiding or stopping bottom-line behaviors include:

1. Avoid isolation.
2. Share feelings and don't bottle them up.
3. Nurture the self.
4. Attend S.L.A.A. meetings.
5. Keep physically active (for example, don't watch television).
6. Replace self-destructive activities with self-affirming ones.
7. Perform daily prayer and meditation to stay focused.
8. Get in S.L.A.A. sponsor.
9. Talk in S.L.A.A. meetings.
10. Read books and program literature on sex and love addictions.
11. Take personal inventory and *don't* take other peoples' inventories.

12. Let go of secrets, shame, and guilt.

13. Plan the day or free time so as to give yourself structure.

14. Remove yourself from people, places and things associated with your addiction.

15. Think of diversionary behavior in advance, for example; how to get your mind off dangerous subjects or how to get out of threatening situations.

16. Think of other things to do with your time and energy like exercise, social contacts, or old or new hobbies.

17. Call your sponsor daily.

18. Call your sponsor, friends in S.L.A.A., or your therapist when in trouble.

19. Prepare for your triggers and avoid them.

20. Reach out.

21. Don't go to cruising areas or public restrooms.

22. Find a balance between work, recreation, rest, and meetings.

23. Avoid getting too hungry or tired.

24. Watch out for anger, and express it quickly and appropriately.

25. Try to find your Higher Power (and remember that it is not you).

26. Develop new acquaintances.

27. Change attitudes.

28. Attend therapy regularly.

29. Maintain "custody of your eyes"; in other words, do not allow yourself to stare or ogle, or to sexualize whom- or whatever you are looking at.

30. Keep a journal.

31. Listen.

32. Grow spiritually.

33. Remember that "this too shall pass."

34. Do things with people in S.L.A.A.

35. Terminate fantasies.

36. Change your thinking.

37. Recognize self-pity.

38. Identify self-delusion.

39. "Keep it green"; in other words, remember how painful it really was to be addicted by listening at meetings, telling your story, or reading.

40. Talk more graphically with your therapist, describing your addiction in detail in order to get out secrets, shame, and guilt, and to open up from seclusion.

41. Talk everything out.

42. Pay more attention to how you dress; some dress is intended to be seductive or is used when cruising or hoping to act out.

43. Try to identify what your "child within" needs; learn how to nurture your "child"; allow your "child" to show, and to be playful and joyful.

44. Get a stuffed animal and nurture yourself with it.

45. Relive the things that you missed in your childhood.

46. Stay where you are safest.

47. Remember that taking care of your "child within" is incompatible with acting out.

48. Bracket events with phone calls or meetings; for example, before, during, and after a stressful event like visiting your family, call someone in S.L.A.A. or go to a meeting if possible.

49. Take someone (preferably from the S.L.A.A. program) with you when you do something that is dangerous or difficult, like going to a mall or attending a wedding.

50. Accept responsibility for oneself.

51. Take healthy risks.

52. Follow the "three-second rule": do not look at or think about someone or something sexual or romantic for more than three seconds.

53. Remember what it felt like to be a "newcomer."

54. Keep centered, focused, happy, content, and serene.

55. Use the "Serenity Prayer": "God, grant me the serenity to accept the things I cannot change, the courage to change the things that I can, and the wisdom to know the difference."

56. Follow God's will, not yours,

57. Make commitments to your program and to therapy.

58. Perform service in and outside the fellowship.

59. Live the Twelve Steps.

60. Remember, "we" belong to a community.

61. Avoid addictive stimuli like pornography, paraphernalia, phone books, club memberships, mementoes, and love letters (get rid of them).

62. Communicate clear, no-contact decisions to people with whom you have been in addictive relationships.

63. Avoid neighborhoods where you tend to act out.

64. Change your job, residence, meeting place, and hangouts, and people that you socialize with.

65. Stop the flirting and "taking rain checks."

66. Do not keep people "on a string" or in reserve.

67. Stop "talking dirty."

68. Be aware of moods that can be triggers, like restlessness, anxiety, having cravings, being preoccupied, feeling cocky, breathlessness, irritability, feeling "horny," and feeling feverish.

69. Stop cruising, mentally and physically.

70. Go to 90 meetings in 90 days.

71. Raise your hand in meetings.

72. Tell the truth.

73. Ask for phone numbers of S.L.A.A. members and make a list. Use it.

74. Every day tell someone in S.L.A.A. the truth about what is going on inside you.

75. List the areas of your life that are unmanageable.

76. Make a list of areas of powerlessness.

77. Rewrite the first three steps as they apply to you.

78. Ask sober S.L.A.A. members to help with your contacts from past addictive relationships.

79. Attend meetings regularly.

80. Get a "home group," which you attend regularly and where you feel comfortable.

81. Get to know people and let them know you.

82. Welcome newcomers.

83. Help set up and clean up after meetings.

84. Help others.

85. Get rid of "stinking thinking."

What is amazing and exciting is that this list is still incomplete. As people continue to grow and recover, they will discover more ways to stop and avoid their bottom-line behaviors. They will share their successes and failures with others, and our wisdom will grow to be even greater than it is today. As our list expands, so too will hope for recovery from this crippling addiction.

One suggestion—the last one—that deserves more attention, at this point, is "getting rid of stinking thinking." Distorted thoughts, obsessions, and preoccupations both enable and initiate the addictive cycle. As sex and love addicts recover they become better able to admit to themselves and to others how they really think. As they do, they begin to share the thoughts they have used to defend, rationalize, and justify acting out on bottom-line and behaviors. Some of these thoughts are:

"I can't help seeing her. We work in the same office."

"One more time won't matter."

"I am entitled."

"No one will know."

"But I love him or her..."

"I've got some sobriety. I can handle it."

"It doesn't hurt anyone but me."

"I should make amends to him or her. My Twelfth Step work requires it."

"I have as much right to be at the party as he or she does."

"Why do I have to be the one to stay away?"

"But I miss him or her so dreadfully."

"This was never one of my bottom-line behaviors."

"It can't be right to be in this much pain."

"It's only a fantasy."

"One day, I will meet my true love. In the meantime . . . "

"I cannot tell the truth to this person."

"We have not seen each other for six months. It's all right now."

"I only want to do this occasionally."

"God wants me to love people."

"It takes me to paradise."

"I need a little oblivion today."

"I cannot stop myself. Let's get it over with."

"If I do this, maybe I will meet the love of my life."

"I have nothing better going."

"I will die if I don't.

"We're just friends now."

"Maybe I am ready for a relationship now."

This is certainly not an exhaustive list, but it does illustrate many of the common distortions in thinking that the sex and love addict uses to keep the possibilities alive for acting out. Some of the thinking is fairly straightforward in terms of its lack of logical consistency, and some of it reflects more so-phisticated mental manipulations, such as trying to incorporate acting out on bottom lines as part of "Twelfth Step work." In order to avoid losing control and falling prey to one's own "stinking thinking," the sex and love addict needs to be able to spot dangerous thoughts and counter them with more healthy and realistic thinking.

For instance, if the sex and love addict tells him- or herself, "I can't stop," then he or she needs to be able to counter, "Yes, I can stop." The newly recovering addict may need to bolster this comeback to the "addict within" by saying something like, "If Jack can do it, so can I," "I will try to stop just for today," or "I may not be able to stop on my own, but with the help of my group and sponsor, I will be able to learn how to stop." Moreover, the addict may need to immediately call for help since he or she may not know how to combat this sort of thought distortion. Cognitive therapy has shown us that irrational thoughts that produce depression can be countered with rational responses that enhance a person's mood. Cognitive therapists who work with addicts help them identify the thoughts that put them in danger and prepare appropriate counter-thoughts that remind addicts why they do not want to indulge their self-destructive, but tempting, impulses. In the program of S.L.A.A., there are a number of informal, less structured ways to accomplish the same task; namely, the development of rational responses to irrational thoughts like "It's only a fantasy." Fantasies are usually triggers for acting out on bottom-line behaviors, and S.L.A.A. members with some sobriety will tend to point to the connection and encourage the newly recovering person to think of why he or she came into the recovery program to begin with: to learn to counteract "stinking thinking."

Triggers

In addition to cognitive triggers for bottom-line behaviors, there are also emotional and external events that can act as initiators of the addictive cycle. These are usually called "triggers." The accompanying image of a loaded gun about to fire is both powerful and appropriate for a sex and love addiction. We have already reviewed how sex and love addictions are life-threatening illnesses, both to addicts and to others who are intimately involved with them. The trigger of a gun is what starts the destructive explosion. Until the trigger is pulled the gun has no power to harm, but once the trigger has been pulled, there is no telling the extent of the damage until the smoke has cleared and the explosion has ended. Sex and love addictions work the same way. They can be dormant, inactive, and cause no harm, but very quickly this seemingly safe situation can explode into a destructive, damaging, and out-of-control binge or ongoing series of acting-out behaviors. Knowledge of the feelings and events that might be, have been, or are triggers for oneself and others can help the sex and love addict (and those who are helping him or her) maintain their bottom-line behaviors and remain safe.

Some research in chemical dependency has indicated that stressful or difficult events account for about 40 percent of reported relapses. Problems with feelings that are overwhelming or that the addict does not know how to cope with in a healthy way tend to account for the other 60 percent of relapses. Some of the events that may act as triggers are:

1. A *Rejection* by a lover, potential relationship, friend, employer, publisher, or even the grocer.
2. A *Humiliating* experience that makes the sex and love addict feel embarrassment, shame, or guilt.
3. A *Confrontational* encounter where the addict is either confronted or else is the confronter and is uncomfortable in this role.
4. A *Diet,* especially if it makes the addict feel deprived, empty, or undeserving of nourishment.
5. A *Fight or Conflict* at work, home, or with a friend.
6. An *Isolating* experience that puts the addict in touch with his or her aloneness, loneliness, and longing for contact with others.
7. *Exhaustion or being Over-Tired,* which makes the addict feel depleted, deprived, unimportant, or used.
8. A *Celebration* like a party, birthday, anniversary, or wedding.

9. *Free Time* like a day off or a vacation.

10. *Holidays* that bring up feelings of isolation or memories of family conflicts, neglect, abuse, or violence.

11. *A Loss,* including a death, the end of a relationship, the loss of a pet, the termination of employment, or moving.

12. *A Performance* such as a concert, play, sport, or lecture.

13. *A Promotion or Job Change* that involves learning a new set of procedures, rules, and relationships.

14. *Danger* like a car accident or close call.

15. *Physical or Mental Illness,* especially one that is chronic or affects someone important to the addict.

Both positive and negative events can be triggers. Most people are sensitized to events such as the loss of a spouse, getting fired from a job, or being humiliated in public. We know that this is dangerous as we will probably look for a quick fix for these obviously traumatic experiences. However, many of us underestimate the potential danger in a successful event such as a job promotion, attending a conference, or going to a party or wedding. For a sex and love addict, successful events can be far more dangerous than troublesome ones. A celebration is a time when people "have fun" and "let down their hair." What better way to have fun than a romantic intrigue or an exciting sexual encounter? With inhibitions down, the sex and love addict becomes more vulnerable.

A sex and love addict with 59 days of sobriety who recently was discharged from an inpatient program, shared the fact that he had been triggered by attending a wedding. He was introduced to a number of single women, and allowed himself to dance with them after the ceremony. A fellow S.L.A.A. member, who happened to be at the same function, even said something to him that dancing might be dangerous. Afterwards, the addict started feeling lonely, went to an A.A. dance, and again began to "check out" the available women. When one began to come on to him, he realized he was getting into trouble and managed to leave. He had not acted out an his bottom line of no sex outside his committed relationship, but felt he had "emotionally acted out" because he was aware of how much he had enjoyed the dancing and intrigue of seeing who was or was not available.

Feelings can also be triggers for acting out on bottom-line behaviors. Most sex and love addicts have numbed their feelings and become easily confused or overwhelmed when they start to feel again, or they have sexualized their feelings so that any feeling means they need sex (for example, if they are angry, they need to relax with some sex). There are a number of potentially dangerous feelings of which the recovering sex and love addict needs to be aware because they might serve as triggers for him or her. These feelings roughly parallel the events just listed, and may be caused by these events. Feeling triggers are:

1. *Pain*—either physical or emotional, like the hurt of rejection.

2. *Shame*—the feeling of being unworthy, having done something unforgivable, wanting to melt into the floor or hang your head; the feeling of intense embarrassment.

3. *Guilt*—feeling like you have done something wrong; feeling like you have hurt or harmed someone else, the embarrassment of being caught.

4. *Hunger*—feeling empty, needing nourishment, craving, wanting to be filled up, needing to stuff or numb some other pain.

5. *Anger*—a most difficult and dangerous state for a sex and love addict; self-pity may be close at hand; frustration and perfectionism are related.

6. *Loneliness*—connects with the sex and love addict's core belief of being unworthy and unlovable, and leads to longings and to wanting comfort from any source, especially physical contact.

7. *Tired*—feeling depleted, exhausted, out of energy, feeling both unable to resist impulses and in need of a reward or fix.

8. *Overworked*—feeling unappreciated, too busy to take care of oneself, unrewarded and unrecognized.

9. *Boredom*—can be quite dangerous because the sex and love addict can yearn for a quick fix; being unsatisfied, feeling unfulfilled.

10. *Neediness*—wanting to belong, feeling disconnected, unrelated.

11. *Depression*—having the "blues"; lacking a sense of hope, of something to look forward to, no happiness, peace, or contentment.

12. *Anxiety*—unwarranted fear, worrying, projecting disaster or failure, rumination, imagining catastrophes.

13. *Unworthiness*—lacking in self-esteem, self-worth, and self-confidence.

14. *Fear*—especially strong in sex and love addicts when they are still holding on to a lot of their secrets and their shame; feeling inadequate and insecure.

15. *Powerlessness*—feeling out of control, unable to direct things and determine the outcome, something that sex and love addicts hate to feel because they might have to change.

With each of these and the myriads of other feelings that we experience, there is the potential for triggering acting out on bottom-line behaviors. Thoughts, events, and feelings can interact in many different combinations to increase the potency of each separate thought, feeling, or event. For instance, a critical comment by a supervisor can trigger the thought, "I've messed up; I'm incompetent," which in turn creates a feeling of unworthiness that the sex and love addict feels compelled to fix with sexual or romantic acting out. Similarly, a positive comment by the same supervisor might stimulate the thought, "I don't deserve that," which generates a feeling of shame at being a fraud or sham. A feeling of boredom may sensitize the sex and love addict to the lack of either positive or negative comments by the supervisor, and can trigger the thought, "I have a meaningless job and a worthless life," which then can start the addict craving for a fix: for excitement, action, meaning, and a sense of involvement and worth. Each addict needs to look at his or her own thoughts, feelings, and life events to determine the possible triggers for his or her bottom-line behaviors.

SECRECY

We start our outpatient groups by saying, "We come together to get honest with ourselves and each other; honesty is the key to sobriety." A common saying in the S.L.A.A. program is, "You are as sick as your secrets." Both these sayings underscore the importance of honesty and eliminating secrecy in the recovery from sex and love addiction. Recovery is not possible without rigorous honesty. This is a tall order since sex and love addicts tend to be the most secretive of all addicts. Nicotine addicts are only beginning to feel uncomfortable smoking in public. Food addicts are obvious because of their size except for bulemics, who secretly throw up what they have gobbled down. Alcoholics drink in public, but as their illness progresses, they often become more secretive, for instance, they may have a few drinks before a party so that they will not appear to drink too much in front of others. Drug addicts are more secretive because what they do is illegal. Sex and love addicts are secretive about their sexual activities, but much of their cruising, use of pornography and prostitution, and dressing to attract sexual and romantic attention is more public than most people would assume. Because most of us are not sensitized to sex and love addictions, we do not think that the woman in the short shorts and tank top or the man renting an X-rated movie may be sex and love addicts. They may indeed be, just as the man who stops for "happy hour" at a bar for a few drinks before going home may be an alcoholic.

When we talk about honesty, it may be important to distinguish between secrecy and lying. Some sex and love addicts think they are being honest when they do not lie. However, if they do not tell the whole truth, they are still guilty of lying by omission. Many sex and love addicts do not see it this way. To them, a lie is making up something, making up a falsehood, like inventing a story about where you were to cover up the truth. Actually, a secret is withholding the truth. You do not have to lie to keep something secret. You just refrain from telling it. This is lying by omission: intentionally not telling the whole truth. If you omit some parts of a story, the listener will not get the whole picture. The part that is exposed may look quite different from the whole. This is why it is a lie, and why it can seriously damage and endanger a sex and love addict's recovery. If your sponsor or therapist does not know the entire story, they may not be able to warn you of potential difficulties or danger areas. Not telling the whole truth is a way of remaining in control and not surrendering, as required in the first three steps. It is playing God, because you are deciding who needs to know what, and not trusting your Higher Power to sort things out for you.

How do we learn to tell lies and keep secrets? First, we learned as part of our normal development that we could lie and get away with it. As very young children we thought that our parents could read our minds because they were able to anticipate our needs, actions, and feelings. They seemed to know, almost before we did, when we were tired, when we were sad, when we felt hungry, when we needed to be changed, when we were embarrassed, when we were angry, and when we needed to use the bathroom. As we got a bit older, we started to realized that our parents were not actually mind readers and that they had just been anticipating things. We discovered that we could fool them sometimes, that we could withhold things, that they would believe things even though they were not true. Some of us had parents who were easier to fool than others. Some lived with naive parents who were embarrassingly easy to "get over on." Others lived with "detectives" who made it their duty and mission in life to know everything that they were up to, and who were very difficult to fool. Still even the most vigilant, most involved, and most skeptical parents could occasionally be duped. As we grew older, we learned that our friends, relatives, teachers, and others could also be fooled. Some of us simply left things out. Others learned to be good liars. Some even became compulsive liars.

Being able to keep secrets was also part of normal development in terms of being able to keep a confidence. During childhood, as we developed friendships, we learned that if we told things that our friends confided in us, we lost our friends. There were some things that our friends needed to share with us that they did not want anyone else to know, or perhaps they wanted to choose who had access to the information and who did not. If we refrained from being blabbermouths and "learned to keep our mouths shut," we could have better, closer, deeper, more trusting friendships. We learned that it is a virtue to be able to keep things to ourselves and not repeat all that we have heard. We found that people admired us for being able to keep a secret. We felt good when we knew something that others did not know, and we felt proud when our friends complimented us on our ability to keep things confidential.

However, lying was not considered a positive attribute unless we were in a peer group that valued fooling adults. Most of us learned that distorting the truth intentionally or fabricating stories was improper behavior. We probably even experienced some consequences when we tried to lie about something about which we were afraid to tell the truth.

While keeping things confidential was a plus, and lying actually was a minus in terms of normal development, some of us learned to keep secrets and to lie as part of a pathological family system. Sick families feel a need to hide their problems from others, and make a point of teaching children that "some things stay within the family." Children get the message—sometimes explicitly and sometimes implicitly—that "What goes on in the family stays in the family." There is a clear "no talk" rule about family business. This usually is directed at keeping family secrets like alcoholism, verbal or physical violence and abuse, and mental illness within the confines of the immediate family. Often even relatives may not know the truth of what is happening behind the family's closed doors. Children may be specifically instructed not to talk about certain things to others, or there may be so much shame and embarrassment within the family that family members get the idea that it would be a mistake to say anything to anyone about the difficulties that are affecting the family. There may be so many secrets within the family itself that even family members do not know the truth about each other. Certainly, if you do not know what is going on in your own family, you will be less likely to expose this sort of dysfunction to others. If you do know the truth, you will probably be intimidated or shamed into silence.

Keeping family secrets can be very destructive to people because such lessons are ingrained quite deeply and carry over even into adulthood. If fact, some adults who have followed a code of secrecy and lying since childhood even lie when it would be easier to tell the truth. Janet Woititz pointed out this irrational carryover in her book, *Adult Children of Alcoholics*. Even if adults from dishonest families do not actually lie, they usually are hesitant and reserved about opening up and telling the truth. They feel compelled to keep up the family image despite the damage that this sort of dishonesty inflicts on them and on the people that they care about.

Carnes's (1988) research indicated that two-thirds of the families of sex addicts are rigid and disengaged. That is, in terms of the family's ability to adapt, it has few resources and tends to fall back on a rigid set of rules and expectations. These families have difficulty being flexible or even structuring themselves without rigidity. Their lack of adaptability can contribute to the tendency to keep secrets. When children from rigid family make a mistake, fail, or do something foolish, embarrassing, immoral, illegal, or wrong, they are afraid to tell their parents because they fear harsh reactions of punishment, rejection, criticism, and shame. As a result, they may try to hide the truth.

On the cohesion, closeness, or love dimension, these families tend to be disengaged. That is, they are more than separate. They do not feel emotionally connected with each other. Each person is not just an island but moreover is a distinct continent unrelated to the others. These family members cannot make each other feel close, loved, or cared about, so love tends to be conditional. This makes keeping secrets almost a necessity to get acceptance and recognition. Having done something you should not have done is only all right if no one knows about it. If family members find out, their tendency will be to pull away even farther and to make the offender feel even worse.

Not all families of sex and love addicts are rigid and disconnected. Some are enmeshed; members are too close and know everyone else's business. Being too tight can create a desire to withhold the truth or keep secrets in order to have a sense of individuality and independence. Some families are more chaotic—the opposite of rigid. These families also can foster dishonesty because they cannot cope with information that is shared. They tend to either over- or underreact, both of which make a person feel like he or she would have been better off not sharing with the families.

The third way that people learn how to keep secrets, besides what evolves normally and under the influence of a dysfunctional family, is through the development of an addiction. Secrecy about sexual thoughts and feelings is taught in the family in terms of normal modesty and privacy. We even call our sexual organs our "private parts" or "privates." Any addiction will create a sense of powerlessness and shame at the loss of control, and thus will foster the tendency to keep it secret and private. A sex and love addiction combines the normal privacy that we feel toward our bodies and bodily functions with the shame and secrecy of behaviors that are unmanageable and out of control, thereby creating an even more powerful motive for hiding and lying about what is really going on.

The purpose of lying and keeping secrets is to protect oneself. Secrecy is a way to avoid feelings of hurt, shame, embarrassment, criticism, rejection, and humiliation. It is a way to keep safe. We use it to defend ourselves from the world. We use secrecy to mask our fears, inadequacies, failures, insecurities, and wrongdoings. We may have even been taught that it is all right to "tell white lies." A so-called white lie is a form of dishonesty that is intended to protect someone else's feelings. For example, if your aunt does not look well and you want to make her feel better and protect her feelings from being hurt by the truth, you might tell her a white lie like, "Gee, you are looking well these days." Such a deception is designed to protect everyone and keep them safe from impact of the harsh reality of real life.

Unfortunately, most of us underestimate and may even fail to understand the damage done by being secretive and dishonest. First, keeping secrets, not telling the whole truth, or lying can increase the distance between the "public self" and the "real self." All of us have an image that we project in public. For instance, we frequently respond to the question, "How are you?" with "I'm fine." Usually this image is a mask, and does not accurately reflect how we really are. The greater the distance between the public and private self, the harder it is for others to know us and to make contact with us in a way that makes us feel genuinely loved and cared about. This split between our mask and our real selves looks something like the figure on the following page.

This can be the basis for the "split personality" of the sex and love addict. The Dr.-Jekyl-and-Mr.-Hyde quality of most addicts is a reflection of the large gap between who they really are and who they can appear to be. Sex and love addicts are usually masters at image and manipulation, and can be quite creative about the way they look in public compared to the way that they are in private, when they are able to remove their masks and show their true character. Actually, the private sex and love addict who is compulsively acting

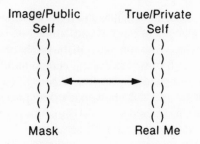

out is only a part of the real person. The rest is the person who is in terrible despair over being unable to get things to work right both within him- or herself and in his or her life. Such people are filled with self-hatred and self-loathing.

The second effect of secrecy, besides promoting a split of the addict's personality into very different public and private selves, is that it destroys self-esteem. Rather than improving self-worth by earning him or her respect for being able to keep a confidence, the lying and secrecy of the sex and love addict damages the addict's self-image because of the reasons for the dishonesty and secrets. Rather than protecting others by respecting their privacy or telling white lies, the sex and love addict is protecting him- or herself from exposure, shame, loss of face, and humiliation. The sex and love addict's motivation and intentions are not honorable, just as the actions and activities they are trying to hide are not worthy of self-respect. Consequently, keeping secrets of this kind gradually destroys self-esteem and encourages self-hatred.

The third effect of secrecy is to increase the sex and love addict's sense of isolation. The farther the true self is hidden from the world, the harder it is for others to make contact with it. If the addict has no one in his or her life who knows the real truth or the whole story of what is going on, which is all too often the case, then he or she has no one with whom he or she can experience genuine contact and true intimacy. Sex and love addicts are good at creating pseudo-intimacy through the medium of sex and love, but, as previously mentioned, this is a poor substitute for real intimacy. Loneliness and isolation are the most painful aspect of the illness, and often lead to increasingly compulsive acting out or suicidal despair.

In addition to losing contact with other people, the fourth effect of secrecy is to increase the sex and love addict's loss of contact with reality. As the addict gets deeper and deeper into the addiction, he or she become more and more detached from real feelings. Everything revolves around sex or romance, and feelings are either numbed or sexualized. Feelings are our major way of keeping in contact with ourselves and the world, and without them we become robot-like, inhuman beings who are disconnected from life.

Sex and love addictions also enhance the addict's distorted thinking processes. As they progress, the addict's thinking becomes increasingly distorted, delusional, and even psychotic; in other words, it loses contact with reality, as with the pedophile who thinks he is not hurting the children he molests and in fact has himself convinced that he is expressing love to them.

The fifth effect of secrecy is that it enables the sex and love addict to continue in the active addiction. Keeping secrets and lying allow the addict to hold onto all or parts of the addiction and keep them underground so that they can resurface when it is safer. It is not unusual for sex and love addicts to have periods of abstinence during which they do not act out. These periods may last for days, weeks, months, or years. The sex and love addiction has not disappeared and the addict has not been cured. Instead, the addiction is just being kept secret, and the addict is lying to him- or herself in saying that he or she is all right without having told anyone the truth of what was going on during the active phase of the addiction. Being dishonest with oneself—"I've finally got this under control" or "It was only a phase and I'm over it now"—is a favorite way that sex and love addicts enable themselves to hang on to their belief that they are all right, that they have no problem, and that they are in control.

The final negative effect of secrecy is that it frustrates any efforts at recovery or therapy. If you withhold or fail to disclose information to your therapist, for example, your therapist will end up treating someone who does not actually exist. The interventions and interpretations will be designed to match a certain person in a certain circumstance, but if this is not the reality of the situation, the efforts of the therapist are doomed to failure. The sex and love addict will, then, have set up the therapist to fail in order to devalue the therapy process and continue to act out in the addiction. Many sex and love addicts hide their problems or the extent of their difficulties because they are ashamed and embarrassed by them. Unfortunately, this can result in many wasted or, at least, less effective hours of psychotherapy than would have occurred if the addicts had been able to tell the truth. For example, one sex and love addict with whom I worked was in group therapy for over a year and spoke a great deal about his insecurity but failed to mention his history of making obscene phone calls or his continuing compulsive masturbation. Consequently, he did not get any help for these problems, and the therapy he did get was based on a false, incomplete picture of who and what he was. He did not talk about his sexual compulsions because he was too embarrassed to admit them, despite being a regular member of S.L.A.A.

What are the steps to change the pattern of lying and secrecy in the sex and love addict's life? The first is the "H.O.W." process, as it is called in S.L.A.A.: by being *H*onest, *O*pen, and *W*illing to do whatever it takes to get well, the addict can begin to reverse the cover-ups developed during the active addiction. The other part of how to change is using G.O.D. In the recovery program, G.O.D. stands for *Good Orderly Direction*. Some people are turned off by the idea of a Higher Power, but recovery from an addiction requires some sort of reliance on wisdom outside the addicts themselves; most of them have already proven repeatedly that they are unable to control their behaviors. In that case, they can use Good Orderly Direction as their G.O.D., at least in the initial stages of recovery or until they are ready to look more closely at spiritual issues. Good Orderly Direction means that the sex and love addict will not indulge his or her urges to be impulsive, take charge, or ignore advice, especially the advice of sponsors and people with some sexual sobriety. There will be order in their decisions and reliance on the direction of those older and wiser than they are in recovery from sex and love addictions.

A second thing that a recovering sex and love addict can do to help improve his or her honesty, openness, and truthfulness is to learn to tolerate some embarrassment. Most of us make great efforts to avoid any situation that might prove embarrassing, and do all we can to get out of an embarrassing situation the minute we find ourselves in one. Actually, embarrassment does not last long if we can learn to live through it. It may last for a few seconds, or a minute or two at the most. Acknowledging our embarrassment can help get us through it. Realizing that we are all imperfect and, therefore, always subject to embarrassing moments, will make them easier to take. Accepting our emotions and not trying to control them or run away from painful feelings will enable us to live with embarrassment more readily.

Third, the recovering sex and love addict can work through some of his or her feelings of shame and guilt in order to have less to hide and fewer reasons to keep secrets. Guilt and shame are serious emotions that can have strong effects. They can be powerful reinforcers for the need to keep secrets and to lie. For example, most families who have a sex and love addict who is known as a "slut" or "philanderer" will keep this a family secret. It will come out in bits and pieces, but the true story will be hidden behind excuses or cover-ups because other family members are ashamed and embarrassed by the addict's uncontrolled sexual or romantic behaviors.

The fourth thing that can be done to remove the pale of secrecy and dishonesty is to break the family's "no talk" rule. This may be impossible in the context of the family, but the sex and love addict can talk to others about the family's secrets and craziness. Initially, the person may feel disloyal and cruel after having disclosed some of the truths about the family, but with time and repetition, it will become easier to talk about these realities that have been hidden so long and so well.

Last, the sex and love addict can start to learn how to have trusting, intimate relationships. Close relationships are greatly prized by sex and love addicts because they do not have them. Building trust requires sharing. You will not trust someone whom you do not know, and likewise, others will not trust you if they do not know you. Being intimate also requires sharing. The public masks need to be removed and the real person revealed for an intimate relationship to develop with another person. This is frightening, and initially may produce a great deal of anxiety for the sex and love addict who is used to creating pseudo-intimacy through sexuality and manipulation. The sex and love addict may know all the right things to say in order to seduce someone into believing that they are in a close relationship, but the addict still holds all the cards by not being real and by being dishonest and secretive about his or her real feelings, thoughts, and motives. In a really intimate relationship, the partners do not have to play games, manipulate, or con in order to get their needs met. All they need do is to honestly share their needs, and their partner will meet them as best he or she can. In an intimate relationship, the closeness generates more love and energy to meet each other's needs, whereas in a secretive, dishonest relationship, the partners compete to see who can garner the most from the limited resources available.

Overcoming secrecy and dishonesty are crucial parts of the establishment of sobriety from sex and love addictions. They are part of the basic ground-work necessary to build a strong and solid foundation. As they say, "Honesty is the key to sobriety" and "You are as sick as your secrets." Work on later-stage issues is predicated on the person's ability to be honest with him- or herself and others.

"WHY ME?"

Most sex and love addicts ask the question, "Why me?" In fact, anyone with a chronic, incurable illness will have a tendency to wonder why he or she has been stricken with the problem when other people are not. Even people who do not have long-term or incorrigible difficulties may ask the question, "Why me?" Whenever we are off-balance or out of homeostasis, we tend to wonder about the cause. Finding the cause can be part of finding the solution, or the way to reestablish balance or equilibrium. This brings us to the motivation for asking this question.

The reasons for asking the question, "Why me?" can vary considerably. For some, this question is the realistic beginning of a search for answers, understanding, and a way to fix, cure, or at least manage the difficulty. If this is the case, the question deserves a serious and considered response. However, often the question, "Why me?" is not posed because of a need for clarification and direction but instead is spoken rhetorically as an expression of self-pity. The sex and love addict is feeling depressed, burdened, and sorry for him- or herself, and wants sympathy and pity rather than truth and understanding. The clue is usually in the person's tone of voice. A clear, firm tone indicates a realistic form of questioning, while a whining, sorry tone shows that the person is seeking some sort of comfort, compassion, or "poor you" response, and really doesn't care about the answer to the question.

Having a lifelong, incurable disease can get a person "down" from time to time. It would be unrealistic to assume that anyone would be able to manage an addiction without occasionally feeling sorry for him- or herself. It is easy to look at others who seem to have no problems and to wish that we were they. This is the syndrome referred to in the saying, "The grass is always greener on the other side of the fence." Staying in remission from an active sex and love addiction requires that the recovering addict make an effort each day to keep the addiction manageable. This means that time and energy must be devoted every day to ongoing recovery. Stopping active recovery means beginning relapse. The saying, "You are either part of the problem or part of the solution," applies to addiction recovery. When a sex and love addict is tempted to feel sorry for him- or herself or to experience self-pity, this can be the start of a slip or relapse. The tone of the "Why me?" question can, then, be a cue to the beginning of backsliding and trouble for the sex and love addict.

The question of why a certain individual gets a certain illness is an important and difficult one. It brings us to the ongoing controversy in health care, and psychology and psychiatry in particular, of nature versus nurture, the debate about the effects of genetics versus environment. Most experts agree that both heredity and upbringing influence our personalities and problems. The disagreement comes in deciding which factors have the strongest effects. A person advocating the genetic model would typically say that 60 percent of a person is biologically determined while 40 percent is the result of training. A person who believed strongly in the importance of nurturing and environment would most likely say that 40 percent is due to heredity and 60 percent is the result of the child's caretaking. There is some debate about the strength of these two major factors in human development, and some people advocate a 75/25 split (some in favor of environment and some the reverse), while others say that 80/20 is more accurate.

Unfortunately, this is a question on which we do not have good scientific evidence on which to base our opinions. My initial opinion, when I began to work in the helping professions, was that nurture or environment was the predominant factor in forming our personalities and problems, and that family backgrounds, especially in terms of the genetic/hereditary factors, was quite small. Therefore, I began with an 80 percent nurture/20 percent nature position. I have since seen that biological factors are stronger than I originally thought, and now tend to see things as 60 percent environment and 40 percent genetics. In my current view, we are "pre-wired" to a fair degree, but there are still many things over which we have control or that we can manage.

When I posed this question to my outpatient program of sex and love addicts, they thought that their families and environment had had a profound impact on the development of their addictions. They tended to see sex and love addictions as 90 percent the result of inadequate nurturing and only 10 percent influenced by heredity and genetics. This indicates that they feel particularly damaged by their early upbringing and, also, most able to do something about their compulsive behaviors. Biological factors do not lend themselves to change other than through chemical interventions such as medication. On the other hand, environmental factors, at least theoretically, should be the most amenable to change through efforts like improved nurturing, support groups, self-help, and therapy.

Our knowledge about the genetic and hereditary factors in addictions comes from our research into the family backgrounds of alcoholics. We know, for example, that alcoholism is two and a half times more likely to occur in people who have alcoholism in their family. The normal rate of occurrence is one in ten. When there is alcoholism present in the family history, the rate rises to one in four. However, we are as yet unable to identify which of any particular four individuals have the disease. In other words, there are no known biological markers or tests that can be given to predict the occurrence of alcoholism.

Alcoholism runs in families. We used to find that 50 percent of alcoholics would say that they had an alcoholic parent, if asked. When we started to ask about grandparents too, the rate of first- or second-generation (namely, parent or grandparent) alcoholism in the family rose to about 75 percent. In adolescent patients, the rate of alcoholism somewhere in the family is more like 90 percent. This supports the nature theory of addiction, and suggests at least an indirect genetic component to the disease of alcoholism. Studies of twins also support the likelihood of a biological factor that genetically predisposes a person to alcoholism if the disease is in their family. Manic/depressive illness (also called major affective disorder) has also shown a tendency to run in families. It is not out of the realm of possibility, then, that sex and love addictions could have a nature/genetic/hereditary/biological factor similar to that found in alcoholism and depression. Other chronic, incurable illnesses like high blood pressure, diabetes, heart disease, and arthritis have a family history factor that can predispose a person to develop the disease. Likewise, sex and love addictions probably have some sort of inherited, biological basis, as yet unknown and unidentified, that may make an individual vulnerable to the illness.

Therefore, part of the answer to the "Why me?" question is, most likely, "Because it runs in your family." Due to the intense secrecy concerning the majority of sex and love addictions, most people will not have access to accurate information about their families. However, if there are people who have been labeled and put down by the family as "runarounds," "nymphomaniacs," or "Casanovas," they are quite likely to have been the families' sex and love addicts. We can still debate the amount of influence of the nature or genetic factor on a given individual: Is it 10 percent, 20 percent, 40 percent, or more? These answers are unknown and may be unknowable.

In addition to the nature factor in the development of a sex and love addiction, there is general agreement that nurture also plays a part in the origin and expression of the illness. In fact, it is impossible to find a case anywhere where nature and nurture are not closely intertwined, so it is often impossible to estimate the power of these two factors with any sort of accuracy or objectivity. Nonetheless, it is possible to identify some of the ways that the home environment makes the sex and love addict vulnerable to the development of the addiction.

The first and most obvious way that upbringing can influence the growth of a sex and love addiction is through role modeling. Social learning theorists have taught us that the model that important people in our lives—like parents—give us is what we usually follow. Behaviors are more significant than words in modeling. The importance of adults as role models to children in terms of their behaviors is reflected in both these saying: "Do as I do, not as I say" and "Actions speak louder than words." Children imitate the adults in their lives whether their actions are healthy or not. Most adults find that they parent their children the same way their parents parented them unless they consciously try to do otherwise.

Consequently, children learn important lessons about sex, coping, and addictions from their parents. If they have had a sex- and love-addicted parent, they may simply be following the model of sex and love with which they grew up, without thinking about what they are doing. A sex and love addict who grew up overhearing his father beg his mother for sex learned that sex was intensely important to a man, that he might have to prostrate and humiliate himself to get it, and that it was a constant source of anxiety and tension.

Sometimes we choose to act the opposite of our parents. In a sense, we are using them as a negative role model, and we do everything the reverse of the way they would. One sex and love addict grew up in a home without any open expression of love, warmth, and affection. As an adult, she found herself constantly and compulsively being overly loving; openly affectionate; and too warm, considerate, and compassionate, to the point where men tended to use her and then leave for someone who was not so "easy." She could not understand why she was abandoned or why she was so obsessed with these relationships. She did not see how extreme her behavior was and how she actually alienated men by being too available, too attentive, and too interested in them, and not independent and self-supportive enough. She came across as swallowing them up when she intended to simply be more loving than her own parents. Her role models were poor, and her attempt to compensate was overdone, probably due to her original lack of nurturing.

Some sex and love addicts have had parents who were bad examples in terms of their own sexual or romantic behaviors. For example, in is not unusual for a male sex and love addict to say that he first masturbated using pornography that his father had bought. Young boys, often find the secret "stash" of their father's pornography and use it for sexual stimulation. One young man told me that all five of his brothers had used their father's "hard core" pornography, and yet they never spoke about it amongst themselves, even after one brother had walked in on him while he was masturbating. Other sex addicts are taught that affairs are "normal" and that it is usual for parents to have separate bedrooms.

Most parents have difficulty teaching their children about sex. However, children learn things about sex and love from their parents even if the subjects are not talked about. One thing they may learn is that sex is to be kept secret. Another thing that children often learn is that sex and love are embarrassing. Moreover, they frequently learn that adults seem unable to cope with these feelings since they cannot even talk about them.

The second way that the environment can influence the development of a sex and love addiction is through a lack of adequate nurturing. Children who are neglected, abused, and deprived will grow up more in need of a fix than children who have had appropriate nurturing. In addition, the former group will be prone to continue the pattern of neglect, abuse, and deprivation with which they have grown up. We know that parents who physically abuse their families were most likely victims of abuse themselves. They continue the cycle of abuse because they are used to it (it does not seem that bad to them), and because they do not have the models or resources with which to do otherwise (they themselves get easily frustrated and lash out, or perhaps they have not learned other ways to cope with their feelings and difficulties).

Family dysfunction can be a significant element in the development of sex and love addictions due to deficits in nurturing that occur when the family is unable to function adequately. Estimates of the number of dysfunctional families run as high as 95 percent. While this means that essentially everyone is from a dysfunctional home and that there are very few, if any, really healthy, functional families, the presence and amount of dysfunction in our families has probably been underestimated. When families function properly, it is the job of the parents to protect, care for, and nurture the children. As a result of this nurturing, the children grow up feeling safe, secure, and self-confident. Children who feel scared and insecure and have no self-worth are vulnerable to developing addictions to cope with these frightening and overwhelming feelings.

This leads to the third way that environment can contribute to the development of a sex and love addiction; self-discovery. Quite often, children find that sexual behavior, especially masturbation and fantasies, can provide the good feelings that they cannot get from their environment. They find they can put themselves to sleep by masturbating, even if they are scared, lonely, or feeling unloved. Some children learn that they can make themselves feel loved and important through fantasies about relationships with other people, often popular celebrities of some sort. Others find that they can get much-needed attention by being flirtatious and seductive. Some children discover that they can have "special" friends when mutual masturbation is involved, and others discover that they can feel "grown-up" by frequenting porno-graphic bookstores or making obscene phone calls. Self-discovery—learning by accidentally discovering the facts rather than being told by anyone else—is a frequent phenomenon, and applies to sex and love as well as many other actions or activities. Children have a natural drive to learn coping skills, or what is sometimes termed "mastery." We feel more confident and secure when we are able to cope with life and when we have mastered how to handle our own needs.

This confusion of sex and love with nurturing is compounded when we learn it on our own without adult guidance or supervision. Especially when we feel bad due to neglect, abuse, or deprivation, we need to learn how to feel good. Sex and love make us feel good. It is a simple step, then, to connect sex and love with filling our neediness, deprivation, emptiness, lack of self-worth, and feelings of hurt.

Abuse—verbal, physical, and sexual—can underscore this confusion. Often, for instance, parents rationalize their abuse by saying that they are hurting children "for their own good." The message the children get is that the parents are acting out of love, and that verbal criticism or physical attacks are forms of love rather than examples of the parents' lack of ability to control them-selves or to more appropriately set limits or give consequences. Sexual abuse, such as incest, gives this confusing message—that sex and love are expressed abusively—even more strongly. Usually, the perpetrator explicitly tells the child that they have a "special" relationship that must be kept secret to maintain its specialness. The child experiences him- or herself as having a unique, and often adult-like, role with the sexual abuser. This close and unusual relationship feels good, especially if the child is deprived or ne-glected, and makes him or her want to keep it despite the abusive aspects of the sexual contact. This may be the only attention this child gets from adults. If this is how adults appear to show love, then the child will learn that sex and love can be expressed through sexually abusive behaviors.

The fourth connection between sex and love addictions and the environ-ment has to do with the family's style of cohesion and coping. Unlike self-discovery, this is something that is done *to* the child, not *by* him or her. Carnes (1988) found that three-quarters of sex addicts identify their families as rigid and detached. That is, the families in which these sex addicts grew up rigidly adhered to their established structure and were not emotionally close to each other. The children typically would feel rather alone, isolated, guilty, and ashamed. Rigid rules make people feel bad due to their inherent imperfection. Detachment makes people feel that they must survive on their own and that "It's everyone for [her- or] himself." Sex and love promise to break down walls of isolation, eliminate terrible feelings of aloneness, cut through feelings of worthlessness, and assuage guilt and shame—what better antidote to a rigid, detached family? This is fertile ground for a sex and love addiction.

The last environmental factor I will mention at this point is our "addictive society." Even if a person grows up in a healthy family without abuse or neglect, our culture's current emphasis on immediate gratification, on the quick fix and the "easy buck," grooms us to become addicted. In addition, our tendency to overvalue sex and underestimate the relational aspects of love makes us vulnerable to developing compulsive, ritualized, obsessive preoccupations with sex and love.

Society has placed a terrible stigma on the label "addiction." No one wants to have one or to be seen as an addict. Nonetheless, our society is obsessed with power, money, sex, and manipulation. It is almost surprising that there are relatively few sex and love addicts in a culture that values the fast, easy, "slick" way to get ahead, and looks down on more traditional values like making an effort, being honest, doing one's best, and caring about relationships with God, family, and neighbors.

What is the answer to the addict's question of "Why me?" The answer is that there is no answer. We know that our biology, genetic makeup, and heredity may have something to do with it. We know that our family, upbringing, and environment are factors in our overall development. Nature and nurture contribute to who we are and the difficulties we experience in our lives. However, at this point in our scientific knowledge, we do not know which factor contributes what or how much, or how to predict who will or will not become a sex and love addict. In short, answering the question "Why me?" will lead to some interesting and challenging facts and theories about human growth and development, but it will not give anyone the key to manage, dispel, cope with, or eliminate sex and love addictions.

How, then, is this topic relevant to treatment and recovery from sex and love addictions? In the initial stage, establishing bottom lines and early recovery, asking the question "Why Me?" indicates feelings of self-pity on the part of the newly recovering sex and love addict. A common response of trained professionals and recovering sex and love addicts to "Why me?" is "What difference does it make?" An intellectual search for a real answer to the question will lead the addict back to his or her starting place: No one knows why, but it is still your problem. Rather than wasting time and energy on this "head game," the newly recovering addict will get more results from trying to figure out how to stay sober today.

Early in the recovery process, the sex and love addict needs to focus on concrete, day-to-day reality rather than an intellectual quest for answers that the best scholars in the field have not yet been able to find. Self-pity, feeling sorry for yourself, feeling abused by the illness, feeling that life is unfair, and feeling that your Higher Power has given you more than your share of burdens are all distorted thoughts that can restart the addictive cycle. This is dangerous territory for a sex and love addict, and needs to be avoided in the beginning. Excessive attention to the question of "Why me?" will make the newly recovering sex and love addict vulnerable to acting out.

In long-term recovery, sex and love addicts may want to spend some time thinking about questions like "Why me?" in order to further their understanding of themselves and their disease. If this is undertaken with a sincere motivation to truly grasp the origin and development of their addictive patterns of thought, feeling, and behavior, it can help to strengthen their long-term recovery.

Asking "Why me?" will require considering the person's relationship with his or her Higher Power. It will also necessitate working on acceptance. In some ways, consideration of this question in long-term recovery will be a review of the first three steps. "Why me?" gets us in touch with our basic powerlessness over so much of what goes on in life both within and outside ourselves. This question spurs us to consider a Power greater than ourselves for the ultimate answer. It also can suggest that the only answer we can get—namely; no answer—leads us to turn our will and life over to the care of the Power that has a better one.

Sex and love addicts who are in early recovery resonate to the question of "Why me?" However, as they develop some sobriety and their lives begin to improve in terms of stability and quality, they start to become more grateful. This "attitude of gratitude" is an indicator of solid recovery. Instead of feeling abused by their addictions and the Higher Power, these recovering sex and love addicts start to count their blessings. In fact, they discover that one of their biggest burdens, their sex and love addiction, is also one of their biggest blessings. This means they have been able to look at themselves and their lives, and to totally reorganize their values, beliefs, priorities, and behaviors to the point where life has become more balanced, happy, fulfilling, and gratifying. They are starting to succeed beyond their wildest dreams, and they realize that they owe it all to their program of recovery from sex and love addiction. Their addiction has become a blessing in disguise, and they begin to ask themselves, "Why not me?"

MASKS AND ATTITUDES

Secrecy and the use of self-pity (like asking "Why me?") are ways that sex and love addicts defend and hide their addictions. Another area of defensiveness common to addictive people is the use of masks and attitudes that keep others from seeing the real person and the truth about what is really going on inside. We all have masks and social roles that we play. For example, when I am at work, I dress and act like a person who is working, while I dress and act differently when I am on vacation. I have different roles when I am being a father and when I am a husband. These are not "phony" just because I am not always showing my entire authentic self. It is not appropriate to share every thought and feeling. People who are too open at times when it is uncalled for have problems with appropriate boundaries. Filling a role or wearing the right mask is not the same as intentionally trying to fool or

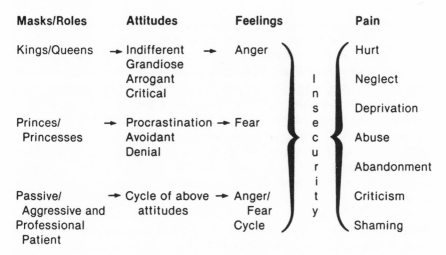

Masks/Roles	Attitudes	Feelings		Pain
Kings/Queens	→ Indifferent →	Anger	I n s e c u r i t y	Hurt
	Grandiose			
	Arrogant			Neglect
	Critical			
				Deprivation
Princes/	→ Procrastination →	Fear		
Princesses	Avoidant			Abuse
	Denial			
				Abandonment
Passive/	→ Cycle of above →	Anger/		Criticism
Aggressive and	attitudes	Fear		
Professional		Cycle		Shaming
Patient				

con someone like addicts try to do. Addicts do not use masks to fit in properly and make things go more smoothly. Instead, they use masks and play roles in order to hide their sex and love addictions.

Sex and love addicts also adopt attitudes in order to accomplish the same end; to conceal the truth about their sexual or romantic acting out. Again, all of us have attitudes like indifference or avoidance which we communicate and use to cope. As with other defenses, these attitudes are self-protective. The purpose of showing an attitude is to keep others from seeing your vulnerability or from hurting you. This may be quite healthy, since not everyone is interested in being open, caring, or close. There are people who are aggressive, hurtful, sadistic, mean, and manipulative, users who will take advantage of us if we let them. Masks, roles, and attitudes can help us keep from getting used or abused.

Sex and love addicts tend to have overlearned these defensive strategies and use them often, even when they are not appropriate or necessary. The extensive use of defenses like masks and attitudes creates distance between the addict and other people, and creates feelings of isolation, loneliness, and alienation for him or her. These latter feelings are dangerous since they often are triggers for acting out on bottom-line behaviors. In general, sex and love addicts start with core beliefs of worthlessness and pain from harmful early-life experiences. This pain creates a profound sense of insecurity, and creates feelings of anger and fear, which are used to cover the deeper pain. Over these feelings, they erect a layer of attitudes, which are covered by masks and roles. These layers look something like the above figure.

While it is an exaggeration to say that all sex addicts fit into one category, in general sex addicts tend to play the King/Queen role with its associated attitudes, while love addicts tend to act as Princes/Princesses, with that category's attitudes and underlying feelings. For example, a "Casanova" type has the King role in terms of feeling all-powerful and needing to be obeyed and catered to by others. He will exhibit grandiose, indifferent, and arrogant attitudes that cover feelings of anger. His anger is used to cover insecurity caused by earlier pain.

Similarly, a nymphomaniac type of love addict is often in a Princess role, and acts as if she should be treated as royalty. Her attitudes include wanting to be undisturbed and to avoid anything taxing. She uses her mask and attitudes to cover her deeper fear, which comes from a profound insecurity related to damage done in her childhood. Most of us react to the outer layers of masks and attitudes, and do not see below the surface. Hiding the reality is, of course, the purpose of the defensive strategy.

In recovery, however, the use of a mask and attitudes can seriously inhibit the change process. It is impossible to grow and at the same time hold on to these old ways of self-protection. What the sex and love addict needs to do, with safe people in a safe environment like an S.L.A.A. meeting, is to take off the masks, stop playing roles, surrender defensive attitudes, and stop using anger and fear to hide his or her insecurity and pain. This is a tall order, and will take time and effort. In order to start the ball rolling, sex and love addicts need to begin to look at themselves when they are playing roles and putting on masks to cover their addictive thoughts, feelings, and behaviors. Then, they need to initiate a process of examining their attitudes. They should ask themselves, "Am I being defensive?" They need to think about their use of fear and anger to cover up deeper, more frightening feelings and past experiences. All this will assist in establishing sobriety and maintaining bottom-lines. Self-examination without sobriety and firm bottom-lines can itself be a defensive and avoidance strategy whereby the sex and love addict can get into the "professional patient" role and fail to initiate any recovery.

Pulling back the layers of defenses is a painful process, and is often done with the help of a professional. Sponsors and people in S.L.A.A. with healthy recovery programs will also be of assistance to the sex and love addict who wants to discover his or her defensive maneuvers and self-protective roles, attitudes, and feelings. In early recovery, this needs to be undertaken with caution and with the one goal of gaining sustained abstinence from bottom-line behaviors. It is possible to uncover too much pain, shame, and hurt, and to trigger a relapse into the pain relief with which the sex and love addict is most familiar, acting out.

The antidotes to defenses are, of course, honesty, openness, and self-disclosure. However, there are some addicts who even manipulate this approach to healing. That is, there are some sex and love addicts who use pseudo-openness as part of their seduction role. There are some who have almost a confessional approach; that is, they disclose their "sins" or acting-out behaviors in what appears to be a sincere effort to change. Actually, they are getting sympathy and caring which they will attempt to manipulate in order to have their romantic or sexual needs met.

The rewards of being undefensive are what will enable the sex and love addict to continue to stay sober and open up. As the recovering person learns to be less defended, he or she will become more open and start to experience closeness with others, genuine intimacy, affirmation, and self-knowledge. These are some of the benefits of sobriety. In other words, the sex and love addict will begin to get what he or she had been seeking all along—meaningful contact with others. As the addict starts to change, so do his or her relationships. While active in their addiction, addicts had nothing to lose when they acted out. As they initiate more real sharing with others, however, they begin to have much more to lose by acting out. These new contacts reinforce the sobriety process.

In short-term recovery, the emphasis is on discovering how being defensive impedes or interrupts establishing and maintaining bottom-line behaviors. Awareness, sharing, and feedback are important aspects of this stage of recovery. In long-term recovery, reducing defenses and eliminating masks and attitudes allows the recovering person to develop a stronger, more authentic self. Listening and sharing are still the vehicles for change, but the results are experienced on a deeper, more personal level.

RELAPSE AND RELAPSE PROTECTION

Chronic illnesses typically have periods of remission followed by relapse. Sometimes relapses are the result of biological changes, but most of the time problems occur because the person has failed to follow the maintenance program fully or did not accurately anticipate the impact of stressors on recovery. Addictions are diseases of relapse, and sex and love addictions are no exception. Most people who suffer from the disease of addiction will experience at least one relapse. Planning and prevention are needed, therefore, if relapses are to be avoided.

Recovery is an active process. Relapse begins when active recovery stops. There is no standing still, taking a breather, or pausing for a rest. When the forward motion ends, the backward motion starts. A recovering addict likened it to the tide: It is either coming in or going out, and it never stands still. Another analogy compares recovery to walking up a down escalator—if you stop going up, you start going down.

As indicated earlier, the recovery rate for addictive diseases is improving from a dismal 4 percent of heroin addicts 30 years ago to anywhere between 30 and 50 percent. Sobriety rates for recovering alcoholics with five or more years of active attendance at Alcoholics Anonymous are over 90 percent (Vejnoska, 1983). Accurate information about relapse and recovery rates for sex and love addicts is unavailable; however, some bits of evidence point to similar rates of relapse as with other addictive diseases. For example, sex offenders with Carnes's level 3 behaviors (rape and child molestation) had a 66 percent relapse rate in less than a year. With improved support systems like S.L.A.A., better trained treatment professionals, and a more educated public, we should be able to improve the one-third recovery rate much as has been done with the alcoholism. Understanding relapse and developing prevention and treatment strategies will help increase the odds in favor of recovery.

Symptoms of Relapse

Many of the indicators of relapse have already been reviewed, but a summary will help to put them all together. The more symptoms present, the more the danger to the recovering sex and love addict.

Dishonesty

As we have frequently emphasized, honesty is the key to sobriety; consequently, dishonesty, even in small amounts, indicates that the person is becoming more defensive and secretive. Dishonesty about sexual or romantic thoughts, feelings, and behaviors is a major indicator of recovery gone awry.

Anger/Frustration

Increased irritability, sarcasm, criticalness, testiness, argumentativeness, and touchiness are all symptoms of problems with anger, which is potentially dangerous to the recovery process and can be a good sign that a relapse is on the way, especially when it persists for more than a day of two.

Exhaustion

Pushing oneself and getting so off balance that physical exhaustion sets in is a clear sign of difficulty. If probably means that the recovering person is trying to do too much and is having trouble setting his or her priorities straight.

Depression

Emotions can trigger relapses in more than half the recovering population. Depression—anything more than the "blues" for a day or so—has been a factor in addiction relapses in anywhere from a third to a half of reported cases. Depression is a serious problem for at least 10 percent of the general population so the odds are that at least 10 percent of recovering sex and love addicts will become depressed regardless of the recovery program.

Self-Pity

Both because of childhood deprivation and abuse and because of the damage done by addiction, sex and love addicts are highly prone to feeling sorry for themselves. Most people with chronic illnesses have this problem, which probably accounts for many relapses. Sex and love addicts tend to overidentify with being victims rather than the role of victimizer and this overidentification can fuel their self-pity.

"Cockiness"/Arrogance/Overconfidence

Overconfidence is a serious problem for addicted people. If they have put some effort into their recovery, they most likely will start experiencing some success and rewards after three to six months. Most of us remember to take our medicine when we feel sick; in fact, we often cannot wait to take it. However, when we feel good, we frequently forget. The sex and love addict's medicine is the Twelve Step program; when sex and love addicts get cocky, they begin to think they need the program less than they did in the beginning. They attribute their success to their own efforts and not the work of their Higher Power and the Steps.

Complacency

Closely related to arrogance is complacency. Instead of developing an overblown ego from doing well in recovery, the complacent sex and love addict gets lazy and content with the status quo, and stops striving to get better. Rather than continuing to be active, addicts start to become passive. Instead of taking charge of their recovery, they only go along for the ride.

Decreased Discipline

For many addicts, recovery involves learning how to discipline themselves rather than indulging their impulses. It means saying "no" instead of "O.K., just this once." Discipline means going to meetings even when you don't feel like it or are not in the mood. Discipline means doing something regularly and routinely, like daily meditation or readings. Something as simple as skipping your morning prayer can start the slide back into an active addiction.

Unrealistic Expectations

Unrealistic expectations of oneself or others can provide a setup for failure and disappointment. Perfectionistic expectations for oneself or others will necessarily create a sense of coming up short and being incapable or incompetent. All these feelings constitute fertile ground for the seeds of relapse.

Ominpotence

Feeling all-powerful is the opposite of steps Two and Three. Grandiosity is a symptom of an active addiction, and is related to the narcissism and self-centeredness that feed the active addictive process. Thinking thoughts like "It can't happen to me" or "I'll do it better than anyone else" are indicative of feelings of omnipotence. An addict who feels omnipotent is an addict without a Higher Power, and an addict without a Higher Power is an addict in trouble.

Lack of or Decrease in Gratitude

Losing or not getting the "attitude of gratitude" is a sign of a poor recovery program. Having the illness remain in remission is an act of grace from the addict's Higher Power, so not being able to feel gratitude means that the addict is secretly feeling resentful or omnipotent. Every day there are things for which you can feel grateful; therefore, the addict who does not feel grateful is out of touch with his or her daily program.

Rigidity

Being too rigid is the opposite of being too loose. The sex and love addict may need to be rigid in the beginning, but there should be a gradual increase in flexibility rather than the reverse. If the addict is becoming more inflexible, something is wrong and relapse is possible.

Fear/Anxiety

Like depression, fear and anxiety are common feelings for sex and love addicts in recovery. Some researchers estimate that a third of relapses are due to unmanaged fear or anxiety. As recovery grows, so should the addict's sense of self-confidence, which should then reduce his or her fear. Anxiety disorders occur in roughly 10 percent of the population, just like depression; consequently, about 10 percent of sex and love addicts will experience problems with anxiety. Some researchers see addictions, obsessions, and compulsions as malfunctioning efforts to cope with anxiety. If this is true, and if the addict cannot find other ways to handle anxiety, then fear will become a problem that can easily lead to relapse.

Sexual Anorexia or Dysfunction

Simply because sex and love addicts have the illness that they do, people tend to think that they know everything about sex and are immune to sexual problems. This is not the case. Some develop sexual anorexia, a total disinterest in sex, while others have some other type of sexual dysfunction like premature orgasm or vaginismus. Needless to say, this sort of problem can easily lead to the impulse to return to acting-out behaviors.

Hypersensitivity

Being overly emotional or overreacting to things can create a lot of tension and difficulties for recovering sex and love addicts, who may find themselves thinking that recovery is not worth it if it means they will be "jumping out of their skin" at the least provocation.

Self-Neglect

Neglecting, abusing, and depriving the self, especially if the person has a history of these experiences as a child, will create feelings of neediness, emptiness, worthlessness, and longing that will strongly connect with the promises of the active addiction, and will therefore be very hard to resist.

Isolation

Self-imposed or undesired isolation will feed the sex and love addict's desire for contact with others. If his or her work or school schedule prevents attendance at meetings or contact with people in the program, the recovering addict will be in serious trouble, and a relapse will be only a matter of time.

Lack of Intimacy

Addicts may have people in their lives yet not know how to get close to them. Most addicts have developed some skills at pseudo-intimacy, but many do not know how to share with others or how to get others to share with them. They need to learn social skills that will give them a sense of being involved with other people. They need to be important to others and to have others be important to them. Without intimacy and love, they are only a step away from active addiction.

Withdrawal from the Support System

When sex and love addicts choose to withdraw from and cease to use their support system, they are in trouble. Their support system is where they will get many of their good feelings, their natural highs. They need to have a source of pleasure that is nonsexual and nonromantic, and their support system should be such a resource. Pulling away from sponsors, friends, and meetings is moving toward acting out on bottom-line behaviors.

These are many of the symptoms of an oncoming relapse. Each slip, each relapse is different, but there are enough aspects in common to be able to see them coming. The problem is not that there are no indicators. The difficulty usually is that no one looks for them, especially the recovering addict. The final segment of this chapter focuses on how to help protect against a relapse.

Relapse Protection

There are no guaranteed ways to prevent relapses in a chronic illness that is prone to them. However, the collective wisdom of treatment professionals and recovering sex and love addicts has identified a number of areas where work can help prevent the recurrence of the active sex and love addiction. Ideas that have already been explained will only be listed, and other suggestions will be outlined.

Actively work the Twelve Steps

H.O.W.: *H*onesty, *O*penness, *W*illingness

Establish bottom-line behaviors

Know your triggers

Avoid secrecy and dishonesty

Talk about feelings of shame, guilt, and embarrassment

Do not dwell on self-pity or "Why me?"

Know your defenses and work at being less defensive

H.A.L.T.: Don't get too *H*ungary, *A*ngry, *L*onely, or *T*ired

S.A.F.E.: Be aware of *S*ecrets, *A*buses, *F*eelings, and *E*mptiness

Do not hang on to resentment

Disassociate from addictive people, places, and things

Make an Assessment

Sex and love addicts can learn to more objectively assess their addictions, personalities, coping and social skills, and early upbringing in order to more rationally judge the quality of their lives, and especially the recovery program. They can also find people in their lives to help them with this task, like therapists, counselors, and spiritual directors.

Educate Yourself about Your Illness

Most addiction treatment and Twelve Step programs advocate education about addictive diseases. The sex and love addict him- or herself is the only one who will be present at all times during recovery. The better educated the addict, the more likely that he or she will be able to identify problems and spot difficulties at an early stage, when something can still be done to avoid a relapse.

Know the Warning Signs

Even if the sex and love addict does not anticipate a problem in many of the areas on the list of symptoms of relapse, if the recovering person is familiar with the broad range of possible warning signs, he or she will be more likely to catch them if they occur. Recovery will take the sex and love addict down many roads he or she never thought to travel, and it is impossible to predict in advance which pitfalls and roadblocks the addict will encounter. Knowing the possibilities improves the odds of preventing a relapse.

Identify High-Risk Situations

Sex and love addicts themselves are best able to anticipate high-risk situations. Most addicts, at least initially, are afraid to think too much about the dangers in front of them. However, when they understand the purpose and the preventive aspect of projecting into the future, they often value the opportunity to think about the situations that could put them at risk for a relapse. By imagining possible problem areas or times, they can also begin to think of how to handle tempting and risky situations.

Develop Coping Skills

Since many sex and love addicts connect acting out with stress reduction, inducing sleep, calming nerves, altering mood, and medicating pain, in their recovery process they will need to find ways other than sexual or romantic acting out to do these things. For some this may be a major task, whereas for others it is a matter of fine-tuning. Thinking about how to cope and learning new coping skills can be a vital way to avoid falling back into the same old rut.

Improving Social Skills

Despite the apparent social skills necessary for an active sex and love addiction—like cruising, intriguing, and scoring—most sex and love addicts feel socially inept or inadequate. Recovery involves many social interactions such as talking to sponsors, participating in meetings, and socializing with program people, which can be quite stressful for someone who feels socially retarded. Learning social skills can, therefore, be a big relief, and can aid in keeping the recovering sex and love addict safe from a relapse.

Knowing about Normal Human Sexuality

Many sex and love addicts know how to act out but lack even the most basic knowledge about normal adult sexual functioning. For example, most have no idea how often an average couple has sexual intercourse (once or twice a week). Learning about normal sexuality can help the sex and love addict think, feel, and act more normal. Some of the excitement, value, and lure of the addiction will fade with an increasing understanding of healthy human sexuality.

Identifying Cognitive Distortions/"Stinking Thinking"

The sex and love addict must be able to spot his or her own "stinking thinking." Often, early on in recovery, more experienced recovering people and professionals will help the sex and love addict see how he or she is distorting thought patterns. However, relying on others is dangerous because they cannot always be there. Consequently, the sex and love addict needs to internalize a thought monitoring system that will trigger an alarm when addictive thinking begins to creep in. Sensitivity to thought patterns can be an excellent early warning system.

Daily Inventory

The Tenth Step calls on the addict to continue to make inventories. Taking a daily inventory of the symptoms of relapse, the preventative steps, and the overall recovery program most likely will help the sex and love addict keep focused and headed in the right direction. Both the addict in early recovery and the seasoned veteran can benefit from self-reflection.

Involving Others/Asking for Help and Consultation

We all need feedback and help on our journey through life. The sex and love addict learns to ask for help and to get others involved from the very beginning. However, we all also have a tendency to go off on our own as things begin to improve for us, and sex and love addicts are no exception. In order to keep on the right track, the sex and love addict must learn to continue to ask for help, feedback, and consultation as he or she travels the exciting, sometimes trying, and always challenging road of recovery.

We now have an idea about relapse and recidivism rates, a cluster of symptoms of relapse, and suggestions about how a sex and love addict can protect him- or herself from a slip or relapse back into the active phase of addiction. A few words about healthy recovery will add on upbeat conclusion to this chapter on short-term treatment.

Essentially, we can get an idea about good recovery from sex and love addiction by imagining the reverse of all the previously listed problems. A strong recovery program involves continual work on the Twelve Steps; daily reflection on the addiction through readings, prayer, meditation, or a journal; regular contact with a sponsor, meetings, and other members of the Augustine Fellowship of Sex and Love Addicts Anonymous; and service work that carries the message of strength, hope, and recovery, such as sponsorship, chairing and speaking at meetings, and holding offices within the S.L.A.A. organization. In addition, recovering sex and love addicts may be involved in their own therapy process to help them grow as persons and strengthen their long-term recovery process.

Sex and love addicts who have made a good initial short-term recovery have usually made their addiction recovery their number one priority. They have become willing to learn about the addiction; to examine the people with whom they associate, the places where they work and socialize, and the things they have collected that are related to addictive acting out; and to change them all. They may also have had to change their jobs or residences in order to secure their recovery. They have made a commitment to work the steps and the H.O.W. program, to be completely honest and not keep secrets; to talk about their feelings, especially their shame, guilt, and embarrassment; to stop feeling sorry for themselves, playing the victim role, and being so defensive; to express their anger and resentment; to H.A.L.T. and be S.A.F.E; and to protect themselves from relapse and recidivism.

In addition to the above actions, sex and love addicts who are in a healthy recovery process also work on eliminating any forms of secrecy or dishonesty in their lives. They are looking to find ways to cope with stress and frustration.

They take care of themselves and try not to get overtired. They seek to be aware of feelings like fear, anxiety, and depression, and to counteract them before they become overwhelming. Recovering addicts avoid self-pity. They seek to reduce their narcissism, grandiosity, self-centeredness, and arrogance. They appreciate feedback about complacency and lapses in discipline. They try to curb high expectations, perfectionism, and feelings of omnipotence, and they work to reduce rigidity and increase flexibility. These people express gratitude and appreciation. They seek to develop healthy sexuality and normal sexual functioning. They attempt to limit hypersensitivity and overreactions. They seek to care for themselves and to eliminate self-neglect, self-deprivation, and self-abuse. Moreover, they are careful about isolating themselves, and look for more contact and intimacy. Finally, they work to build and maintain a healthy support system.

Of course, all recovering sex and love addicts do not do all these things all the time. After all, they are in an addiction recovery process, not a program for sainthood! However, the point is that there is much to learn and attend to in the first six to twelve months of recovery.

5

Long-Term Treatment and Recovery

Chapter 4 emphasized the tasks involved in short-term recovery from sex and love addiction. The primary focus was on establishing initial sobriety, identifying and applying personal bottom lines, learning about triggers for acting out, and developing awareness about the recovery program and possible roadblocks. Areas like honesty and secrecy, feelings like fear and depression, defenses like denial and anger, hang-ups like guilt and self-pity, problems like shame and abuse, and difficulties like resentment and loneliness were reviewed, with the hope that recovering sex and love addicts, along with professionals and people who care about them, can use these ideas, suggestions, and warnings to develop a workable sobriety program for the first 6 to 12 months.

Chapter 5 will examine what happens next. Long-term recovery and treatment issues are different from early recovery and treatment concerns. Short-term recovery involves building a foundation for the life that will follow. If the foundation is rushed or poorly constructed, then eventually the whole building will collapse, and the sex and love addict will be plunged back into an active phase of addiction. Long-term recovery and treatment concerns creating a life after sobriety has been firmly established. For some addicts, this will be a concern in the latter half of the first year; however, this is rather unusual, and most often involves addicts who come into sex and love addiction recovery with experience in another Twelve Step Fellowship like Alcoholics Anonymous, Narcotics Anonymous, Overeaters Anonymous, or Gamblers Anonymous. In most cases, the issues examined in this chapter will not arise for the recovering sex and love addict for at least a year, and some addicts will not be ready or able to work on these concerns until two or three years into their recovery.

Addicts like the quick fix. They are narcissistic, grandiose, self-centered, and egocentric. They love to do things fast. They want to be the best. They like to think of themselves as ahead of others or exceptions to the rules. Consequently, addicts do not want to hear that recovery and treatment take time, and that they may not be ready to deal with some things for a year or two. They want it all, right now. They want to it their way. Support people such as other members of the S.L.A.A. Fellowship, sponsors, significant others, and professionals need to encourage the sex and love addict to take things one at a time and to be patient with the treatment and recovery process. "Trust the process" is something I often tell my clients when they appear eager to "get things over with."

Long-term recovery and treatment differs from short-term treatment and recovery in many ways. The issues are not the same. The timing is different. Concerns are delved into more deeply. The pattern is more consistent; in early recovery you may jump, whereas in long-term recovery you maintain a focus over time. The quality of life and change are more profound. The issues that are dealt with can go way back into the person's past, and are more like root causes than immediate triggers for acting-out patterns. Integrating healthy coping and social skills and developing appropriate interdependencies are emphasized. Concerns like healthy sexuality, boundaries, self-support, and self-affirmation are worked on with the idea that this is establishing a lifelong program that will continue long after any formal psychotherapy has ended.

Lifelong recovery is the focus of this section of the book. Patterns that will continue over time and are part of the person rather than expectations of the program or authority figures are the concern. With some sex and love addictions, the question of lifelong recovery is crucial not only to the recovering sex and love addict but to society as well. People whose sex and love addictions have involved sexual activity with children, for example, need to be safe and sober not only for the period of treatment or supervision but also for the rest of their lives. A relapse for them places more children at risk as well as the addicts themselves. Long-term recovery looks at what might make a person vulnerable to relapse and how to address these issues. The concerns of establishing an initial recovery program and maintaining sobriety need also to be continued.

SELF-AFFIRMATION

One of the hardest and most important jobs of long-term recovery is to learn to be self-affirming. Early in recovery, sex and love addicts get affirmation from their peers. The process begins at the first meeting when the new person introduces him- or herself and is immediately greeted by the group. After that, there are many examples of affirmation by individuals and the S.L.A.A. program. Anyone who has been to an S.L.A.A. meeting or spoken to someone in the recovery program can attest to the wonderful, non judgmental encouragement that people receive just for trying. Attendance at the meetings is celebrated just as much as sobriety anniversaries are. The message is one of unconditional love: We are just as happy that you came tonight as we are that our speaker has had two years of sobriety. Recovering sex and love addicts know that being affirmed is essential to getting sober.

What is affirmation? To affirm someone is to acknowledge their existence and celebrate their being. It is not recognizing achievements or honoring accomplishments. Affirmation is enjoying someone's presence and letting them know how you feel. Affirmation is appreciating someone's uniqueness and the gift of their life to all who encounter them. Affirmation is singing praise and dancing for joy that a person is with us. It is *not* getting something from someone before you give something back. It is *not* needing people to prove themselves or earn your respect or admiration. It is *not* holding back your feelings for fear that you will be hurt, disappointed, or abandoned. Affirmation is trusting your Higher Power and loving your fellow human beings. Affirmation is celebrating life in all its forms. Affirmation is having the strength to tolerate the pain, losses, and sadness, as well as the courage to be happy, to live, and to love.

Obviously affirmation is both a gift and a big job. Most of us find self-affirmation quite difficult and even painful. This is even more true of recovering addicts. Most of us are much better able to affirm others than to affirm ourselves. (We will explore the reasons for this shortly.) In short-term recovery, most recovering sex and love addicts depend on the affirmation of sponsors, therapists, friends, members of the S.L.A.A. Fellowship, spouses, and family. Unfortunately, many of these people are not yet ready or able to be affirming due to their anger, hurt, or lack of understanding of the sex and love addict, so instead the primary sources of affirmation will be found within the S.L.A.A. program and from understanding professionals. Then, in long-term recovery, the sex and love addict needs to transfer his or her dependence on affirmation from others to a dependence on self-affirmation. Affirmation from others becomes frosting on the cake rather than the cake itself. The positive reinforcement that the sex and love addict once got from outside becomes integrated into him- or herself. Additional affirmation from outside is welcome, but it is only "gravy," not the "meat and potatoes." Self-affirmation becomes essential to the addict's life, and he or she no longer needs external verification in order to feel good about him- or herself.

Barriers to Self-Affirmation

There are basically three sources of interference with the capacity to be self-affirming: the sex and love addiction and its affects on self-esteem, the person's childhood, and people's socially or culturally based fears of becoming too egotistical or self-centered. Some recovering sex and love addicts may only have problems from one or two of these sources, but most have problems from all three. In fact, these three areas tend to interact and to reinforce self-critical thoughts, feelings, and behaviors rather than those that are self-affirming.

The sex and love addiction contributes greatly to low self-esteem, and to treating the self with hatred, loathing, disgust, criticism, neglect, deprivation, and abuse. I have listed all these nonaffirming reactions because they are so frequently articulated by sex and love addicts even after they have begun to get sober. Inflicting pain on oneself is considered a sign of a serious and severe mental and emotional disorder. Sex and love addicts are constantly beating themselves up about their failures, limitations, defects, and short-comings. Fortunately, in the S.L.A.A. meeting rooms there are other recovering people who are highly sensitive to this (they do it too), and who make a concerted effort to counter this self-destructive habit.

In one recent group session, a sex and love addict was describing how he had acted out after having had twelve days of sobriety. He could not look others in the eye, mumbled his words, sat slumped over, and sounded hope-less and forlorn. A fellow group member commented, "You seem to be beating yourself up." The first speaker reacted with surprise because he had been totally unaware of his self-rejecting, self-critical, attitude. Then, he be-came confused because he did not want to give himself permission to act out more, and was afraid that if he and the group did not "beat him up," he would feel free to continue to break his bottom-lines. He saw affirmation as self-indulgence. Many sex and love addicts are confused because they have been, on the one hand, totally self-indulgent and undisciplined, and, on the other hand, terribly self-critical and harsh. They do not know how to be loving and still set limits on themselves. They get this from the people in the program in early recovery. At this stage, they need to start learning to do this for themselves.

The dishonesty, lying, manipulations, secrecy, and deceit of their active addictions has reinforced all the negative thoughts and feelings about them-selves that addicts may have developed while growing up. It is impossible to live through an addictive illness without also suffering from low self-esteem. A sex and love addiction eats away at self-worth like a cancer. Even if you came into an addiction with fairly healthy self-esteem, you would not have it when you were finished. Sex and love addictions make liars out of honest people, manipulators out of genuine people, and immoral actors out of moral people. Self-esteem cannot survive this sort of damage.

When I did a study of chemically dependent people, I was surprised to discover how poorly they rated themselves on stereotypically masculine and feminine items. Most people think of themselves as slightly above average. When asked to rate themselves on a scale of 1 to 10, controls typically gave themselves a 6. The scoring even had to be adjusted to account for this normal overrating. The median split or exact halfway point was almost 6 rather than 5, as it would have been if controls did not typically think of themselves as a little bit better than average or a cut above the rest. However, the alcoholic and drug addicts who took the test had much lower scores than normal. They were not even close to 5. The women scored slightly above the men, but their addictions were active for a shorter time, and they still did not see themselves as average or as being as good as others. The obvious interpretation is low self-esteem. The most likely cause is chemical dependency.

Most sex and love addicts who are chemically dependent say that the sex and love addiction is harder to kick than the alcohol or drug addiction. The logical consequence of an addiction that makes people feel more powerless and less able to stop is even lower self-esteem. In addition, sex and love addictions typically involve more secrecy, lying, and dishonesty than other addictions, which would also contribute to lower self-worth. When core beliefs like "I am a bad person" and "No one would love me if they really knew me" are combined with neglectful, abusive childhoods (which most sex and love addicts report), the chances of a sex and love addict having low self-esteem are almost universal. Sex and love addicts have taken normal drives and emotions like sex and love and perverted them. They feel like perverts, and are filled with self-hatred and contempt. In this context, the job of rebuilding self-worth to the point where self-affirmation is possible is a major task indeed.

The sex and love addict's childhood, to which we have already alluded, can be a significant contributor to difficulties with self-affirmation. Children incorporate or internalize their parents. Some call this internalization of the superego. Some simply refer to it as our "parent part" (as opposed to our adult and child parts). We tend to parent ourselves as we were parented, just as we parent our children as we were parented. If as a child the sex and love addict was treated with neglect, deprivation, or abuse, then he or she will be neglectful, depriving, and abusive with him- or herself. They may even make an effort not to parent their own children the way they were parented because they are sensitive to the damage their parents did to them, but when it comes to the way they treat themselves, addicts often repeat the lessons learned in childhood. They do not really feel worthy of care, love, and attention. Quite often, they can give it to others but cannot tolerate being on the receiving end themselves. Affirmation is something for which these people starved as children, long for as adults, and fear getting because their need is so great. They have not internalized any good models for nurturing and loving, so the task of self-affirmation seems beyond them. They may also have leftover resentments, and refuse to give to themselves because they are still waiting to get what they deserve from someone else.

Less obvious but just as detrimental to self-esteem are parents who are perfectionists or are preoccupied with how others see them. These other-directed, image-conscious parents can overemphasize achievement and will provide only conditional love. Their children get the message that they are worthless if they are not the best, like the sex and love addict whose father got angry at him when he got only three hits in four at bat in Little League baseball. All he heard about was the time that he failed to get a hit, and not the three times that he was successful. Those parents have good intentions, but they can still fail to build positive self-worth by failing to affirm their children for being alive rather than for what they do, how well they do it, or how much they accomplish. These children never feel good enough. They too long for external affirmation. They need to get it before they can either give it to others or to themselves.

The rigid, disengaged families that Carnes (1988) reports parenting sex addicts also harm their children in terms of failing to help them develop a healthy sense of self. Their lack of flexibility makes the children feel unworthy and bad because they cannot follow all the rules or live up to all the expectations. The lack of love, warmth, and contact makes the children feel unlovable and unwanted. Adults who still feel like bad, unworthy, unlovable, and unwanted children cannot affirm themselves or treat themselves with softness, gentleness, and love. These adults tend to be rigid and detached with themselves, and uncomfortable with caring or affirming thoughts, feelings, or behaviors. As with children who have been abused, they may even be able to affirm others, like their own children, yet have a double standard when it comes to caring for themselves. With themselves, these addicts are harsh, demanding, critical, and conditional. Affirmation to them feels like being soft, "wimpy," and weak. Nonetheless, they may be silently, angrily, waiting for justice to be done and for someone "out there" to recognize, acknowledge, and affirm them before they can affirm themselves.

The third barrier to self-affirmation can be a social/cultural expectation that has become ingrained; in other words, people have the idea that if they are positive about themselves, they will be guilty of or will quickly become conceited, self-centered, egotistical, and narcissistic. Many addicted people with whom I have spoken harbor this fear. Even when they know the value of being self-affirming, they shudder at the concept of saying nice things to themselves. Such people typically cannot tolerate compliments or positive feedback from others. They usually have terrible guilt and shame about their addiction, and often feel they have embarrassed and disgraced their families and friends. They can be hard workers in recovery and helpful to others, but when asked to return the favor and help themselves, they become paralyzed. These individuals do not have an obvious history of neglect or abuse, nor do they come from families that are terribly rigid or perfectionistic. They tend to have good morals, values, and judgment, and to come from supportive, caring families. However, when the chips are down, they can not, and sometimes will not, affirm themselves. The most reasonable explanation, then, is one of social or cultural learning. People are taught in church, in school, or in their neighborhood that it is wrong to think or say positive, affirming things about oneself. Unfortunately, they learn their lessons well, and the new task of learning how to be self-affirming in recovery is a difficult one for them.

What Can Be Done?: Ways to Become Self-Affirming

The Twelve Steps provide the initial direction in developing self-affirmation. Steps Four and Five, Six and Seven, and Ten have to do with building self-worth and the capacity for self-affirmation. Taking inventories and allowing your Higher Power to remove your defects of character are essential aspects of these Steps and of improving your sense of worth and affirmability.

Taking an inventory requires assessing both negative and positive qualities. Making a list of only your deficits is like a storekeeper identifying only what has run out and ignoring what is present. In a person's evaluation the list of positives should clearly outweigh the negatives, even in the case of a sex and love addict. If we believe that people are basically good, then we must look beyond the problems and see their healthy side. Step Four teaches us this and Step Five teaches us to share with God, ourselves, and another human being the results of our inventory process. Most of the time, when recovering addicts ask for help with Step Four or ask me to do their Step Five with them, their list of negative qualities exceeds their positives, or at best they can only come up with a list that is exactly even. We then work together to make the positive, affirming list longer than the deficits or defects list.

Steps Six and Seven focus on humility, surrender, and willingness to allow God, and not ourselves, to remove our character defects. The addict's temptation is, of course, to jump into the driver's seat and act like God by attempting to fix these difficulties without the assistance of his or her Higher Power. Part of the affirmation in these Steps is that we are acceptable as we are and not only as we would like ourselves to be, and it is up to our Higher Power to choose which defects to remove and which to leave. Usually addicts are surprised at the defects that remain. Did they expect perfection? Probably they did, but their Higher Power does not. Progress, not perfection, is what should be sought in life, and especially in recovery from sex and love addiction. The Steps teach us this if we will learn. This is unconditional love, which is the foundation of affirmation. Self-affirmation, then, requires developing the capacity for unconditional love directed toward oneself.

The Tenth Step encourages daily inventories and promptly admitting to wrongdoing on our part. This is a continuation of the growth established in the earlier steps, and suggests integrating this form of honesty and integrity into daily living. Again, this is the foundation for building ongoing self-esteem and self-respect. Self-affirmation should be easier to achieve once this has been established.

In addition to the steps, there are other things that recovering sex and love addicts in long-term recovery can do to develop the capacity to be self-affirming. Here are some ideas for growth:

Look at Yourself in the Mirror

Say nice things to the person you are looking at. Many sex and love addicts cannot look other people in the eye, and never really see themselves when they look in the mirror. The idea is to really look at yourself with caring, not critical, eyes. If you are going to develop the capacity to be affirming to yourself or anyone else, you need to be able to see the good in them, to see the real person, to see why their existence should be celebrated. See if you can get excited about your existence. Isn't it great you're alive? Aren't we all blessed that you were born? These are the affirming thoughts and feelings that a healthy parent has toward his or her child. Such a parent does not need achievements to feel thrilled about the child's being.

Talk to Your Child Within

There are a variety of ways to do this. You can visualize yourself as a child in your mind, and talk to him or her. You can get an empty chair, picture yourself as a child sitting in the chair, and talk to this child. You can get a pillow or some other soft, large object, imagine that this is you as a child, and talk to the object. We spoke earlier about developing the parent part of yourself. Now you will be connecting this parent part with the child part that is within us all. Many recovering sex and love addicts have connected with the idea of a child within themselves that they need to recognize, attend to, love, and affirm. They find this image very powerful in terms of helping them understand how they need to relate to themselves, especially the part of them that has been neglected and damaged by the addictive process.

Learn to Brag

As mentioned before, many recovering sex and love addicts are self-deprecating and incapable of saying positive things about themselves, especially in public. If they do give themselves a compliment or "toot their own horn" a bit, they quickly add so many disclaimers that the positives are lost. No one follows you around in life, so many times other people do not know about the good things you have done or the positive qualities you possess. Let them know. The idea is not to score points or win awards but rather to affirm your essential goodness. You need to acknowledge and recognize yourself since others do not always know about, see, or understand your healthy thoughts, feelings, and actions. Of course, some people brag too much already. This advice is not intended for them, as they are the ones most likely to abuse this suggestion.

Care for Yourself as a Good Parent Would

Get in touch with what an affirming, unconditionally loving parent would be like, and try to treat yourself accordingly. Do not just do it for others:

Share the wealth. Allow yourself to get what you give to others and know that you yourself need. Do not feel sorry for yourself. Do something: Give yourself what you need and expect from others.

Being a good parent means eating and sleeping right, getting exercise, being happy that you woke up in the morning, celebrating your birth, making a fuss over yourself, and taking time to be with yourself. Do not wait for others to do it for you. Take the initiative. Be gentle with yourself. Give yourself boundaries. Be compassionate. Be understanding. Encourage your-self to express your thoughts and feelings. Acknowledge your good deeds and help yourself make corrections when you miss the mark. Do not expect perfection, but do not expect nothing either. Strive for a healthy balance in all things.

Say, "I Love You" to Yourself

Too many of us have grown up without this affirmation. We need to tell ourselves that we love ourselves. If we do not love ourselves, knowing our-selves as well as we do, how can we expect others to love us? Do not make the mistake that many parents make, they cannot put their love into words, so they say, "He knows I love him because I do X for him." Do not leave it to chance. Say the words "I love you." If you are uncomfortable at first, stay with it. You will improve because practice makes perfect. Self-affirmation requires self-love. If you try one without the other you will fail because you have not been genuine. Affirmation is not phony, and it cannot be put on. It needs to be real or it is worthless.

Treat Yourself to Good Things and Provide Yourself with Healthy Rewards

A good parent enjoys giving his or her child both treats and rewards. The first is a celebration just because the child is him- or herself. The second is an acknowledgment of the things that he or she does. Most sex and love addicts have grossly distorted the ideas of treats and rewards. They have frequently rationalized and justified acting out as giving themselves treats and rewards. For instance, they think, "I deserve this because of...," "I need a reward because of enduring...," or "I have been under such stress that I need..." In early recovery, the rewards have involved gaining sobriety and developing a support system. In long-term recovery, the sex and love addict needs to take responsibility for his or her own rewards and treats. They cannot be left to others or to chance because this will lead the addict to feelings of neglect, deprivation, and eventually to acting out as a treat or a reward.

Ask for Acknowledgments When You Deserve Them

Don't be shy. Don't wait for others to notice. If you have done something that is worth noting, let other people know. This seems like bragging, but instead it involves asking for what you need from other people. In recovery, some sex and love addicts become passive and wait to be noticed by others. This too can lead to feelings of abandonment, neglect, or isolation, all of which can be dangerous for the recovering person at any stage of recovery. We should not assume that other people are as aware of or tuned-in to our lives as we are. This is impossible. Being a good parent to ourselves means getting praise and recognition from ourselves when we deserve it. Having the self-confidence to ask for an acknowledgment when you deserve it is a sign of healthy self-esteem and an important element in self-affirmation. You deserve recognition for both being and doing. You need not neglect the doing simply because you want to be affirmed for being; the two go hand in hand. Self-affirmed people enjoy life and spontaneously do things for others. Doing for others can be affirmed.

Give What You Need—Affirmation

On of the profound truths of recovery is that you get what you need by giving it away. This is true for affirmation as well. In order to give to others, you must be able to see what they need or lack. If you can develop this skill with others, you can also learn to use it with yourself. See what sort of affirmation others need, and give it to them. In the process, you will also start to discover what affirmations you need for yourself.

Meditate on Your Gifts, Not Your Burdens

Finally, the process of becoming self-affirming requires us to see our gifts. If we focus on our trials and not our blessings, we will not see the whole picture. Actually, when we meditate on our burdens, the things that get us down, the hassles that we experience, and the stressors in our lives, we find that these are the same things that we have to be thankful for and that give our lives joy and meaning. If my job is a pain, it is also a source of rewards and fulfillment. If recovery is annoying, it also saves our lives. Self-affirmation requires that we see and acknowledge our gifts and blessings. In short-term recovery, these are often unclear to us. In long-term recovery from sex and love addiction, we need to see the whole picture and accent the reality of ourselves and our lives.

With joy and gratitude, we can be alive today, and we can live this day sober of sex and love addiction. This is our affirmation. When others celebrate our triumph it is nice, but recovering sex and love addicts also need to be self-affirming to maintain long-term sobriety.

SUPPORT SYSTEMS

Many of us, especially recovering sex and love addicts, confuse support with dependency. In short-term recovery, a lot of emphasis is placed on giving up the old supports that were used, like acting out and "people, places, and things," and developing new supports like sharing and relationships with sponsors, therapists, and members of the Augustine Fellowship of Sex and Love Addicts Anonymous. In lifelong recovery, having a strong, working support system is essential. Some people accuse recovering addicts of simply switching dependencies from sex and love to the S.L.A.A. program. What these critics fail to see is that the recovering sex and love addict has grown to the point where he or she has changed an unhealthy dependency on sexual or romantic acting out to a constructive, healthy, supportive interdependency with other people who are sympathetic and who understand the nature of the illness and the struggles of recovery.

The difference between dependency and support is crucial because it can help the addict and others to comprehend the distinction between healthy and unhealthy dependence on others. Dependency implies that the dependent person cannot survive alone. For instance, we depend on food, water, and air to survive, and we cannot live without them. When addicts are dependent, they feel they cannot survive without one specific thing (acting out sexually) or person (acting out romantically). They need sex or love to exist. They need sex or love to take care of their loneliness, emptiness, worthlessness, shame, guilt, fear, confusion, anxiety, and other needs. They need a caretaker or a fix. The relationship they have with this activity or person is an unequal one. The behavior or partner is the superior and the addict is inferior. The sex and love addict is in a childlike position with regard to the addiction. He or she needs the acting out or the romance, while the sexual or romantic interest will not unless he or she is also a sex addict, which is not uncommon. The roles are dominant and submissive, victim and victimizer, parent and child. The addiction is in control, and the addict is powerless. This is a dependency.

Supportive relationships with behaviors or people are quite different from a dependent relationship. In a supportive relationship there is equality and mutuality. Support involves sharing, opening up, being honest and genuine, and taking responsibility. One person or activity does not need the other to survive: The two sides are independent and interdependent. Sexuality and romance can be present, but they are not essential, they are sufficient but not necessary, and the behavior or partner can stand alone or in relationship. Supportive actions and connections involve sharing, compassion, understanding, and caring. The relationship is adultlike rather than childlike. There is a sense of being equal partners with shared rights and responsibilities, so that the partners feel supported by each other rather than dependent.

Part of understanding the difference between support and dependence involves understanding interdependence. Independence and dependence are opposites. Interdependence is an integration of these two polarities that is stronger than either is alone. Both total dependence and total independence are unhealthy states for an individual. Healthy people have a combination of independence and dependence in their lives, which is termed interdependence. For example, mature adults do not depend on others for their basic needs like food, shelter, clothing, and activity. However, they do depend on others for relationship, caring, and love. A person's relationship with his or her Higher Power is similar: It involves both dependence and independence. We do not depend on God to run our everyday affairs, but we do depend on our Higher Power for love, direction, and caring.

In early recovery, dependence on the program and other recovering people is encouraged. As recovery progresses, more independence is expected in terms of day-to-day functioning. Eventually recovering people even allow others to depend on them, for example: as sponsees. Long-term recovery is characterized by interdependence, not independence. If every recovering person became totally independent, who would run the S.L.A.A. program and to whom would newcomers look for guidance and direction? Obviously S.L.A.A. would not exist without independent, responsible recovering sex and love addicts who were willing to give their time and energy to helping others with the same difficulties. The "old timers" know that newcomers need to hear from them as well as from professionals about how to stop their devastating obsession and compulsion.

Normal Support Systems

In terms of normal development, children get their initial support from their families, then move on to peers, and finally connect with people from the world of work. In the beginning, the family is the basic unit from which the small child receives support. Ideally, the family unit is the place where people can be most themselves. The family provides basic physical nurturing like food and shelter, and it also provides the basic emotional nurturing that makes a child feel loved, lovable, and worthwhile.

From this safe and supportive environment, the child starts to venture forth to make contact with the wider world. At first these forays are short, and the child quickly returns to his or her supportive parents. After awhile, the child makes stronger connections with peers and needs less support from his or her family. During adolescence the child makes greater separation, and may even appear to totally reject the family in return for the support of his or her peer group.

In young adulthood the person grows even farther from the family unit, becomes integrated in the world of work, and begins to establish his or her own family. Peers remain very important, but the young adult also begins to shoulder some responsibility and starts to develop self-worth, confidence, and support from coworkers and accomplishments.

For the so-called normal person, then, there are three main arenas for getting support. They build on one another and are not mutually exclusive. The family is a core source of support. Peers become and continue to be essential. Finally, coworkers and relationships in the work world can add to the support system on which a healthy individual counts for love, encouragement, compassion, understanding, recognition, praise, and help.

Recovery Support Systems

In recovery, the sex and love addict's support system is usually the reverse of the normal person's support system as outlined above. The sex and love addict gets most of his or her support, especially in the beginning, from the people who will tell him or her to "work your tail off," the people in S.L.A.A. Then, the recovering person usually has some nonrecovering friends who become supportive. Finally, in most cases the family brings up the rear.

As has been emphasized over and over in this book, the sex and love addict needs to get a sponsor and friends in the Augustine Fellowship of Sex and Love Addicts Anonymous or a similar Twelve Step organization. Without this sort of 24-hour-a-day support network, recovery is almost impossible. Many addicts have tried, and most have failed. A salesman who consulted me was horrified at the suggestion that he attend some meetings. He said he wanted to "do it on [his] own." Therefore, in order to test his resolve, I asked him to do some homework between sessions. He briefly scribbled a few lines on a piece of paper the day of our next session because he only remembered his assignment at the last minute. When I confronted him about his lack of effort, especially because he *had* found time to act out for a few hours, he became angry and withdrawn, and did not return the next week. He returned three months later, in worse trouble, after having again tried to "do it on [his] own." He needed the support of other recovering people but was too embarrassed, and secretly too proud, to ask for their help. His recovery would require his willingness to change this false pride and fear of humiliation.

The sex and love addict in recovery needs to build a new support system based on relationships with people in the S.L.A.A. program. A sponsor is essential. Many people who relapse had made this fatal error: They never got a sponsor or they stopped using him or her. The newcomer also needs to make friends with other people besides his or her sponsor because there will be times when he or she will need to talk or will need some other form of help and the sponsor may not be available. Some people have more than one sponsor. Others simply have a phone list and use it. Whatever the arrangements, the S.L.A.A. program members are the recovering person's family.

Other recovering people provide the sex and love addict with what the normal family provides the normal child: love, caring, nurturing, safety, and a sense of worth. In the meetings and with program members, sex and love addicts are safe. Even if they want to try to act out with sober people, they will be accepted, encouraged to "talk about it," and directed to other ways to meet their needs besides sexual or romantic acting out. They will be allowed to be themselves. They will be encouraged to open up and share with others in an environment that fosters strength, hope, and recovery, just as the normal family environment does for normal children.

At the next level, the recovering sex and love addict will establish supportive relationships with professionals, like therapists and counselors, and nonrecovering friends. As recovery takes hold, the sex and love addict becomes more available to and capable of engaging in other nonaddictive relationships. Prior to recovery, many sex and love addicts have addictive relationships with their therapists: They have exaggerated dependencies, they fall hopelessly in love, they sexualize the relationship, or want to continue in therapy forever. Most do not have healthy relationships with peers or friends. In fact, in early recovery most sex and love addicts feel like adolescents who are just learning how to have and to be friends, especially with nonrecovering people. In later recovery, developing a circle of supportive friends is a major part of protecting one's recovery with a working support system.

The last group of people the recovering sex and love addict usually accepts as support are family members. This is just the opposite of the normal process. Most families do not understand addictions, especially sex and love addiction. They cannot be supportive of something they do not understand and often feel quite uncomfortable about. Most families do not understand addictions and recovery in general, unless they have had some personal exposure to this process. When the addiction in question is to sex or love, most families become embarrassed, frightened, and distant. They may verbalize some sort of support for the recovering sex and love addict, but they generally cannot provide the same sort of support that S.L.A.A. program members and professionals can give to the newly recovering sex and love addict. Many sex and love addicts find this fact sad, frustrating, and confusing. Sometimes they make great efforts to inform and enlist family members in their support system without many results.

For example, at a recent education session for family and friends of sex and love addicts in our outpatient program, only a few family members even attended. One who did come said, "I do not really know why I am here," despite two years of treatment and recovery for his addicted brother. One sex and love addict had had a promise from his parents that they would attend only to have them make excuses at the last minute for not coming. Another addict came with her parents and sat between them. They had pushed her to go into treatment, but she was not ready for treatment for herself, despite being in a love dependency that had driven her to physically assault her boyfriend, and she refused to follow through with her own therapy.

Family support, then, usually comes last in the newly recovered sex and love addict's support system. Many family issues are best dealt with in long-term recovery due to the family's lack of motivation and understanding as well as the potential of these powerfully charged relationships for making the addict vulnerable to a slip or relapse. Developing support among therapists and friends comes first, after the sex and love addict has initiated his or her recovery process with a Twelve Step Fellowship. The support of S.L.A.A. members, especially sponsors, is crucial in establishing a strong foundation for recovery.

How to Develop New Supports

The following are a number of suggestions about how to foster a new support system or enrich one that has already been established. These ideas are not all-inclusive, but they will give some direction to recovering people who need to examine their support systems, especially as an aspect of a lifelong recovery program.

Regular Attendance at S.L.A.A. Meetings

This seemingly simple and obvious suggestion is the one with which most people seem to have the greatest difficulty. In early recovery there are lots of excuses why attendance is not possible. Once the recovering sex and love addict has overcome his or her early resistance and begun a pattern of regular attendance, another problem begins to surface; complacency. After they have found some stability, most recovering addicts begin to think about having less contact with the program, and often decrease the number of meetings they attend. Frequently they lose sight of what regular attendance at meetings does for them by exposing them both to support and to the dangers of recovery, showing others their commitment and reliability, and "keeping it green" in terms of reminding them of the "cunning, baffling, and powerful" addiction from which they suffer.

Share at Meetings

Attending but not talking is insufficient for recovery. Especially in the beginning, some people are afraid to speak, often because they are intimidated by the group. In long-term recovery, "getting current" at meetings by sharing immediate feelings, thoughts, problems, and impulses is essential. No amount of sharing, reading, talking to therapists or reflection that a recovering sex and love addict does will replace sharing at an S.L.A.A. meeting. Unfortunately, too many sex and love addicts only find this out by experiencing a slip or relapse. In long-term recovery, the sex and love addict him- or herself needs to take responsibility for examining and monitoring his or her program in terms of both attending and sharing at meetings.

Get Involved with the S.L.A.A. Program

In addition to attending and speaking up in meetings, the sex and love addict can become more involved in the S.L.A.A. program by "taking commitments." This means that the person agrees at a business meeting to take on certain functions like chairing a meeting, working on a committee, or volunteering to answer the phone. There are lots of other jobs that must be done to keep the program working, like setting up chairs, making coffee, selling literature, and cleaning up after meetings. Doing service work is part of recovery, especially after the initial struggle to maintain sobriety. At this stage of the game, the sex and love addict gets by giving. Attending meetings, personal sharing, and showing a willingness to work will attract new people to the recovering person's support network because they will see the healthy side of the addict's personality.

In their active addictions, many sex and love addicts were involved in seducing, soliciting, cruising, and manipulating others to get what they thought they needed. In recovery, they tend to be overly suspicious of their own motives for developing relationships, and question themselves mercilessly about why they want to have a relationship with someone. While addictive attractions can sometimes be the basis for a desire to get close to another person, this is not the only reason for wanting to have friends. The recovering person at times loses sight of his or her own healthy side and need for relationships. Therefore, sex and love addicts tend to be overly suspicious of their own attractions. Likewise, they are quite suspicious of the motives of others. Often they do not realize they are sending off a different signal. In other words, instead of "I'm available for fun," they are communicating, "I am working hard at this," which will attract a different type of person than they had attracted before while on the make or looking for action.

Come Early. Stay Late. Go for Coffee

In order to develop or firm up a support system, the person needs to let others know that he or she is available. If you rush in and dash out of meetings, people may get the idea that you are very busy, important, or overly committed, and they will not get the message that you are lonely, needy, isolated, and vulnerable. A recovering sex and love addict may be the former, but will definitely also be the latter, and he or she must find ways to let other people know that he or she needs their caring and support. This may be an extremely difficult task for the recovering person, since he or she probably is accustomed to wearing an "I don't need anyone" mask and appearing to be self-sufficient and independent. One way to give the message, besides telling others that you need to build relationships with them, is to attend the meetings and socialize before and after. Going for coffee after meetings may be the difference between having friends and being isolated.

Use the Phone. Stay in Touch

While some sex and love addicts have used the phone as part of their acting out (for obscene or long, romantic calls), most sex and love addicts seem to develop a "phone phobia" during recovery. They feel afraid to call people to talk, they feel embarrassed to need to talk, and they feel self-conscious about what to say. They become overly shy, tongue-tied, and aloof, as if they didn't need to call as much as others. They feel awkward and "stupid." In other words, they have a million reasons why they don't use the phone. However, the phone is a lifeline to sobriety. In long-term recovery, phone use can be a barometer to warn of returning self-centeredness and addiction, much the way meetings can. That is, when addicts stop calling, they are getting into trouble.

Keeping in contact with other people is another important part of healthy living, and a good recovery program for a sex and love addict. Often this is accomplished by meeting in person or talking over the phone, but if these are not possible, sex and love addicts can keep in touch through writing letters, notes, and postcards. All these actions will give others the idea that you care about them and that they are important in your life.

Ask for Help. Share Hurt and Vulnerability

Many of the first five suggestions involve behavior. The following are implied or specific suggestions for verbal actions as well, but the idea becomes even more concrete. In order to build support and a mutually helping relationship between two people, you need a helper and a helpee. Hopefully, in a good relationship, these roles will be reversed at various times. To begin with, however, if you want to feel that someone will be or is a support to you, you must let them know you need help. Again, the masks of aloofness, arrogance, self-sufficiency, and independence tend to cut us off from others who do not perceive us as being needy. Actually asking for help can break down this barrier.

Sometimes people find asking for help so difficult that they must practice on small things and build up to bigger ones. For instance, you might ask someone to pour you a cup of coffee or help you fill out a form. Before "moving up" to asking for help with your life, you may need to ask for help getting to work or completing a project at home. Learning to ask for help should be something that happens with asking for a sponsor. If the sex and love addict does not have a sponsor, he or she obviously already has a problem with asking for help. Sometimes early recovery is less difficult, so the addict does not feel an intense need for a sponsor or for late-night phone calls. Nonetheless, at one time or another, most of us will need help, and we must have a support system to turn to when we do. The sex and love addict in long-term recovery is asking for failure by not asking for help.

In order to get support, the sex and love addict not only needs to ask for help but also needs to let others know what he or she needs help with; in other words, to express his or her pain or vulnerability. Sharing the hurts, the embarrassments, the anxieties, and the confusion will enable another person to really know you, and thereby to offer help and support that is meaningful and useful. Without the truth about the pain and tenderness in the sex and love addict's heart, other people can only guess at how to be supportive and caring. Only by revealing oneself fully can you allow others to be there for you.

Trust: Give What You Want to Get

Another way to expand and improve on your support system is to give what you want to get from others. Trust is a crucial issue for most recovering sex and love addicts. They need it, yet they find it in short supply because they have not given it to others (in fact, they may have taken advantage of others' trust) and are not certain that others are trustworthy (perhaps others are living two lives too). Instead of taking a passive approach and waiting for trust to develop in a relationship, a recovering sex and love addict can take the initiative by trusting others with the truth about him- or herself. Addicts can share, ask for help, and be a trusting confidant for others. Many sex and love addicts have become cynical and suspicious, and need to counter this tendency in themselves by taking the responsibility to start the trust process by giving trust when they need to get it.

Watch Your Expectations of Others

In addition to giving trust in order to get it, the recovering sex and love addict needs to be aware of his or her expectations of others. "Taking inventories" (being critical) of others is fairly commonplace, and addicts must be reminded that the S.L.A.A. program suggests only taking an inventory on oneself. While being critical of others can interfere with developing a support system, most people realize the dangers involved. Often, however, the difficulties we encounter because of our expectations of others are not as clear to us. If we expect things that others cannot deliver, we will be disappointed, and we will feel hurt, and possibly resentful. Usually we are not aware of our expectations unless we make a specific effort to reflect on what we expect from others.

A major area of difficulty is expecting others to read our minds, and to thereby know how we feel, what we are thinking, and what we need. Small children expect their parents to read their minds because most of the time parents put a great deal of effort into trying to figure out what the child feels and needs since he or she cannot communicate his or her needs verbally. As adults, many of us regress into this sort of mind-reading expectation, especially with people we trust, care about, and feel close to. In long-term recovery, problems may continue in our support system because of expecting things from others of which they are not aware, that they cannot or will not give, or that they do not feel comfortable giving or doing. If we can at least bring our expectations out into the open, we can negotiate to learn which can be met and which cannot. This will, hopefully, prevent some hurt, confusion, and disappointment with the support system of the long-term recovering sex and love addict.

Hold Back on Sarcasm and Criticism

A quick way to push people away is to be angry, sarcastic, or critical with them. Many sex and love addicts in their active addictions have become experts at pushing people away, and sarcasm is one of their favorite tools. They can be quite perceptive in terms of seeing other people's vulnerabilities and weak spots since they have often used them to get what they wanted. In recovery, they begin to change the way they relate to others by replacing manipulation with genuineness, dishonesty with truth, and anger with love. The process is frightening, however, so defenses like anger and sarcasm are often retained after they have outlived their usefulness. At times the recovering sex and love addict can be insensitive to the isolating character of sarcasm, and will need to be reminded of his or her own intense sensitivity to any sort of criticism or rejection. In long-term recovery, fine-tuning relationships will involve looking at behaviors that push people away and make the support system weaker, such as sarcasm and criticism.

Accepting the Humanness and Vulnerability of Others

As well as no longer pushing people away, the recovering sex and love addict needs to welcome people into his or her world. To be a part of a long-term support system, a person needs to be accepted for who and what he or she is, not who or what he or she should be. Like expectations, acceptance can be superficial when it is not given wholly and with an open heart but is instead conditional and temporary. If the recovering sex and love addict is to have a support system that includes people, he or she will, then, have an imperfect and fragile system indeed. The strength of the system does not come from the inhuman perfection of any one individual but instead from the interdependence and vulnerability of a group of individuals who are connected with each other.

Again, this is a lesson from the First Step—surrender—and involves giving what you need to get—acceptance. By accepting the humanity of others and their essential vulnerability, the recovering sex and love addict will be better able to accept these characteristics in him- or herself. In long-term recovery, as in the last three steps, the focus is on working at a daily program of awareness, surrender, and giving that will keep sex and love addicts in tune with their addiction and with their need for support, in order to manage their illness and their lives.

Support is not dependency. A recovering addict's support system does not parallel the normal support system of family, peers, and outside world. For the recovering sex and love addict, support starts with the Twelve Step Fellowship, expands to professionals and friends, and only later may include family. Developing a new or improved support system is difficult, and involves changes in behavior and attitudes. Suggestions for change include attending and sharing at S.L.A.A. meetings, going early and leaving late, using the phone, staying in touch, asking for help, trusting, being careful of expectations and sarcasm, and accepting our humanness and that of others. Obviously, there are many other ways to build support systems. As sex and love addicts continue to grow and recover, the accumulated wisdom and experience will be passed on, just as these suggestions have been shared to date.

FAMILIES

We all deal with family issues all the time. Some of us work on them, and others avoid them. Some of us are getting better, and others are getting worse. Some of us live with them, and others live as though they did not exist. Some of us seek to free ourselves from the chains of the past, and others seek to return to the comfort of our childhood, however imaginary or real. There is no question that our relationships with our families—parents, siblings, grandparents, and other relatives—have a profound effect on us in both our developmental years and the years that follow. Many of the influences are good, but some are terribly destructive.

In earlier chapters we referred to the debate about how much nature (genetics and biology) and how much nurture (families and environment) contribute to the way we are. Most researchers and clinicians agree that both have affected us, and that the debate is over how great a part each plays. Some say nature has the upper hand, 60:40. Others say the reverse, that nurture accounts for 60 percent of who and what we are and that nature represents only 40 percent. However, some sex and love addicts feel that 90 percent of their personality and problems come from their childhood.

In early recovery, issues concerning the family of origin can be dealt with only in a limited way. Some therapists have used a family therapy approach to the treatment of addictions, but this has not been demonstrated to work to any degree to date in sex and love addiction. I have no doubt that we will learn much about this approach in the near future, but at this point, families have instead been involved in education about the disease and how to help, treating co-dependency problems that contribute to continued acting out, and working with the sex and love addict him- or herself to identify family issues that interfere with the recovery process, such as ongoing conflicts or repressed experiences of victimization. Efforts to work on these deeper issues are done with great caution in early recovery because of their potential to create difficulties as well as resolving them. Later in the recovery process, family issues can be addressed in order for the sex and love addict to understand him- or herself better, and to thereby strengthen his or her personality, thus building a stronger outer core to protect him- or herself from relapse.

This section is geared toward identifying and working on family issues that may influence long-term recovery from sex and love addiction. Many of these issues may be problems in early recovery, and they may have been the topic of some therapy at an earlier point in order to firm up the initial part of the recovery process. Later on, the pain and conflicts of early family life can be handled in more depth, and with more resolution than could have been accomplished earlier. This is due to the sex and love addict's increased self-confidence and self-worth that derive from building a foundation of sobriety. Without the strength from a successful period of sexual and romantic sobriety, real, in-depth family work cannot be done. As sex and love addicts progress in their recovery, many of them seek help with these difficult family issues because they too have the sense that cleaning up their "old garbage" will make them better able to continue the journey that they have begun.

An example of how family issues can become relevant to long-term recovery is the sex and love addict whose family expressed compassion and under-standing when they found out about his problems, which he had kept a well-guarded secret, but were unable to support him in his efforts to become more independent and connected with people outside the family. For ex-ample, even after more than two years of not acting out on his bottom line of sex with minors, his parents suggested that he not go to church while he was at home for a visit. They couched it in terms that implied it was "for his own good," but the addict got the message that it was to help them avoid feeling embarrassed by his public presence. They never visited him in his inner-city home, and he was afraid to ask them because he anticipated their horror at the knowledge that he lived in a neighborhood that was largely black. They would not see his neighborhood as a consequence of his sex and love addiction, which it was, but rather would encourage him to see himself as being victimized by some outside authority. He was working on his overdependence on his parents, their infantalization and overprotection of him, and their projection of blame or responsibility on outside forces like God. He wanted healthy, interdependent relationships, and to be an equal among adults. He did not feel the need to blame others, even God, and wanted to be able to feel strong enough to cope with life on his own.

While this section in many ways cannot do justice to a topic that could easily fill several books, a brief review of how family issues can be problematic and can also be dealt with by professionals and recovering sex and love addicts is the purpose of this segment of chapter 5. The first part will look at dysfunctional families. The next section will focus on "looking-good" fam-ilies that have masked their dysfunction behind a good-looking facade of functionality.

Dysfunctional Families

The concept of dysfunctional families has become quite popular in the past decade, and increasingly more literature deals with this important concern. The idea has its roots in the conception of the alcoholic family. As we have grown in the treatment of the disease of alcoholism, we have included more and more people in the treatment process. For instance, we discovered that alcoholics did better when spouses were included in the recovery process through Alanon and therapy. Later, we began to understand more clearly from a systems point of view that the excess drinking of the alcoholic affected all of the family members. Children of alcoholics, and then adult children of alcoholics, were increasingly understood, helped, and studied. Even the intergenerational issue of grandchildren of alcoholics has received attention. As this information and help has become more public, other people have started to identify with the issues being raised.

Other addictions have not been looked at as closely in terms of family issues, but most experts believe that much of what applies to alcoholic families also describes the dynamics of other addicted families. Even people from families without identified addicts connect with many issues discussed in addicted families; hence, the term "dysfunctional family." This descriptor is broad enough to include any sort of illness or dynamic that interferes with the normal functioning of the family. Unfortunately, some therapists think that most families are dysfunctional, at least in some ways, which tends to water down the concept's meaning. What I address in this section are families that have had some sort of breakdown in the basic family functions outlined below. Most often this loss of functioning is due to an addictive disease like chemical dependency, but it can also occur because of other factors like a chronic medical illness, extreme rigidity and perfectionism, or abuse.

In order to understand the idea of dysfunction, it is important to identify what normal family functions should be. The five functions outlined below parallel the five areas of functioning that addictive diseases affect in the individual—physical, mental, emotional, social, and spiritual. A healthy family will provide structure and support for the development of the family members in all these areas. An unhealthy and, therefore, dysfunctional family will have difficulties in one or more of these areas.

Physical

The core function of a human family unit is to provide *safety* for the family members. This means in its most basic form that the members must be physically safe. In our era, physical safety includes the provision of food, clothing, and shelter. It also involves protecting the members from physical harm from violence, whether from intruders or within the family itself (namely, domestic violence such as spouse or child abuse). In a functional family, all these basic, physical needs are met consistently, and are often unquestioned or assumed rights by family members.

In a dysfunctional family, basic, physical needs are not met. Food, clothing, shelter, and safety from physical violence and abuse are not assumed or taken for granted. These things may be provided at times and not available at other times, or they may never be present in sufficient quantities to give family members the confidence that they will be there in the future. These families live in an unsafe world, and even basic necessities cannot be taken for granted. Physical abuse is common when parents will not guarantee physical safety.

The lack of physical safety produces fear in the family members. The fear centers around basic survival issues, like having enough food, clothing, and shelter, and being protected from physical harm and abuse. The pain and hurt inflicted by physical abuse and the lack of basic needs creates anger and distrust. Children who live in families like these are hurt, scared, needy, and furiously angry.

Mental

The family is the initial translator of *reality* to the child. The family unit has the function of teaching its members about how the world works. Our basic grounding in reality comes through our experience within the family context. Accurate perceptions, logical thinking, the relation of cause and effect, and the principles of how reality works come from our contact and training in the family. In a healthy family, basic input and rational processing are taught almost unintentionally.

In the dysfunctional family, perceptions are distorted, illogical thinking is modeled, and the relation of cause and effect is confused or denied. Defense mechanisms like denial, minimization, rationalization, and projection are used and treated as if they truly were reality. Children learn to deny and distort in order to fit into the family system. For instance, if one parent's abnormal sexual behaviors, such as incest, are ignored, kept secret, and denied, the children will learn that reality can be distorted in these ways.

In families where basic mental functioning like reality testing are distorted, the family members will be confused, frustrated, anxious, and illogical. They will not be able to solve problems well nor will they be able to communicate well with others because their perceptions of and experience with reality is different from the norm.

Emotional

Families are responsible for the *emotional well-being* of family members, and failures in this area produce profound insecurities and low self-esteem. Emotional caretaking or nurturing is an essential function of the human family. Unlike other animals, we humans need more than physical safety to survive. Even good reality contact is not sufficient, because we are emotional as well as rational beings. In fact, despite our emphasis on intellect, much of what human's do is based on our feelings and not our thoughts. Such deep human emotions and drives as love and sex have an enormous effect on our day-to-day living.

In a healthy family, the emotional life of the members is recognized as essential, and nurturing is seen as needed and appropriate. Love is not given conditionally, but rather is unconditional. Affirmation, recognition, acceptance, and celebration of our beings are encouraged and supported. The feeling life of family members is as important as their life of achieving and accomplishment. A healthy emotional climate in a family is seen as an indication of success, just like other indicators of success such as financial stability and social status. Emotionally healthy families like themselves as well as the individual family members.

In the dysfunctional family, feelings are dangerous. They go out of control, and cause pain and suffering. The emotional life of the family is a roller coaster in some families and an empty wasteland in others. There is no healthy balance of love, nurturing, affection, affirmation, and caring. These families are either too close or too distant emotionally, and their feelings frightening and confusing.

This lack of emotional stability or integration produces insecurity in the family members. They have a deeply rooted sense of anxiety, and wonder if they really belong anywhere. They do not feel they deserve to be loved, cared for, and nurtured. They may become narcissistic in defense against deprivation or emotional abuse. Because they feel unloved and unlovable, they may learn to appear close and loving, but what they really do is incorporate a pseudo-intimacy along with a secret distrust of others. They have deeply damaged self-esteem, and feel like bad people.

Social

As well as providing basic reality testing and security, the family unit is the primary *social* unit for the family members. Social rules, norms, and expectations are learned in the family system. Ways to make and keep friendships and relationships are modeled in the interactions within the family. Basic social skills are taught and reinforced on a daily basis, especially in early childhood, when infants encounter few other human beings.

In the healthy family, members are able to make initial contacts, share feelings and experiences, express conflicts and resolve them, and give and receive love and nurturing. Relationships are seen as a source of joy and gratification, not as a means to an end. Relating is part of the meaning of life, and an essential ingredient to a satisfying and fulfilling existence.

In dysfunctional families, social interactions are quite problematic, and serve as poor models for future living. There are often conflicts that never get reconciled, important events and feelings that are not shared, and awkward or inadequate contacts. Relating is troublesome and confusing. Interactions seem unpredictable and inconsistent.

This lack of adequate, healthy relations creates a lack of confidence in family members. Rather than being a source of happiness and support, social interactions are feared and seen as potentially dangerous or complicated. Dysfunctional families produce people who are isolated, overly dependent, aggressive, and inappropriate in behavior. They feel inadequate and insecure in social situations due to a lack of comfort and insufficient confidence in their social skills.

Spiritual

The final essential function of the family unit is *spiritual* development. The family environment provides the mold for physical, mental, emotional, social, and spiritual issues in the lives of its members. Basic concepts and practices in spiritual areas are established in the early years of a child's life. In a healthy family, an active spiritual life will produce feelings of hope and optimism in its members. Life will be fuller and more meaningful if it has a spiritual dimension.

In the dysfunctional family, spirituality is neglected or, frequently, non-existent. Sometimes these families do practice religion, but with such rigidity and perfectionism that people feel diminished and sinful. Other times, spirituality is seen as a joke and a foolish sign of dependency or a childishness. Cynical and pessimistic attitudes toward life are common, and promote hedonism, materialism, and living for today.

Families can be dysfunctional in many areas—physical safety, mental clarity, emotional security, social confidence, or spiritual hopefulness. After some sobriety, sex and love addicts often report that they grew up in a dysfunctional home. Physical, emotional, and sexual abuse are frequently identified as experiences that were destructive and that contributed to their later fear, thinking distortions, insecurity, lack of confidence, and hopelessness. Angry, hurt, needy, confused, anxious, isolated, self-centered, and pessimistic children possess fertile ground for the roots of a sex and love addiction. This type of family of origin is not necessary for or causative of addictive behaviors, but it can be a strong contributing factor, and can fuel the fire once it has ignited.

In long-term recovery, the task of sex and love addicts is to identify areas of weakness or vulnerability and to strengthen themselves in these areas in order to reduce the risk of a slip or a relapse. Tracing feelings back to issues concerning the family of origin can help to identify, clarify, and focus the work that must be done. For example, if a sex and love addict has achieved a year or more of sobriety and still finds him- or herself feeling cynical or pessimistic about life, he or she should question the roots of this spiritual malaise. For such addicts, spiritual development may have been stifled, neglected, or abused as children.

Feelings of isolation, neglect, or discomfort in social situations may be related to improper social skills taught in the family. A lack of self-confidence or insecurity may have to do with the social or emotional functioning of the sex and love addict's family. Difficulties with reality testing and distorted thinking or perceptions could also have their roots in family life. Fear, anger, and distrust may have been founded or fostered in an unsafe home life. All of these and many more thoughts, feelings, and behaviors can have a dysfunctional family as their source.

Janet Woititz, in her book *Adult Children of Alcoholics*, identified 13 characteristics of people who had grown up in the dysfunctional situation of trying to cope with an addiction to alcohol. Many people who read her book but did not come from a home with an identified chemically dependent person can still identify with these characteristics. The dysfunctional nature of the families of these individuals was in some way similar to the destructive force of alcoholism. These adult children relate to Woititz's characteristics such as guessing about normality; having difficulty following a project through to the end, lying when it is just as easy to tell the truth, judging themselves mercilessly, having trouble having fun, taking themselves too seriously, having difficulty with intimate relationships, overreacting to changes over which they have no control, constantly seeking approval and affirmation, being extremely responsible or irresponsible, showing extreme loyalty, and tending to be impulsive and to lock themselves into a course of action. Children who grew up in families with other dysfunctions, like perfectionism, workaholism, sex and love addiction, religious fanaticism, overeating, compulsive cleaning, gambling, chaos, chronic illness, disability (whether physical or mental), unpredictability, arbitrariness, denial, and/or physical, sexual, or emotional neglect or abuse, find they can relate to these feelings and reactions.

Some family theorists have proposed that children in alcoholic families tend to take on certain roles as a systemic way of coping with the family dysfunction. In alcoholic families there is often a *hero* (frequently the oldest child), who is an overachiever in school and at home. Often family heroes get good grades and come home and take over adult functions such as cooking, cleaning, laundry and child care. The second child is frequently the *rebel*, who acts out all the anger and resentment in the family system. The rebellious child does not follow the rules and refuses to be told how to live at home or in school. The rebel is the focus for the obvious problems in the family. The third child frequently is a quiet, withdrawn person who keeps to him- or herself and causes no problems. These children are *lost* children because they go unnoticed and get no love or attention. The last child is the fun-loving *mascot*. This child is an entertainer who can be counted on for a laugh or a distraction when things start to get tense. Often the "baby" of the family, the mascot will keep things moving and make sure that the mood is light. Obviously, not every alcoholic or dysfunctional family has four children, and even the ones that do will not exactly fit into these broad categories. Often children of dysfunctional families can relate to more than one of the roles—hero, rebel, lost child, and mascot—at various times in their lives or under various circumstances. These are not intended to be rigid pigeonholes, but rather are general examples of how dysfunctions can affect family roles.

Again, the job of the recovering sex and love addict in long-term recovery is to identify the characteristics or roles to which he or she can relate and to begin to trace them back to the family of origin. The point of working on these sorts of family issues is to clean up old business so that it will not intrude into the present and cause the recovering person to overreact or to feel hurt or vulnerable .

An example of how a sex and love addict works on family issues differently in short-term versus long-term recovery is a young man who grew up in a home with an alcoholic, "looking-good," successful father, and a dependent, overprotective, co-dependent mother. He was raped by his father at age 8, and began compulsive masturbation using his father's pornography at age 12. By age 14 he was going to adult bookstores, engaging in anonymous sex, abusing alcohol and drugs, and cruising by hitchhiking and going to parks where "the action was." His initial treatment focused on establishing sobriety and developing his sense that he was worth saving and that he deserved to live without acting out sexually. Family issues were addressed in terms of his neglect and abandonment by his parents due to their own sickness. His deeper issues concerning sexual assault and rape were left for long-term recovery. He needed to develop ego strength, self-worth, and success with sobriety in order to cope with his profound feelings of rage, violation, and abandonment. He already was an angry, critical, explosive person, so he did not need to experience more of his rage early in recovery. Later, with some sense that feelings can be resolved and that he would be supported by others, he would be ready to work on the deeper family issues of emotional and sexual neglect and abuse. Dealt with in long-term recovery, these issues would provide him with additional strength and reserves to prevent relapse over the long haul.

The young man described above was a combination of the rebel and the lost child. He identified problems knowing what normal is, problems following through on things, judging himself without mercy, taking himself very seriously, difficulty with intimacy, seeking approval, and being extremely loyal. Some of these problem areas needed to be addressed in order to establish sobriety, including being rebellious, isolating, following through, being merciful, seeking approval, and loyalty. However, the depth of resolution of even these problems was more superficial than would be possible after sobriety had been established for at least a year. At that point, his child within, his questions about normalcy, his lack of intimacy, and his choices or relationships could be addressed at a deeper, more long-lasting level as a part of his plan for maintaining long-term sobriety through developing himself more fully.

Looking-Good Families

In addition to the damage done by dysfunctional families, some sex and love addicts grew up in families that looked good on the outside but were still quite destructive on the inside. These families lack some of the more obvious forms of dysfunction like sexual or physical abuse, or the more common causes of dysfunction like alcoholism or other addictions, but they suffer from their own form of dysfunction, which is called "looking good." In one of her lectures, Ann Smith of the Caron Foundation has identified this type of family, and has outlined their pathology in a way that helps clarify the nature of the dynamics and the damage.

A looking-good family is primarily concerned with its image and public presence. Looking good on the surface, is all that counts, and whatever is going on underneath is ignored and repressed. Families that are concerned with looking good are superficial; they promote a pseudo-intimacy that appears to be the real thing but it lacks the genuine depth and caring that characterizes true intimacy. In a looking-good family, you can appear to belong but feel like a stranger; you can appear to be loved yet always feel alone; you can fit in while feeling like a misfit.

Your family is supposed to be the place where you feel most at home. In your family, you should be physically, mentally, emotionally, socially, and spiritually safe; You should be able to be truest to yourself, to be "real," to be able to "let your hair down," to be your least inhibited and phony. This is not possible in the looking-good family. In such a family it is not safe to be yourself. You do not have to live in fear of physical abuse, because physical abuse "wouldn't look good." Therefore, in these families the abuse and neglect goes underground and takes subtler forms. It is much harder to identify, to see, and to believe, even though the feelings of being unloved and unlovable, unaccepted and unacceptable, and unworthy and worthless exist seemingly without any reason. There is no closeness, but the illusion of closeness is created for public consumption, and even fools the family members themselves. Trust and sharing do not occur, revealing oneself is too dangerous due to the fact that self-revelations can "come back to haunt you" and be "used against you."

Looking-good families are comfortable with a high level of activity, stress, and even crisis. Rather than crumbling under the strain, the looking-good family rises to the occasion and proves to the world by surviving under duress and acting happy how capable, loving, close, and successful it really is. These families are quite co-dependent, and accept victimhood as a chance to once again prove their worth.

In looking-good families, feelings are repressed. Being honest, open, and real, especially with feelings, is a high-risk endeavor. Open expression of any sort of negative feeling like anger, hurt, rebellion, or frustration will be met with rejection, abandonment, and possibly abuse (of the verbal, cutting, and subtle sort). There is no support for any kind of messy, uncomfortable, disturbing, or unsettling feelings. These must be "stuffed." Clearly, repression is the name of the game.

Needless to say, looking-good families need compulsive behaviors to reduce their anxiety and numb their pain. Addictions, compulsivity, rigidity, obsessiveness, and perfectionism are commonplace. Compulsive use of drugs (preferably looking-good prescriptions) and alcohol, shopping, cleaning, working, eating, praying, and "healthy" activities (such as athletics) are how these families live. They need to self-medicate their pain. They have problems dealing with anger, resentment, and frustration. They rush to fix things without ever working them out.

Looking-good families are run by perfectionistic parents who try too hard. They are determined to avoid the mistakes their parents made (like being addicted to alcohol). They are overly determined and achievement-oriented, and want the world to know how successful they are as people and as parents. Perfectionistic parents cannot acknowledge difficulties with their children because they want to prove they can do a better job than their parents did with them.

These are individuals actually running from the past, a topic they avoid. They cannot talk about the past, and keep family secrets. They create a "no talk" rule about their childhood traumas and pain. They are devoted to doing the opposite of what their parents did to them but unfortunately, they go to the other extreme, and end up equally out of balance with their own issues.

Looking-good families are prone to a series of subtle abuses. For instance, they make love conditional. They give out praise for achievement, for actions that reflect well on the parents, and for looking good in public. They do not give unconditional love, which is love without any strings attached. They do not affirm, recognize, acknowledge, and accept their children for the people that they are rather than the people they want them to be.

These families tend to be rather rigid and controlling. They are unable to be flexible. Challenges to their rules are seen as personal assaults rather than the normal questioning of childhood or adolescence. Parents want things done "my way or the highway." Abandonment, rejection, and criticism are the rewards of asking for changes, flexibility, or compromise. The rule is, "Let's compromise—do it my way."

There is "silent violence" in looking-good families. Some arguments become heated, but there always seems to be an air of civility even when tempers are at their worst. However, the rage will be expressed in the form of withdrawal, isolation, and "the silent treatment." If debating and rational fighting fail, outright physical violence will be avoided by withholding and backing off.

The parents in looking-good families are not able to adequately meet the needs of their children, whom they emotionally neglect. These parents are too needy themselves to give much to others. They are experts at hiding their neediness, but their inability to nurture themselves or their children reveals the truth about their emotional bankruptcy.

These looking-good families are parent-centered. The activities and events of family life are geared around the needs of the adults rather than the needs of the children. The children learn to be "people pleasers." The children's natural business and exploration is curtailed for the sake of the adults. Children are asked, for example, to "keep the peace for Dad." The activities and entertainment of the adults takes precedence over the activities and entertainment of the children.

These families tend to have boundary issues. The limits are either too close ("smothering") or too far (detachment). Looking-good parents can be quite moody, and children learn to be great adaptors to the mood swings of their parents. Such parents are poor role models for healthy adjustment, balance, and appropriate contact between people. They go to extremes that are confusing, invasive, isolating, and anxiety-producing for their children.

One chemically dependent adolescent recently came to me complaining that her parents were not accepting of her and her friends. They were rigid and controlling, distant, argumentative, unable to listen, neglectful, and easy to fool in terms of her drug and alcohol use and sexual acting out. These are not unusual complaints for a teenager, especially one who is drug-dependent and sexually active at age 14. However, I became much more sympathetic when I met her overachieving, looking-good parents. They were both highly trained professionals, constantly on the go, well-off financially, and good-looking. They were extremely rigid; for example, the mother refused to allow her other daughters to miss a couple of hours of school in order to come in for a family session. They aggressively attacked their daughter's friends despite saying they were concerned about her loneliness. The mother frequently came to the point of tears, but could not let herself cry. When her daughter screamed, "I hate you," in her face, the mother did not react, and instead went on with the logical extension of the preceding discussion. She expressed no concern or anxiety over having gone back to work two months after her second daughter was born. She could find nothing that she or her husband, the girls' stepfather, had done to create the anger, hurt, and distrust that her daughter was expressing toward them. The mother needed to look good even in treatment, and could not let her guard down or express her feelings. Her husband supported her in her blindness to their looking-good lifestyles.

Another instance of looking good at the expense of being real, genuine, and authentic with each other was the family of a sex and love addict whose bottom lines included masturbation and compulsive calling of "900" sex-talk phone numbers. As he began to look at the people in his family of origin, he discovered that they were unable to express their feelings and were particularly uncomfortable with anger. They were rigid and devoted to their religion. They appeared close but never expressed affection, touched, or talked about their feelings. They compulsively overate to cope with their feelings of anxiety, insecurity, and inferiority. They felt victimized, and were comfortable with the stress of always feeling behind and trying to catch up. They were co-dependent, and tried to fix things without really going into the deeper feelings or the true meaning for the individual. He was afraid to talk to them about his problems because of their lack of closeness, understanding, and acceptance. Initial recovery involved recognizing how his family felt and beginning to see the looking-good problems of repression of feelings, rigidity, victimhood, compulsive self-medication with food, difficulty with anger, and habits of avoidance. Long-term recovery will provide an opportunity to work on the deeper feelings of abandonment, isolation, rage, deprivation, and poor modeling. These latter issues could jeopardize early recovery because of the intense feelings they generate, the lack of self-worth existing in the sex and love addict, and his or her need for improved social and coping skills to handle the thoughts and feelings related to early family experiences.

Family issues—whether from dysfunctional or looking-good behaviors— certainly need to be discussed and understood in early recovery, but the in- depth, working through, therapeutic process is more the business of long- term recovery. As sex and love addicts grow stronger in their recovery, they become more capable of coping with feelings related to early experiences of abuse, neglect, deprivation, and abandonment that surface during in-depth work on family issues. This work needs to be conceptualized as part of developing the addict's outer layer of protection from relapse rather than as eliminating the cause of the addiction. Working on family issues too early or too much can obscure the addiction and give the message that if these issues were resolved the addiction would disappear. Later in recovery, the sex and love addict will have learned that recovery is a lifelong effort and that no amount of therapy or resolution of early traumas and conflicts will ever take the addiction away. Work on family issues will make lifelong sobriety easier and more livable, but it will not eliminate the sex and love addiction or pull it out by its roots.

BOUNDARIES

Boundary issues are a common problem in recovery, and are obviously related to family issues since most of us learned our boundaries in our families of origin. Boundaries have to do with deciding what is too close and what is too distant. Each of us has boundaries, whether or not we are conscious of them. Most of the time we become aware of our boundaries when someone crosses them (an invasion of our space) or is overly respectful of them (a feeling of isolation).

Boundaries define our personal space. We have a sense of how close we will allow others to approach. If another person gets too close, we feel violated. This may occur if they get "in our face" or actually intrude in our body by raping us. We can feel raped even when there is no physical pen- etration if the other person has penetrated the boundaries of our personal space. We even feel raped when someone breaks into our car, house, or apartment, or goes into our personal belongings, because they have violated our personal limits. When we lock our car or house; put our things in our desk, pocketbook, or room; or say, "You are getting too close," we are establishing our boundaries, our personal space, and our limits. When others transgress these limits, cross our boundaries, and come into our personal space without a specific invitation, we feel violated. As people, we have the right to set our limits and boundaries, and we have the responsibility to maintain them and inform others of what they are. We instinctively respond to boundary violations with anger and aggression as part of our survival reaction.

Boundaries have to do with intimacy and relationships. Being able to establish clear boundaries can promote trust and closeness because the partners are able to become intimate without being either too close or too detached. Both people feel respected and valued when clear boundaries and mutuality have been established. Having boundaries promotes both giving and getting love, attention, affection, contact, closeness, and intimacy by allowing people to know what is appropriate and what is not.

A simple example is the difference between giving and taking a hug. A person with boundaries that are too distant and rigid will be uncomfortable with physical contact and will not hug, or else will freeze when someone tries to hug him or her. A person with healthy boundaries will inform others of what he or she is doing ("You look like you need a hug"), and will ask permission to cross personal boundaries ("Do you want a hug?"). Proper limits are maintained when a person asks for what he or she needs ("I need a hug"), and gives the other person a choice ("Can I have a hug?"). Inadequate boundaries exist in a person who gives or takes a hug without permission, without giving the other person a choice, or without disclosing either his or her needs or what he or she is doing. Sometimes it is easy to identify this intrusive action because it feels like a violation or rape. Sometimes, if the other person is a good manipulator, the boundary violation, intrusion into your space, or violation of your limits will be less obvious. The transgression may only be discovered in retrospect as you investigate the source of the uncomfortable feeling that you have just been violated yet don't know how. Someone asked to give you a hug, possibly because you "look[ed] like you need[ed] one," and you walked away feeling like a hug actually had been taken from you without you having had the satisfaction of giving it away.

Sex and love addictions aggravate whatever boundary difficulties the sex and love addict derived from his or her family of origin. As the sex and love addiction progresses, the addict becomes increasingly self-centered, narcissistic, infantile, demanding, and egotistical ("His or Her Majesty the Baby"). As the disease progresses the significant others who live with and care about a sex and love addict become increasingly co-dependent, centered on meeting the addict's needs, other-directed, parental, giving, and selfless. Healthy boundaries, if they ever existed, gradually—or sometimes quickly—erode, and personal space, individual integrity, and proper limits cease to be important.

Families of origin also contribute to boundary problems for sex and love addicts and co-dependents. Dysfunctional families tend to set poor boundaries, have loose limits, and be unable to say "no" or establish personal space. These families can be too close. They are enmeshed and smothering. They do not allow members to separate and develop as individuals because they find distance frightening and uncomfortable. They are overprotective, and project harm and danger onto the rest of the world. The parents always remain parents, and tend to intrude into the lives of their children even when grown.

In dysfunctional families, there is a tendency to parentify children (i.e., make children parents). For instance, a child can become the confidante and friend of one of the parents rather than his or her child. The child is, therefore, treated as an equal, even before being developmentally ready to take on adult roles and responsibilities. These children are the family heroes, and often perform adult jobs in the household. Their needs for normal growth and developmental experiences are invaded in the name of the overall good of the family.

Incestuous relationships—whether overt or covert—are extremely intrusive and damaging invasions of children's boundaries. Unfortunately, adult perpetrators are so driven by their own needs and desires that they cannot see the harm of this sort of sexual contact for the child. Even when they do know it is wrong and hurtful, their own ability to say "no," to set limits on themselves, and to keep boundaries, is so poor that they cannot stop. In fact, there appears to be a strong quality of sex and love addiction to incestuous relationships between children and parents. Unfortunately, incest victims grow up with profound damage to their own sense of what is an appropriate touch, how to be close, how sexuality fits into intimacy, and how to have healthy boundaries and limits in relationships.

Looking-good families and families whose dysfunction has to do with being too rigid and detached tend to create people with boundaries that are too rigid, distant, detached, and superficial. They have too many boundaries, and are unable to get close to others or allow people to get close to them. They are uncomfortable with touching and being touched. While starved for affection, attention, love, and nurturing, they are unable to give any of these things to others, nor can they receive them. They feel alone, abandoned, worthless, and abused. They tend to experience themselves as victims and to view the world as neglectful, hostile, and dangerous. They take care of their own needs and tend to overwork and overachieve. They do not trust that their needs can or will be met by others, and they make sure that they are as self-sufficient as possible.

Both boundaries that are too close and those that are too distant create problems. Some families have an odd combination of both: There may be smothering from one parent and isolation from the other, or there may be incestuous behaviors from one parent and detachment from the other. These conflicts can be extremely confusing to children.

Recovery from sex and love addiction requires the establishment of boundaries and limits; for example, saying "no" to sexual or romantic impulses and setting bottom-line behaviors. Long-term recovery entails developing the capacity to have healthy relationships that involve intimacy and contact. Interdependence and getting close with other people is essential, both in early recovery and over the long haul. Boundary issues, therefore, are an important aspect of the recovery process from sex and love addiction.

In short-term recovery, some addicts are too rigid with their boundaries, and need to learn how to be firm without being harsh, punitive, and self-destructive. For example, one sex- and love-addicted teacher came from a rigid family and tended to have strict, inflexible boundaries. In his addiction he gave himself no boundaries or limits whatsoever. During early recovery, he would become enraged whenever anyone suggested a strict boundary such as no relationships for a year. However, on his own he was not able to follow the boundaries he set up for himself, such as not going to a woman's apartment on the first date, and ended up continuing to act out with casual sex and masturbation. He needed to learn how to set a boundary he could follow without being either too rigid or too loose. This came about through expressing the caring and love that lies behind limit setting rather than the criticism and guilt he had experienced as a child.

Another sex and love addict had a tendency to have loose boundaries and could not set limits on himself. He was sexually and emotionally abused as a child by both parents in an alcoholic home. In other words, he grew up with people who were incapable of setting appropriate boundaries and could not control their own impulses despite the harm they were inflicting on their child. To him, boundaries felt like the neglect, deprivation, abandonment, and isolation that he had experienced. To him, limits told him he did not deserve to be taken care of and that he was worthless. He needed to learn that boundaries and limit setting are forms of loving through saying "no" to destructive impulses and behaviors.

In long-term recovery, some sex and love addicts need to become firmer with their boundaries while others need to be less rigid. The roles of their addictions and their family of origin need to be sorted out so that each can be worked on to improve the person's balance of contact and detachment. Healthy boundaries involve both structure and flexibility. Appropriate limits can be set and changed without causing trauma or chaos.

An instance of boundary work in long-term recovery is the recovering alcoholic who later discovered and worked on his sex and love addiction. He tended to be overly rigid with his boundaries and therefore left himself isolated, lonely and without much personal closeness or contact. He was uncomfortable with touch and affection. He felt abused by feedback unless it was positive. He could not allow others to nurture him and was distrustful and critical. This addict achieved sobriety but was not happy. He ruled his impulses with an iron will, and his rigidity spilled over into his interpersonal relationships. He did not have a sponsor. He took other people's inventory; for example, he complained that others in S.L.A.A. did not work the Steps, yet he did not work them either. He only befriended people younger than himself. He needed to become softer, more loving, more open, less rigid, more flexible, and less structured. He needed the firmness to establish his sobriety, but the task of long-term recovery was to improve the overall quality of his life, especially in terms of his interpersonal relationships. He needed to learn how to be close, intimate, and sexual in the context of a caring, committed relationship.

Another sex and love addict was still loose and out of control even after establishing his sobriety. He tended to be narcissistic and grandiose, and to overdo everything with which he was involved. His boundaries were not strong enough. He became overly dependent on others in his recovery process, and needed to learn how to separate and individuate. He grew up in an enmeshed family where "everyone was in everyone else's business." He was able to learn how to say "no" to his sex and love addiction bottom lines, but he still was troubled by feelings of abandonment, neglect, and abuse by others when they were not overly affirming and supportive. He had to firm up his boundaries in order to be truly interdependent and not simply switch his dependency from sexual acting out to a love addiction.

Family and boundary issues, then, are important in both short- and long-term recovery. The emphasis on what is worked on and how can change dramatically as the sex and love addict progresses in recovery. Initially, the addict may need to learn how to establish firm boundaries and clear limits. As he or she grows and becomes more comfortable refraining from acting out, the task of lifelong sobriety may include becoming balanced by being less rigid and more flexible without losing control or becoming chaotic. Sometimes the opposite is true. The early recovery process may involve gradually establishing boundaries and being less harsh, rigid, and punitive. After some time in recovery, such a sex and love addict may need to learn how to become firmer and stronger in his or her boundaries and limits in order to have an optimum balance and quality of life.

NURTURING AND DISCIPLINE

The concept of boundaries and limits relates to the issues of nurturing and discipline. Both are needed in life, especially in a recovery process. Sigmund Freud once said that the important things in life were "to love and to work." Stereotypically, in the United States, loving and nurturing have been the mother's task, while working and discipline have been the jobs of the father.

The child needs both contributions in order to grow and live with a healthy balance. In fact, observers of group dynamics have identified these two aspects of healthy and productive group functioning and have labeled them the *task* and *maintenance* aspects of group process.

The study of sex roles has taught us that mothers can be both loving and disciplining just as fathers can be both nurturing and task-oriented. Some theoreticians have posited that a healthy human being should have both qualities, and have labeled people who are high in both areas as androgynous. In this section, then, when I refer to "mothering" or "fathering," I will be discussing the generic activities of nurturing and disciplining, and not stereotypical concepts of gender or sex role behaviors. I do this because I find that some people can relate better to the idea that we need to have internal "mothers" and "fathers" (as well as our inner "child") than to the concept that we need nurturing and disciplining parts in ourselves. Other people have the opposite reaction, probably because their mothers or fathers were so damaging that all associations with these words are negative. In any case, I encourage the reader to use the idea that is most comfortable. We all have internal aspects of ourselves that act to nurture, discipline, and joy. Some call these our ego, superego, and id. Others call these parts our adult, parent, and child. They can also be described as our mothering, fathering, and child-like parts. The point is that in order to be whole, healthy, balanced, happy, and fulfilled, we need all these aspects of ourselves to be alive, functioning, and working together.

Since we tend to integrate the parenting that we experienced as children without much discrimination (and seem to "swallow our parents whole"), we usually parent ourselves the same ways we were parented. We also continue to live as the child we were unless we find ways to continue our own growth and development as adults. Consequently, if you had a smothering mother and a distant father and were a people pleasing child, you will continue to give to yourself and expect from others a smothering type of nurturing, a detached type of discipline, and a perfectionistic type of enjoyment. Each of these aspects, in its own way, is damaging. Smothering creates anxiety and insecurity. Detachment fosters loneliness and feelings of worthlessness. Perfectionism engenders feelings of failure and hopelessness.

To be a healthy, balanced person, we need all three of these qualities in ourselves: nurturing, discipline, and enjoyment. We need a supportive, caring, affirming part in ourselves. We need a structured, limit-setting, achievement-oriented aspect of the self. We also need a fun-loving, playful, excited element to our being. Mothering or nurturing ourselves refers to loving ourselves unconditionally. It means accepting ourselves for who and what we really are without pretense, exaggeration, or grandiosity. It means being able to recognize ourselves as we are. It means feeling joy in the mere fact of our existence without the need for proof of our worth or accomplishments to show our basic value. Nurturing is encouragement to try things and comforting when we feel hurt, neglected, or abused. With our mothering part, we feel safe to be ourselves and to be real, and we know we will be accepted with all our limitations, imperfections, and failures. We feel supported but not smothered. We feel cared about but not strangled. We feel appreciated but not put on a pedestal.

Fathering or disciplining provides us with structure and limits. Being able to discipline ourselves means we can say "no" to our inner child or our impulses if they have the potential to be harmful or destructive. Fathering and disciplining leads to feeling safe and protected, having the strength to resist and the courage to fight. With our fathering part we seek to explore the world, achieve things, and conquer new territories and experiences. We look to do things, we seek accomplishments, and we look for tasks and jobs to complete. A good father sets achievable goals, and offers praise and recognition for reaching the goal or at least trying. Fathering also means being able to break things down into achievable parts and building on what has been accomplished. Discipline is a combination of effort and control. Disciplining means doing things within limits and manageability. It means providing structure and consequences for not following the limits, it means obeying and being responsible, and it means following direction.

Being childlike is the third aspect of this parenting dynamic. Children have a great capacity for joy and excitement in all elements of life. They do not need great achievements or fancy toys to enjoy themselves. They are able to see and feel without the many complications that adults bring to every situation. They live life simply, and in the here and now. They are present-oriented rather than always looking to the future. They are not preoccupied with what others think of them or with trying to impress anyone with their talents or abilities. Children express their feelings with a genuineness and openness that adults tend to cover up and hide from the rest of the world. As adults, we need to have a healthy child within who is taken care of by healthy mothering and fathering parts of ourselves.

In recovery from sex and love addictions, these healthy elements are also needed. In fact, the dynamics and structure of the S.L.A.A. program include all three in large measure. The First Step speaks to nurturing, discipline, and the childlike state. The First Step begins with "We"—a nurturing, caring, and inclusive identification. The step continues with the idea of "powerlessness," which is a childlike state, and "unmanageability," which indicates a lack of discipline.

Families of origin and addictions can both cause problems with nurturing, disciplining, and being able to be childlike. Detached mothers tend to create in their children feelings of being uncared for, isolated, and worthless. An absence of nurturing or cold caretaking makes children feel alone, empty, and hopeless. On the opposite end of the spectrum, enmeshed mothers seem to cause children to feel smothered, have low self-confidence, and be narcissistic. Because these children are overprotected, overnurtured, and over-cared for, they do not feel capable of coping on their own. They feel anxious and fearful if left to their own resources, and expect the rest of the world to cater to them as their mothers have.

Fathers who overdo their job by being too rigid, too demanding, and too conscious of limits also damage their children. They create feelings of anger, resentment, and being overly controlled. Their children resent authority and limits, and do not feel cared about by efforts to provide discipline. They become sadistic, withholding, and passive/aggressive. At the other extreme, children whose fathers are absent, unavailable, or disinterested in setting limits suffer from an inability to control their impulses, poor boundaries, and inadequate inner discipline. They seem not to care about rules, limits, or expectations. They do not respect authority figures or see the need for discipline or order.

There are, of course, many different possible combinations of parental nurturing and discipline. In general, sex and love addicts who came into the S.L.A.A. program with various types of damage or deficits in terms of nurturing and discipline will react in different ways. If, for example, a sex and love addict had a detached, unnurturing mother, he or she might respond very favorably to the warmth, caring, and contact of the fellowship. If the mother was enmeshed and overly involved, the addict might have the opposite reaction and be repelled by what appears to be the smothering, overly intimate contact of the S.L.A.A. program. If the sex and love addict had a rigid, controlling, overly disciplined father, he or she might react to the structure of the program and the steps with anger and resentment because they feel too much like the inappropriate fathering experienced at home. A person with a chaotic, disorderly childhood might, on the other hand, love the direction, order, and advice of the program, and feel cared about and helped for the first time in his or her life.

Many reactions to the program, then, are due to the nature of the nurturing and discipline that the sex and love addict experienced at home. In early recovery, many of these reactions may need to be pointed out and even interpreted in order that they not interfere with the person's progress in recovery. In long-term recovery, these issues concerning the family of origin can be worked on in more depth, so that the nurturing and discipline that is learned from the recovery process will be truly integrated into the person in terms of developing new mothering and fathering styles within him- or herself.

Sex and love addictions themselves contribute to and damage a person's ability to nurture and to discipline him- or herself. People may come to an addiction relatively intact. They may have had adequate parents, and they may have some real strengths in terms of their abilities to be a mother and father to themselves. However, as the disease progresses, these abilities become increasingly distorted and nonfunctional.

In an active sex and love addiction, nurturing is seen as sexual or romantic.

Sexual or romantic acting out comes to be the addict's source of nurturing, good feelings, caring, and support. He or she becomes overly dependent on these thoughts, feelings, and behaviors, to the exclusion of others. Nothing can be as nurturing as a sexual fix or a romantic hit. Relationships start to take a back seat to acting out on bottom-line behaviors. The addict takes care of him- or herself by becoming overly dependent on sexual or romantic obsessions and compulsions. Authentic nurturing ceases to exist. Mothering is sexualized and romanticized.

Likewise, genuine discipline or fathering is lost in an active sex and love addiction. It becomes less and less possible for the sex and love addict to say "no" to these powerful impulses, which become compulsions that cannot be stopped. The sex and love addict continues to break the limits and boundaries that he or she sets. For instance, if a sex and love addict has promised herself not to go out with married men and then does so, she has violated one of her own boundaries. As she continues to do this, she finds it becomes increasingly easy to be undisciplined. Fathering, limit setting, and establishing boundaries may become the enemy of wild, unbridled passion and even a challenge to overcome.

The child within the sex and love addict is also damaged in the course of the illness. The child in the sex and love addict becomes spoiled, overindulged, and pampered. Sex and love addicts become self-centered, childish, narcissistic, demanding, egotistical, and selfish. They resent efforts by others to control them, and are constantly challenging rules, limits, and expectations. They may be open about this rebellion against convention, or they may be quite secretive and manipulative. However, in their hearts, they will know they have no interest in healthy nurturing or discipline. They have discovered the excitement and seeming fulfillment of romance and sexual activities which they imagine will fill all their needs, emptiness, and longings. Nurturing to them seems phony, and discipline appears restrictive and harmful.

Consequently, when a sex and love addict enters a recovery program, there are many variables that go into his or her reactions to the nurturing, discipline, and care of the child within offered by the S.L.A.A. program and treatment professionals. Consequently, different sex and love addicts will need different things from the program and their treatment professionals. At times this may create some confusion, anxiety, and concern on the part of the S.L.A.A. members and the professionals, all of whom are trying to help. Some sex and love addicts need nurturing first and discipline second. Others need the reverse, and still others need a combination of both at the same time. Often, it is quite difficult to determine what is needed and when because of the sex and love addict's lack of openness about both the addiction and the family of origin. Caring people and helping professionals need to try to ascertain the sex and love addict's deficiencies in terms of nurturing, discipline, and enjoyment so they can foster the mothering, fathering, and childlike attitude that will help the addict to grow in recovery.

Recently one sex and love addict questioned me about my method of treatment because he was struggling with controlling his acting out. He had had four months of sobriety after residential treatment, but was only able to attain a few days at a time after his initial slip. In treatment, we had initially focused on learning how to identify times when he was vulnerable, was triggered, or felt compelled to act out and plan coping strategies. Once I was clear that he knew what to do, I began to focus on building his sense of self-worth and to put less emphasis on the discipline of sobriety. This was because he knew what to do but was not doing it. I decided he would come to a point where he would decide to stop for himself (initially, he was staying sober for me) because he would feel he deserved to live a life free of the chains and humiliation of his addiction. Consequently, I stressed nurturing and contacting the child inside him rather than discipline. From his life history and attendance at therapy, I could see he was able to be disciplined when he determined that it was worth it. Therapy, therefore, focused on developing his belief in himself and his own worth; that is, on nurturing and supporting his child part. In long-term recovery, he would have to examine in more depth his rage, anger, and resentment toward his father, and the overly controlling, harsh, judgmental side of himself that was asking me to punish him for his lack of willpower to resist the addiction.

Another sex and love addict came from a smothering mother and a distant father. In his sex and love addiction, he had become quite isolated, and acted out through frequenting pornographic bookstores and through masturbation. He was highly distrustful of nurturing and, at the same time, he put potentially nurturing people on a pedestal. He sexualized attention and was more needy of attention from men than from women. In initial recovery, he needed to learn how to establish a healthy relationship with his therapist and to have appropriate boundaries that did not smother him but also did not allow him to be too distant and detached. Later, in long-term recovery, he would work on issues of hurt, anger, and resentment toward his distant father, who taught him discipline but not love.

Another sex and love addict did not have much nurturing or discipline at home from either parent. He had gotten some training in discipline in school, but his deficits with nurturing were left untouched. He worked on both nurturing and discipline initially, but in his long-term recovery, the issues involved with being able to nurture himself and allow relationships to nurture him were the major focus of his work.

Another sex and love addict had had deficits in both areas. She received a great deal of support and nurturing while in early recovery so she did not have much trouble loving herself. However, what she lacked in long-term recovery was the ability to set limits, to establish boundaries, and to say "no" and mean it. She was able to do this somewhat with herself in that she could maintain her sobriety, but it was nonetheless an area of vulnerability for her.

She needed to work on her fathering and disciplining part in order to be whole and satisfied with her life.

A final example is a sex and love addict who was quite deprived and abused at home, and who needed both love and control when he came into recovery. He had learned to discipline himself as a child, so this aspect of recovery came most easily for him. On the other hand, his ability to be in relationship, to be nurturing to himself, to let others care for him, and to be close to others was the most damaged by both his family of origin and his addiction. In lifelong recovery, learning to care for himself in healthy, noncompulsive ways and to let others into his life in nurturing relationships were his biggest tasks.

Issues of nurturing, discipline, and being childlike come from family life and from sex and love addictions. In each individual the issues are different, and therefore the timing will differ in terms of which issue is most important to work on and when. Both nurturing and disciplining are necessary for recovery. The child in the sex and love addict needs both inner parents to help him or her in both short-term and long-term recovery. All areas need to be developed. Some aspects have never existed while others have gotten repressed or lost in the addictive process. Nurturing, discipline, and being able to be childlike are aspects of getting better that need differing emphases at different times on the road to health and a balanced life.

All the concerns in the sections on dysfunctional and looking-good families, boundaries, and fathering and mothering, influence the sex and love addict in terms of vulnerability prior to the development of obsessive/compulsive behaviors and the damage done by the active sex and love addiction. They are all attended to in various ways in treatment and recovery in Sex and Love Addicts Anonymous, both in the early phases and in the long-term aspects of recovery. In long-term recovery, there is an emphasis on the prevention of relapse by building the person's strengths and removing his or her deficits. Working through family of origin issues concerning dysfunction or looking good, and working on nurturing, discipline, a childlike attitude and boundaries, is painful and can be dangerous to the newly recovered sex and love addict. However, once sobriety has been clearly established, work on these issues will improve the sex and love addict's sobriety and the overall quality of his or her life.

POST-TRAUMATIC STRESS DISORDER (P.T.S.D.)

Family and boundary issues are dealt with to some degree in early recovery, but in long-term recovery these issues can receive more attention and be worked on in greater depth. Addicts need time and strength to tackle traumas like physical, sexual, and emotional abuse and neglect in a way that promotes true healing. Therefore, any real, in-depth work with these issues requires some clearly established sobriety on the part of the recovering sex and love addict. At least a year, and probably two years, of abstinence from bottom-line behaviors are needed in order to be able to delve into such areas of intense pain and hurt from the addict's past. Some addicts choose never to deal with these issues. However, others are forced to face them because they are experiencing a condition called post-traumatic stress disorder.

Post-traumatic stress disorder (P.T.S.D.) came into our awareness and vocabulary out of the Vietnam War experience. Vietnam veterans showed aftershocks from the traumatic events of the war. Sometimes these effects did not appear right away but rather came on long after the veteran had returned to the United States—hence the use of the designation "post." The reactions were to the horrifying experience of war—hence the term "traumatic." After the trauma of war, these veterans were showing signs of suffering from stress such as nightmares, unwanted recollections, flashbacks as if they were reexperiencing the events, and even dissociative states. Anniversaries seemed difficult. Some veterans went out of their way to avoid any memory or association with the war. Some became isolated, distrustful, hostile, angry, and even paranoid. They exhibited symptoms like difficulty in sleeping, problems with concentration, irritability, excessive startle reactions, and sweats. All these reactions are common to stressful situations. However, the stress had already occurred, so the concept was developed that these Vietnam veterans were having post-traumatic stress.

Ever since this idea was developed in relation to war veterans, other groups have begun to be identified as having similar patterns of symptoms. Survivors of incest and sexual abuse often have these same experiences. They were not previously identified because they rarely spoke up (so their symptoms were attributed to other causes) and because there was no appropriate frame of reference other than traditional mental health diagnostic categories. Many of these victims were labeled with illnesses like depression, anxiety disorders, and adjustment reactions. As professionals became more familiar with the post-traumatic stress disorder, however, they began to see that victims of incest and sexual abuse were having stress reactions after the event or trauma that resembled the syndrome of the war veterans. Now we know that incest and sexual abuse victims can and often do experience post-traumatic stress, and that its onset can be considerably delayed, especially if there is an active addictive process in the individual.

We are seeing that children who are physically abused have symptoms that resemble this disorder. Often adolescents on our inpatient unit who are aggressive, hostile, distrustful, tough, angry, and defensive are victims of physical abuse. Sometimes they do not know how to tell us or are afraid to tell us because they feel the need (or, have been specifically instructed) to protect the abuser. They expect to be abused again, so they take an aggressive approach to solve the problem. After they have come to know us and realize they will not be hurt, they usually share other symptoms like problems with sleep, concentration, memories, association, nightmares, and sweats. They have been through their own "war" experience, and have a similar set of stress symptoms related to the trauma that they lived through in the past.

Until we had a concept and a label around which people can organize and share their experiences, it was not possible to see the extent or nature of the ongoing impact of stressful events from past life. We knew that childhood traumas affect us deeply, but our ideas were vague and did not lead to a comprehensive or helpful approach. Now that we have begun to understand the post-traumatic stress disorder, we can begin to see how this may apply to recovering sex and love addicts and to understand how P.T.S.D. fits into treatment and recovery.

Before looking more closely at this concept in terms of sex and love addiction, let's review the definition of Post-Traumatic Stress Disorder as it has been developed by the American Psychiatric Association in its *Diagnostic and Statistical Manual—Revised* (1987).

The symptoms need to occur substantially after the traumatic event. Usually, there must be at least six months between the experience and the development of symptoms. The symptoms are related to a traumatic experience, shock, or other experience outside the realm of usual human experience that is harmful, disturbing, or distressing, or that is upsetting to most people. A car accident, a robbery, and a mugging are traumatic, although not as damaging as a long-standing trauma like war or chronic neglect or abuse. An experience that is more hurtful, such as a rape or stabbing, is more traumatic than an experience that is intrusive but does not include physical harm, like an obscene phone call or having your home burglarized. The amount of trauma and the length of its duration combine to increase the amount of harm and, therefore, the extent of stress that will develop later.

Most shocking or traumatic experiences take time to process. When we are emotionally overwhelmed or overloaded, we detach and shut down; in other words, we go into shock. After the trauma has ended, we eventually begin to thaw out and start to experience the thoughts and feelings related to the event that we had closed off at the time. We can reexperience these reactions by recalling the event, dreaming about it, talking about it, having "flashbacks," and reacting to things that remind us of the shock. We learn to resolve these feelings so that the trauma no longer takes center stage in our minds but rather recedes into the background where it belongs. The trauma is part of our past, and thus accessible to memory, but it no longer intrudes into our current experience and distracts us from our day-to-day lives. The past trauma no longer rules our present experience. However painful the past has been, we know it is over and can live our lives in the present without being paralyzed by these traumatic experiences or preoccupied by their memories. The more we can settle the issues of the past, the more fully we can live in the present.

Many of us fail to recognize everyday signs of stress, not to mention stress symptoms that are the result of past traumas. Common signs of stress include increase or loss of appetite, sweating or dry mouth, rapid or slowed heartbeat, rapid or shallow breathing, muscle tension, nervousness, hyperactivity, and sleeping too much or too little. Indicators of chronic stress include physiological problems like ulcers, colitis, high blood pressure, chest pain, headaches, poor circulation, weakness, dizziness, shakes, and asthma. Worry, anxiety, depression, rumination, anger, irritability, feeling victimized, and even paranoia are psychological symptoms of stress. Withdrawal, procrastination, passivity, drug and alcohol abuse, compulsive behaviors, competitiveness, hypersensitivity, and polyphasic activity (doing many things at once) are often related to stress.

Post-traumatic stress symptoms are often the repeated and persistent reexperiencing of the trauma through recollections, dreams, nightmares, and flashbacks. The experience of feeling as if the trauma was happening again may be like an illusion or a hallucination. At times, it may even be a dissociation or feeling of being there but not being there, like an out-of-body experience where the person observes from a spot outside him- or herself. An extreme form of dissociation involves a complete separation mentally such as occurs in multiple personalities. Another recurring or persistent form of reliving the trauma may be stress experienced in relation to symbolic events such as anniversaries, similar events, such as movies, or related things such as music or clothing that remind the person of the trauma.

Another cluster of symptoms of post-traumatic stress disorder has to do with avoiding the painful recall or related stimuli, or actually numbing oneself. Some people make an effort to scrupulously avoid any thoughts, talk, activities, situations, people, or things that might trigger some form of recall or recurrence. Some actually cannot recall the trauma, and have a form of psychological amnesia. Others experience a decrease in interest in important activities and feel detached or estranged from other people. Some individuals just cut off their feelings and become unemotional about everything; for example, they are unable to cry or feel joy. Others cut off their sense of the future and do not experience hope or anticipation with regard to future events or relationships.

The opposite of numbing and shutting down like the symptoms just listed is to become more sensitive, alert, and aroused. People who react to post-traumatic stress with these symptoms have trouble falling asleep or cannot stay asleep. They tend to be tense, irritable, hypersensitive, and angry. There may be problems with their ability to concentrate and focus their attention for long periods of time. They tend to be on the lookout, hypervigilant and even paranoid. They often startle easily and with little obvious provocation. They can psychologically overreact to symbolic events, and experience stress symptoms like sweating or dry mouth. Appetite, energy, enthusiasm, and vitality all can be either constricted or overactive.

No one individual has all these symptoms of post-traumatic stress disorder. Most of us tend to react in one extreme or the other: We either "clam up" or fall apart. Consequently, those who clam up will most likely have the P.T.S.D. symptoms related to avoidance, numbing, controlling, and tightening up, while those who usually fall apart will have the P.T.S.D. symptoms related to being overly attending or feeling, losing their grip, and being out of control. Some people, of course, will have a combination of these, since no one is exactly alike. However, in order to have P.T.S.D., there must be a cluster of symptoms rather than only one or two isolated indicators of the disorder.

The traumas that sex and love addicts tend to identify from their early life experiences include sexual abuse, incest, rape, physical abuse, emotional abuse, neglect, and deprivation. Other significant early life stressors include losses like death and divorce, poverty, discrimination, frequent moving, isolation, smothering, and overprotection. Chronic illnesses, disabilities, addictions, and mental illness can also create stress in early life if they occur in the individual (for example, learning disabilities and related school and social problems), or the family (such as an alcoholic parent or chronically ill grandparents).

Addictions themselves are stressful, and can create symptoms similar to P.T.S.D. In its active stage, a sex and love addiction can be extremely demanding in terms of its own urgency as well as the amount of covering up that is required. Many examples have already been given to show how all-consuming a sex and love addiction can be. A person who has both early childhood trauma and the trauma of a sex and love addiction has had a double dose of trauma, and may experience intensified symptoms of post-traumatic stress as recovery progresses. Professionals, informed friends, and addicts themselves can help recognize P.T.S.D. by becoming familiar with the concept and the symptom cluster associated with the syndrome.

Before work on previous trauma is undertaken, a firm grasp on sexual and romantic sobriety is necessary. One sex and love addict consulted me determined to find the cause of his compulsion to visit prostitutes for oral sex. He was certain it had something to do with his relationship with his father. He was more successful than his father, and he was afraid that his acting out was an unconscious way of sabotaging himself so he would not prove superior. However, under scrutiny this analysis did not match the facts, because my client went to prostitutes to celebrate his sales successes and also when he felt overwhelmed with stress and needed a break. Usually, when an unconscious motivation is made conscious through analysis, the power is removed from the unconscious mind and placed in the control of the rational, conscious mind. In this case, no matter how much he talked about his competition with and love for his father, my client continued to feel out of control of his bad habit. Resolving early life conflicts, therefore, is not effective in controlling obsessive/compulsive behavior patterns. Awareness of the trauma in his relationship with his father did not enable this sex and love addict to stop visiting prostitutes.

In fact, any real work on early life trauma is not effective until the addiction is under control; otherwise, new learnings will not be integrated. The sex and love addict described above had repeatedly gone over this material about his father with no improvement whatsoever. Actually, he now felt worse and more depressed because he had convinced himself that if he could figure out why he did these things, he could stop them. Since this analytic approach to problem solving was not working, he began to feel increasingly hopeless. He could not take in the alternative information I was giving him about control of compulsive behaviors and the need for support in order to achieve sexual sobriety.

Working on issues of the post-traumatic stress disorder needs time and stability. In early recovery, this time and energy are needed for the initial involvement in the recovery process. Unless it is absolutely necessary, the resolution of early life traumas should be postponed until the sex and love addict has grown in sobriety. This does not mean that these experiences or difficulties cannot be talked about. Quite the contrary is true. Talking about early pain will help develop the sex and love addict's ability to be honest, open, and willing (H.O.W.). Talking about these issues and traumas is, however, different from really working them through to the point of resolution and forgiveness. Professionals and S.L.A.A. members with some experience in the pitfalls of recovery can usually serve as good guides through the minefield of early life experiences.

A sex and love addict who had lost a marriage to his addiction had been bullied while he was growing up. He had suffered a great deal of unresolved trauma from these experiences, and he began to get sober when he started to see that his addiction was bullying him and that he needed to learn to stand up to bullies, including the disease. The deeper pain of this physical and emotional abuse could be worked on only after this addict had become more confident and less vulnerable to the call of his sex and love addiction. One sex and love addict with some years of sobriety came for some psychotherapy because he realized that his temper was related to his early life experiences of neglect, deprivation, and abuse in his family. In order to be in better balance in his everyday life, he chose to work on the issues that were causing symptoms of post-traumatic stress disorder like irritability, difficulty sleeping and concentrating, overeating, compulsive working, feelings of estrangement from others, numbing of feelings like sadness, and tension related to conflict situations. He was not at risk of acting out yet, but in order to protect his recovery and improve the quality of his current life, he chose to dig into these early life experiences which were still influencing him.

One sex and love addict who had achieved almost two years of recovery decided to attend an Incest Survivors Anonymous (I.S.A.) group because she was planning a trip home over the summer. She had actively avoided contact with any events, discussion, or activities that might bring up her memories of sexual abuse and emotional neglect in childhood. She was detached, tense, and irritable; had trouble sleeping at times; had nightmares and unwanted dreams of her past; and tended to run away from stressful situations. Her exposure to the courage and sharing of the people in I.S.A. brought out a great deal of pain and sadness which she was able to begin to deal with for the first time in her life. She might not have been able to contact her family had she not begun to resolve these old traumatic memories, because her impulse was still to avoid her family and run away. This addict almost backed out, but proved able to go on the visit, which was difficult but a much more real visit than any visit she had ever had before. After she returned, for the first time in her life she began to miss her siblings and to feel sad that they did not have more contact, especially since they had become so close while surviving the same traumatic childhood.

The concept of post-traumatic stress disorder can be helpful to sex and love addicts in order to clarify and label their experience. The timing of talking about and actually working through these issues is important, and therapy needs to be undertaken with care. Some sex and love addicts can get the wrong message that early life experiences cause sex and love addictions, and that once they have been worked through, recovery will be easy. Other addicts are in so much pain that they must put some things to rest before they can feel they deserve to live and have a recovery at all. The impulse to dive into all these issues needs to be resisted, and time must be taken with post-traumatic stress disorders. The most appropriate time seems to be during the sex and love addict's lifelong or long-term recovery program.

HEALTHY INTIMACY: "WHEN CAN I HAVE SEX/LOVE?"

Sex and love addicts are obsessively concerned with their future sexual and romantic status, so the most common and most urgent question that I get about the recovery process is either "When can I have sex?" or "When can I get into a relationship?" There is a need to know up front about the period of abstinence and the promises of the future. This is both understandable and proper, although the addict's current attitudes about the answer may not reflect much sober thinking.

The goal of recovery from sex and love addiction is to return the person to a normal state. Normally, adults are interested in and involved with committed relationships, and engage in sexual relationships once or twice a week. There is a balance in their lives in terms of their intimacy needs and their sexuality. In the Augustine Fellowship of Sex and Love Addicts Anonymous, the suggestion is that sexual activity occur in the context of a committed relationship. Romantic and sexual activity are healthy and encouraged, but care must be taken that the excesses of the past are not triggered and that a relapse does not occur.

Some professionals and others seem to have the mistaken impression that the concept of sex and love addictions will somehow foster a repressive, regressive attitude toward sex. They seem to fear that an awareness of this segment of out-of-control sexual and romantic thoughts, behaviors, and feelings will bring on a new era of Victorian and Puritanical attitudes toward sex. In those days, sex was a taboo subject, and was considered dirty, base, sinful, disgusting, and animalistic. Love and romance, on the other hand, were idealized, put on a pedestal, and considered holy, uplifting, spiritual, and sacred. This separation created a great deal of pain and trauma for people because of the coexistence of sex and love. In our current era we have been able to make sex and love an acceptable topic and a more realistic concept. Sex and love addiction treatment and recovery build on this foundation of growth and understanding about our sexuality, our intimacy needs, and our views of love and romance. The fears about this approach to the problem of obsessive and compulsive sexual and romantic thoughts, feelings, and behaviors are ill-founded and based on a lack of understanding or misinformation about the disease concepts of sex and love addiction and the Twelve Step approach to recovery.

Let's go back to the original question, "When can I have sex/love?" The flaw in the sex and love addict's thinking, feeling, and behavior is imbedded in the question itself. Do you *have* sex or love with someone or do you *share* it? Is sex or love a commodity that you give and take, that you have or don't have, or are sex and love part of an intimate relationship that has other dimensions as well? "Having sex" implies that sex can be an objectified and self-centered act on the part of the persons involved. This suggests the addict's narcissistic, egocentric, demanding, self-serving attitude toward sex and love. I am certain that many people who use the phrase "having sex" are not addicted and do not intend to objectify sex or love into a commodity that is exchanged without real contact or intimacy. Still, the seeds of the addictive style of phony intimacy and of impulsively and urgently using others to get a sexual or romantic fix can be seen behind this often-used phrase.

The proper question a recovering sex and love addict should be asking about sex and love is: "Am I ready and able to share in an intimate relationship?" All of us can experience sexual and romantic thoughts, feelings, and actions in the context of a committed relationship. When we can be best friends with another human being and truly love that person and ourself, then loving and sexual expression of that intimacy can and usually does happen unless the partners choose to do otherwise (for example, they have other primary commitments like a spouse or a vow of celibacy). Corollaries to the question of "Am I ready and able to share in an intimate relationship?" include, "Can I be open, honest, and trustworthy?" "Am I a safe person?" "Can I invest?" "Am I responsible?" and "Can I make a commitment?" All these are aspects of intimacy. Love and sex should follow intimacy, and not the other way around, as the sex and love addict has been trying to do, saying; "After we have had sex, we can decide if we like each other."

In the S.L.A.A. program, there is a tradition that the program is one of attraction, not promotion. Sex and love addicts in their active addictions have been promoting the idea that they are great lovers, wonderful companions, superior sexual athletes, driven by passion, and/or capable of tremendous intimacy or sexual activity. They can give and take more than most. They have been promoting the primacy and priority of their sexual and romantic needs to others, but mostly they have been convincing themselves that they cannot live without sex and/or love. The fact is that they can. We all can; we may not want or choose to, but we are able to survive without sexual and/or romantic activity for fairly long periods of time. Some people even choose to live celibate lifestyles, like marriages without sexual contact or religious lives, although these people do not usually choose to live totally without intimacy, love, or closeness with other people. The point is that physical and emotional contact should follow spiritual closeness. When kindred spirits find each other, love and sex can grow naturally from their sharing. The attraction of human spirits is the basis for a committed relationship, and therefore is the context of sexual and romantic thoughts, feelings, and behaviors.

In order for this sort of spiritual connection to be made, the sex and love addict needs to be in recovery. In their active sex and love addictions, addicts have sought out a high from sexual or romantic activities rather than intimate or committed relationships. Their pursuit of the high was driven by many needs such as boredom, anxiety, insecurity, low self-esteem, isolation, loneliness, fear, anger, feelings of neglect and deprivation, resentment, longing, stress, and avoidance of pain. The pain and despair after acting out only seemed to push them deeper into their addictions. Sex and love addicts became willing to substitute the fix of pseudo-intimacy, temporary good feelings, some sort of physical contact, the illusion of closeness, and the fantasy of some future success for the true good feelings of love, closeness, trust, safety, intimacy, and commitment. Most felt incapable or unable to get the real thing, so they settled for what they could get. They did not know how to get what they really wanted, and some were not even sure what that was. Many became cynical and hopeless about the reality of hope, meaningfulness, and real contact because of their childhoods. The more their addiction progressed, the more they became convinced that reality was an illusion and that the pseudo-intimacy of their sexual or romantic acting out was the best that they could find. Some never knew they were in pursuit of love and acceptance, and only discovered this in their recovery.

A sex and love addict with whom I work had a strong spiritual drive that he found antithetical to his sexual acting out. He compulsively masturbated and had anonymous sex in pornographic bookstores and other public places.

He was sexually abused, emotionally deprived, and rejected and abandoned by his alcoholic father and co-dependent mother when he challenged their attitudes and lifestyle. He was desperately in need of a love that he never got, even from his five siblings, but he saw himself only as seeking sexual gratification. He had so repressed his need for intimacy, relatedness, contact, closeness, and love that he was unaware of the depth of his desire for an intimate relationship. Another sex and love addict had been physically disfigured due to a birth defect and overprotected as a child. He too sought satisfaction in pornographic bookstores and anonymous sex, but also had had some sexual contact with people with whom he did have some sort of relationship. He was repeatedly surprised and disappointed that every time sex entered a relationship, it ended. He was unaware of the fact that these relationships lacked intimacy and commitment. There was some initial trust developing, but it was not based on complete openness, honesty, and in-depth sharing. In fact, he manipulated the trust of others in order to set up his sexual acting out. When sober, this man felt incapable of establishing close friendships characterized by intimacy and mutuality. He did not trust himself to be a safe person, and constantly second-guessed his own motives in starting a relationship with someone.

What is intimacy? What are the characteristics of an intimate relationship? Intimacy is human beings sharing at the most personal, private, and deep level possible. To reach this level of contact, the participants need to feel safe being themselves. In order to feel safe, they need a feeling of trust, acceptance, equality, and mutuality. There needs to be a give-and-take, a back-and-forth sharing that reflects an evenness in terms of power and self-disclosure. When there are differences in power or disclosure, the relationships will be unequal and trust will be one-sided. Rather than establishing partnerships, unequal relationships resemble, and may even recall, parent/child, teacher/student, or employer/employee relationships. While they may involve a type of trust, it is different from the trust that is engendered by mutual sharing. In an intimate relationship, the participants feel like partners with an equal investment and responsibility for the success of the venture. Each person feels safe to be who they are, and they accept their companion for who he or she is, without requiring changes or modifications.

Safety and trust are basic aspects of intimacy and commitment. Eric Erickson (1950) made "basic trust" his first stage of development and the foundation for all that came afterwards. He was it as an essential ingredient to authentic relationships and to feeling whole and real as an individual. Parents build basic trust for the child by protecting, caring for, and nurturing him or her. When any of these elements are missing or when abuse is present, the child will have a profound sense of distrust and isolation. As adults, we can foster trust by making ourselves safe people and making our interactions open, accepting, and committed; in other words; we act as our parents should have acted in terms of being responsible for the protection and safety of the relationship.

Developing intimacy, providing safety, and establishing trust is a risky business. Even when we have had a solid foundation from our early life experience, being open, mutual, and equal involves taking risks. Many people are afraid to take the risk of building an intimate relationship. They fear abandonment, rejection, or betrayal and broken promises. This may be due to experiences in early life. Certainly, in an active sex and love addiction there will be experiences of abandonment, rejection, and betrayal. When the person lacks self-confidence and self-worth, these fears will be magnified. Since sex and love addictions destroy self-esteem, the recovering addict will be afraid of developing intimate relationships because of the hurt and pain associated with loss, being pushed away, and seeing promises and hopes destroyed. These may be compounded for the recovering person by damage done in early life. Intimacy then becomes even more threatening, even impossible.

Another aspect of intimacy is commitment. In order to build a relationship, the partners need to be willing to make an investment. In this case, it is an emotional investment in sharing, opening up, and being honest with each other. Commitment requires responsibility on the part of those involved. They need to be willing to act as adults and not children; they need to be willing to initiate actions and to accept their consequences. Finally, they must be willing and able to set priorities and to change them as needed in order to foster the growth of the contact and closeness.

Sometimes, even when people are willing to take the risk and responsibility, make the commitment, and invest in the relationship, intimate and committed relationships do not develop. This can be due to a poor choice of partners, inappropriate expectations, or an inability to express feelings. For example, the partner that a sex and love addict would choose while in active addiction might not be capable of having an intimate relationship. Often, sex and love addicts choose each other. One recovering sex and love addict who was feeling lonely and needy on a Saturday night picked up his old phone book (a "thing" in the "people, places, and things" category that the S.L.A.A. program recommends you drop) and called a number of women in it. He was surprised when he began to fall back into his addictive thinking and actually made a date with a sex and love addict who was not available for two weeks because she had so many other relationships in progress. It took him four days to become convinced he had made a poor choice of partners.

Another problem in establishing intimacy and trust is the expectations that we hold of others. Often problems occur when the expectations that we have of a person or relationship are not expressed directly or are unrealistic. Sex and love addicts have spent a great deal of time in their own heads in fantasy and preoccupation. They have grandiose images of dramatic romances or intense sexual encounters that are impossible for ordinary human beings to live up to even if they want to. Addicts are also used to keeping things secret and not disclosing the truth about their thoughts and feelings. In order to get clarity about expectations in an intimate relationship, these hopes, dreams, desires, and needs must be brought to light. Many times the partners will be happy to comply, and may even find that these once-hidden expectations enhance the commitment and openness of the relationship. At other times, the source of conflict, anger, disappointment, and distance can be determined when expectations are voiced and examined. One sex and love addict expected her husband to be romantic and sexual during the week and felt rejected and abandoned when he could not perform sexually. She did not tell him what she expected and he did not share his expectations with her. He was annoyed and felt overwhelmed by her sexual overtures because he was overtired. They were both expecting their partner to read their mind and became resentful when the partner did not. They expected that such mind reading would be the result of their intimacy and commitment to each other, and did not think realistically about the need to inform each other about their thoughts, feelings, needs, and expectations.

Inability to express feelings can also inhibit the process of developing an intimate, committed relationship. Again, this can be due to the repression of feelings in an active addiction, the need to hide emotions in early childhood, or both. When partners do not share feelings, genuine intimacy is not possible. Expectations are often intellectual, but feelings are subjective and emotional events. They need to be reported openly and accurately for your partner to truly understand and accept you as you are. If feelings like sadness or anger are deemed unacceptable by the person or by his or her partner, an entire aspect of their relationship will be hidden, and their trust will be damaged to the degree that either person will feel the need to keep his or her feelings secret. When a person represses, numbs, or covers up feelings, he or she is essentially lying. This is an example of lying through omission rather than commission. Regardless, the result is the same: The other person gets a false impression of his or her partner. He or she will not see the whole picture, the whole truth, or the whole person. One sex and love addict felt the need to hide from her husband her anger for his refusal to be sexual with her due to her fears that she would be abandoned and lose her "best friend." Her husband, on the other hand, was only motivated by fear and threats, so he felt comfortable having affairs while she stewed. Only after she had shared her anger and the relationship was on the verge of collapse did he admit the truth of his own acting out.

Intimate, committed relationships are needed for recovering sex and love addicts to enjoy romantic and sexual feelings and activities. Intimacy and commitment involve sharing oneself; taking risks; dealing with fears of abandonment, rejection, and betrayal; being responsible; making an investment; and having the right priorities. They also require the person to make good choices of partners, to be open and honest about expectations, and to reveal feelings. Doing all these things will make you a safe person. Seeking safety for yourself and your partner is quite different from searching for the illusive safety of an overly dependent love addiction or a physically charged sex addiction. Mutuality, equality, sharing, and give-and-take characterize an intimate, committed relationship.

A person's recovery from sex and love addiction will foster development of the characteristics needed for intimate, committed relationships. In working the Twelve Steps, talking at meetings, using a sponsor, and being involved in a therapy process, a sex and love addict will learn how to take risks. Even asking for help the first time is a risk. The recovering sex and love addict will learn to overcome his or her fears. He or she will begin to experience real acceptance and love in the Fellowship of S.L.A.A. Addicts will begin to become responsible, to keep their promises, and to invest themselves. Their priorities will be challenged, as will their thinking, their expectations, and their avoidance of showing feelings. They will be encouraged to share, be honest, open up, and learn to trust. These efforts will be rewarded with a kind of closeness, intimacy, and contact that they may never have experienced before. The tools for healthy intimacy lie in the recovery program. Working a recovery program will lead to sobriety, intimacy, commitment, and, eventually, the expression of love and sex in the context of committed relationships.

These are the promises of recovery. Some sex and love addicts do not want to do the work needed to achieve these rewards. These are the only sex and love addicts among my clients who have not succeeded. One sex and love addict in his mid–30s came for help but did not follow any of the advice or direction that he was given. For example, it was suggested to him that he get a sponsor and call that person daily. The addict did not do it. It was suggested that he keep a daily journal, have daily prayer or meditation times, and do daily readings. He did not. It was suggested that he work on the Twelve Steps and identify examples of powerlessness and unmanageability. He did not. He complained of being mistreated by his father and having been spoiled by his mother. His immaturity and hope that someone else would be able to fix him kept him from entering a recovery process and developing the capacity for intimate, caring relationships. He was most interested in the question, "When can I have sex?" but least willing to make the effort to change in order to get himself to the point where he would be capable of being close and intimate.

Another sex and love addict, who was into exhibitionism and compulsive masturbation with pornography, was also eager to know when he could have sex. He too, however, was unwilling or unable to commit himself to his own recovery process. He saw the suggestions of therapy and the program as extensions of his mother's nagging. She had devoted herself to fixing her son of his sexual problem, which had been uncovered when he was 16, and had neglected her other children in the process. She did not help him, but he was so angry, embarrassed, and humiliated by her efforts that he was highly resistant to even the most gentle, supportive approach should it require any consistent effort on his part. He would not attend meetings regularly, allegedly because of his work schedule. He would not use the phone to call a sponsor (although he did use it to make obscene phone calls). He would not keep a daily journal or a record of triggers, which might have helped him identify what he needed to do to stop his compulsive acting-out behaviors. He ended up back in jail, where he continued to act out even while being confined for exhibitionism. He eagerly looked forward to the part of recovery that included sex, but he overlooked the effort required to build healthy, intimate, committed relationships. If he had shared, gotten close to the program members, opened up, and allowed others to support and direct him, he would have been able to learn that recovery does not lead to "having sex or love," but rather that relinquishing a sex and love addiction will bring a person to the point where he or she can commit him- or herself to an intimate relationship that will have love and sex as an important part of the sharing.

Traditional sex therapy has focused on the area of sexual dysfunction in males and females. Sex therapists emphasize the importance of relaxing, reducing stress, and eliminating performance pressure in sexual relationships. In order to reduce tension, they often suggest a period of abstinence followed by slow, gradual increases in touching, sensate focus, communication about what is or is not enjoyable and talking about expectations and feelings. These same techniques describe what many sex and love addicts learn to do to reintroduce healthy sexuality in their relationships once closeness and commitment have been reestablished. They have learned the value of patience, of taking things one step at a time, and of sharing, caring, and openness. They have developed trust and confidence in themselves, and seek to rebuild it in the relationships that mean the most to them. They see healthy intimacy and sex in the context of a committed relationship and as the task of long-term recovery.

Bibliography

American Psychiatric Association. *Diagnostic and Statistical Manual of Mental Disorders*, 3rd ed., rev. Washington, D.C.: American Psychiatric Association, 1987.

Augustine Fellowship, Sex and Love Addicts Anonymous. *Sex and Love Addicts Anonymous*. Boston: Augustinian Fellowship S.L.A.A., Fellowship-Wide Services, 1986.

————. *Suggestions for Newcomers*. Boston: Augustine Fellowship, S.L.A.A., Fellowship-Wide Services, 1987.

Black, Claudia. *Repeat after Me*. Denver: Medical Administration Co., 1985.

Carnes, Patrick J. *Out of the Shadows: Understanding Sexual Addiction*. Minneapolis: CompCare Publishers, 1983.

————. "From intuition to reality: Research progress in sexual addiction." Second National Conference on Sexual Compulsivity/Addiction. Minneapolis, MN: September 17, 1989.

————. *Contrary to Love: Helping the Sexual Addict*. Minneapolis: CompCare Publishers, 1989.

————. *A Gentle Path through the Twelve Steps for All People in the Process of Recovery*. Minneapolis: CompCare Publishers, 1989.

Covington, Stephanie, and Liana Beckett. *Leaving the Enchanted Forest: The Path from Relationship Addiction to Intimacy*. New York: Harper and Row, 1988.

Earle, Ralph, Gregory Crow, and Kevin Osborn. *Lonely All the Time: Recognizing, Understanding and Overcoming Sex Addiction for Addicts and Co-Dependents*. New York: Pocket Books, 1989.

Erikson, Eric. *Childhood and Society*. New York: Norton, 1950.

Forward, Susan. *Men Who Hate Women and the Women Who Love Them*. New York: Bantam Books, 1986.

Hope and Recover. Minneapolis: CompCare Publishers, 1987.

Hunter, Mic. *The First Step for People in Relationships with Sex Addicts*. Minneapolis: CompCare Publishers, 1989.

Institute for Behavioral Medicine. "Diagnostic criteria for sexual addiction." Golden Valley, MN: Institute for Behavior Medicine.

Larsen, Ernie. *Stage II Recovery—Life beyond Addiction*. San Francisco: Harper and Row, 1985.

Norwood, Robin. *Women Who Love Too Much: When You Keep Wishing and Hoping He'll Change*. New York: Pocket Books, 1985.

Peele, Stanton, and Archie Brodsky. *Love and Addiction*. New York: Signet, 1975.

Schaeffer, Brenda. *Is It Love or Is It Addiction?* Center City, MN: Hazelden Educational Materials, 1987.

Schneider, Jennifer P. *Back from Betrayal: Recovering from His Affairs*. Center City, MN: Hazelden Educational Materials, 1988.

Twin Cities Sex Addicts Anonymous. *Abstinence and Boundaries in S.A.A.: Tools for Recovery*. Minneapolis: Twin Cities S.A.A., 1987.

Vejnoska, Jill. *Growth of AA, Treatment Cited over Past 15 Years*. NIAAA Information and Feature Service, IFS no. 104, February 1, 1983, p. 2.

Wegscheider-Cruse, Sharon. *Another Chance: Hope and Health for the Alcoholic Family*. Palo Alto, CA: Science and Behavior Books, 1981.

Woititz, Janet. *Adult Children of Alcoholics*. Pompano Beach, FL: Health Communications, 1983.

Index

abandonment, 99, 107, 113, 140, 159, 183, 184, 185, 187, 189, 190, 191, 206, 207, 208

abstinence, 95, 135, 198, 203, 210

abuse, 48, 52, 61, 62, 64, 80, 99, 106, 111, 113, 120, 128, 141, 142, 144, 145, 148, 151, 160, 161, 162, 178, 179, 184, 185, 187, 191, 193, 197, 199, 202, 206

acceptance, 132

addiction cycle, 84, 89, 119, 120, 125, 127, 143

addictive personality, 31-32

adolescents, 71, 72, 99, 139, 168, 170, 185, 198

affairs, 208

affirmation, 90, 92, 108, 117-18, 134-35, 136, 147, 150-51, 155, 182-84, 188, 189, 190, 191, 194, 204, 205, 206, 210

AIDS, 3, 5, 7, 50, 56, 64, 70, 72, 73, 74, 87, 103

Alanon, 26, 178

Alcoholics Anonymous, 2, 5, 6, 7, 40, 44, 45, 51, 53, 55, 61, 76, 77, 79, 87, 92, 101, 116, 147, 157

alcoholism, 5, 6, 7, 13, 19, 20, 39, 40, 41, 43, 44, 47, 50, 51, 54, 55, 58, 63, 65, 67, 69, 76-77, 82, 87, 101, 106, 130, 131-32, 139, 147, 148, 161, 177-78, 182, 183, 184, 185, 190, 200, 201, 205

amends, 106, 110-14, 125, 126

American Medical Association, 5, 7, 10, 36, 199

androgyny, 192

anonymous sex, 58, 93, 111, 121, 183, 205, 206

attitudes, 144-47

bibliotherapy, 52, 92, 149

binges, 49, 65, 74, 80, 82, 119, 127

bookstores, 58, 93, 96, 114, 121, 142, 177, 191, 205, 206

bottom lines, 89, 118-27, 129, 143, 145, 146, 147, 151, 152, 157, 160, 190, 195, 198

boundaries, 158, 165, 186, 187-91, 197

bragging, 164, 165-66

caffeine, 81

Carnes, Patrick, 1, 2, 52, 81, 83, 84, 90, 132, 142, 148, 162

Caron Foundation, 184

"Casanova," 139, 146

ABOUT THE AUTHOR

ERIC GRIFFIN-SHELLEY is an attending psychologist who leads a dual diagnosis team on the Adolescent Service Unit at Charter Fairmount Institute. He directs the intensive outpatient program for sex and love addicts of G-S Counseling Associates. He has worked clinically, conducted research, and performed administrative duties in addiction settings for over 20 years. He has written more than 20 professional articles concerning his theoretical and research findings in addictions and has presented at national, state, and local conferences, as well as on television and radio programs.